T0178833

IET CONTROL, ROBOTICS AND SENSORS SERIES 130

Transparency for Robots and Autonomous Systems

Other volumes in this series:

Transparency for Robots and Autonomous Systems

Fundamentals, technologies and applications

Robert H. Wortham

The Institution of Engineering and Technology

Published by The Institution of Engineering and Technology, London, United Kingdom

The Institution of Engineering and Technology is registered as a Charity in England & Wales (no. 211014) and Scotland (no. SC038698).

The Institution of Engineering and Technology
Michael Faraday House
Six Hills Way, Stevenage
Herts, SG1 2AY, United Kingdom

www.theiet.org

British Library Cataloguing in Publication Data
A catalogue record for this product is available from the British Library

ISBN 978-1-78561-994-6 (hardback)
ISBN 978-1-78561-995-3 (PDF)

Typeset in India by MPS Limited
Printed in the UK by CPI Group (UK) Ltd, Croydon

This book is dedicated to my granddaughter Tilly.
When I am long gone, I hope that together we will have made the
world a better place for you to live.

Contents

Related Publications

The following is a list of published works related to this dissertation.

1. Wortham, R.H., Theodorou, A. and Bryson, J.J., 2016. What Does the Robot Think? Transparency as a Fundamental Design Requirement for Intelligent Systems. *IJCAI-2016 Ethics for Artificial Intelligence Workshop*, New York, USA.

2. Wortham, R.H. and Bryson, J.J., 2016. A Role for Action Selection in Consciousness: An Investigation of a Second-Order Darwinian Mind. *CEUR Workshop Proceedings*, 1855, pp. 25–30, December 2016.

3. Wortham, R.H. and Theodorou, A., 2017. Robot Transparency, Trust and Utility. *Connection Science*, 29(3), pp. 242–248.

4. Theodorou, A., Wortham, R.H. and Bryson, J.J., 2017. Designing and Implementing Transparency for Real Time Inspection of Autonomous Robots. *Connection Science*, 29(3), pp. 230–241.

5. Perez Vallejos, E., Wortham, R.H. and Miakinkov, E., 2017. When AI Goes to War: Youth Opinion, Fictional Reality and Autonomous Weapons. *CEPE/ETHICOMP 2017*, University of Turin, Italy, June 2017.

6. Wortham, R.H., Theodorou, A. and Bryson, J.J., 2017. Robot Transparency: Improving Understanding of Intelligent Behaviour for Designers and Users. In: Gao, Y., Fallah, S., Jin, Y. and Lakakou, C., eds. *Towards Autonomous Robotic Systems: 18th Annual Conference, TAROS 2017*, Guildford, UK, July 2017. Berlin: Springer, pp. 274–289 (Lecture Notes in Artificial Intelligence; 10454).

7. Wortham, R.H., Theodorou, A. and Bryson, J.J., 2017. Improving Robot Transparency: Real-Time Visualisation of Robot AI Substantially Improves Understanding in Naive Observers, 2017. *2017 26th IEEE International Symposium on Robot and Human Interactive Communication (RO-MAN)*, Lisbon, Portugal, August 2017.

8. Wortham, R.H. and Rogers, V., 2017. The Muttering Robot: Improving Robot Transparency Though Vocalisation of Reactive Plan Execution. *26th IEEE International Symposium on Robot and Human Interactive Communication (RO-MAN) Workshop on Agent Transparency for Human-Autonomy Teaming Effectiveness*, Lisbon, Portugal, September 2017.

9. Wortham, R.H. and Bryson, J.J., 2018. Communication. In: Prescott, T.J., Lepora, N.F. and Verschure, P.F.M.J., eds. *Living Machines: A Handbook of Research in Biomimetic and Biohybrid Systems*. Oxford: Oxford University Press, chap. 33.

10. Wortham, R.H., Gaudl, S.E. and Bryson, J.J., 2018. Instinct: A Biologically Inspired Reactive Planner for Intelligent Embedded Systems. *Cognitive Systems Research*, 57, 207–215.
11. Gjersoe, N. and Wortham, R.H., 2019. What Behaviours Lead Children to Anthropomorphise Robots? *Movement That Shapes Behaviour 2019, AISB Convention 2019*, Falmouth, UK, April 2019.
12. Rotsidis, A., Theodorou, A. and Wortham, R.H., 2019. Improving Robot Transparency: An Investigation With Mobile Augmented Reality. *2019 28th IEEE International Symposium on Robot and Human Interactive Communication (RO-MAN)*, New Delhi, India, October 2019.

List of figures

List of tables

About the author

Robert H. Wortham is a Lecturer in Robotics and Autonomous Systems within the Electronic and Electrical Engineering Department at the University of Bath. He completed an M.Eng. in Electrical and Electronic Engineering at the University of Bath in 1986 and in 2018 also completed his PhD in Computer Science (Intelligent Systems) at Bath. Robert investigates how human natural intelligence (NI) interacts with AI and how engineers and designers can make the behaviour of AI systems more understandable through transparency. Robert studies both the risks and benefits of AI and how we can maximise the benefits of autonomous intelligent systems, whilst minimising the risks.

Previously, the Founder of RWA Ltd, a major international company developing IT systems for the leisure travel industry, Robert is a proven leader in the analysis, design and delivery of large and complex IT systems. Robert is also a Director and Treasurer of The Society for the Study of Artificial Intelligence and Simulation of Behaviour (AISB). He is a Chartered Engineer, Member of the IET and Fellow of the British Computer Society.

Preface

Though applicable to a wider audience, I have primarily written this book as an engineer, for engineers. We engineers are interested in solving problems by making things. We have many design decisions to make during this process and we have physical, practical, financial and legal limitations to consider. In this book, I introduce some special additional considerations that are relevant to complex decision-making systems. I hope that you will not infer that I wish to stifle innovation, but rather that these considerations will help us achieve *better* solutions. Better for the people that design them, better for those that work with them or interact with them in their daily lives, and better for wider society.

Over recent years, there has been considerable academic and public concern over the proliferation of increasingly powerful 'AI' (artificial intelligence) – computer systems that have been designed to make 'intelligent' decisions as they operate. These concerns are wide ranging, from issues relating to the privacy of our personal information, to the use of these systems for manipulation of electoral outcomes. In response there have been many efforts to understand, structure and combat these perceived risks. At the time of writing, many organisations, including well-established standards organisations, regulatory bodies and even transnational governmental organisations are engaged in serious efforts produce principles, guidelines, standards, regulations and laws related to AI.

There are also fears, bolstered by talk of 'Artificial General Intelligence' and 'the Singularity', that machines – broadly computers and robots – will become 'super-intelligent'. At this point, so the story goes, we will no longer be able to understand their decision-making and will have no option other than to submit to their will. Given the current state of AI and robotics, there is no evidence to support such ideas, but nevertheless they have significant traction, not only in the media, but in serious academic debate and well-funded research effort.

During my doctoral studies, I became interested in why this was the case. Why do we humans fear that which does not exist? Why do we build complex narratives and arguments to support bodies of often inconsistent ideas that have no empirical basis? Why do we jump to normative positions so quickly and then find ourselves unwilling to change our views, even in the light of new evidence? It quickly became apparent that evolutionary theory provides the key to understanding not only our misunderstanding and unfounded fears about AI and robots, but also to build systems that avoid these pitfalls. One of the unexpected outcomes of my PhD studies was a much deeper interest in subject areas that have been historically unrelated to engineering and computing, but which are now essential for the successful design and deployment of AI and robots.

Evolutionary biology helps us understand *why* we perceive and relate to each other, the world around us and our artefacts in the way we do – including the AI systems and robots that we build. We are evolved as *hyper-social* animals, and we have a strong tendency to understand the world around us in terms of human behaviours, desires and intentions. Psychology and neuroscience further boost our understanding and today offer a wealth of carefully and rigorously justified experimental data, together with a body of well-argued, empirically based theory. Moral philosophy (ethics) provides tools to structure, recommend and defend concepts of right and wrong behaviour relating to the design and use of AI. We need to embrace all these disciplines if we are to best develop engineering solutions.

I remember sitting in a research talk given by an impressive young woman, Dr Angelica Lim, who declared that we should be 'Renaissance people'. What I think she meant was that to be effective, we should no longer categorise ourselves solely as engineers, psychologists or legal experts, seeing knowledge outside of our particular discipline as simultaneously irrelevant to our endeavours and beyond our cognitive grasp. Rather we should see all knowledge and understanding as useful, valuable, attainable and most importantly 'joined-up' in some sense. The design of AI and autonomous intelligent systems requires elements from all these disciplines and more. Whilst we cannot be experts in everything, we can nevertheless be enlightened by ideas, evidence and tools from a wide body of knowledge. Working with specialists in these other fields, we can engineer systems that are sophisticated and intelligent, but most importantly genuinely useful yet well-designed to reduce risk.

In this book, I have not attempted to review or even mention all of the principles, guidelines, standards, regulations and laws that currently proliferate on a weekly basis. Such an endeavour is simply not possible by a single author, and in any case this would not be a suitable focus for a book – it would inevitably become rapidly outdated and therefore obsolete. Such cataloguing and monitoring endeavours are already undertaken by many research groups, and several well-maintained examples exist on the web. Rather, in this book I have attempted to unpack our concerns about AI and robots and offer some suggestions for how we might reduce legitimate risks through the use of *Transparency*. I have described in some technical detail how we can build complex decision-making physical systems that are amenable to being made transparent, and I discuss how other forms of AI based on current machine-learning approaches can also be made transparent.

We humans love to signal that we are smart. One way we do this is to build systems that seem to be impenetrably clever: *"Joe is a super-smart guy, he builds these robots that only he can understand"*. For robot, substitute self-driving car, smart speaker or any other artefact that demonstrates AI. For super-smart guy substitute guru, wizard or even investable corporation. My argument in this book is simple: let us make these things do the job we need them to do without seeming so smart. Let us make their inner workings transparent. Then we will understand them, trust them appropriately and use them wisely. We will be more able to see through them when they are not working as we would like, or when they are being used by others to our detriment.

Transparency is generally agreed to be a fundamental characteristic of democratic governance. It underpins the generation of our laws, the operation of our governments and the judgements made by our judiciary. I similarly argue it should be a fundamental consideration for the design and operation of AI and autonomous intelligent systems.

Historically, we the engineers have been considered by some to be relegated to the building of appliances. We should leave discussions about the moral, societal and sometimes even legal implications of our work to others. I hope you do not believe this to be the case, and as a professional engineer I hope you share my view that we are indeed responsible in the widest sense for the products and systems that we create. In this book, I draw on ideas, theories and evidence from other professional disciplines. We engineers can learn a great deal from others, to the extent that they no longer seem like 'others' – just part of a wider team effort to advance civilisation for the good of humanity. That may sound like a very grand opening to this modest book, but why not? We should have grand aspirations and reach for all the tools we have available to achieve them. It is no overstatement to say that our entire species is now reliant on its technology for survival, and it is the responsibility of engineers to deliver that technology. It is our obligation to become as widely informed as we can and draw on the entire breadth of human knowledge in the pursuit of technological solutions.

Acknowledgements

I am indebted to many people who have encouraged me to write this book and supported me during the process.

I would like to thank my supervisor, Prof Joanna Bryson. During my doctoral studies, Joanna constantly challenged and extended my understanding. Her knowledge and insight continue to be invaluable, and she taught me what it is to be a scientist and academic.

I have learned a great deal from many people in our Computer Science and Electronic & Electrical Engineering departments at Bath and at many other institutions, too many to name individually; I have probably learned something from everyone I have met. However, I would particularly like to thank Dr Swen Gaudl for taking considerable time to help me understand action selection in general, and POSH in particular. I must also mention the considerable helpful advice, insight and support of Dr Paul Rauwolf, Dr Leon Watts, Dr Marina de Vos and Dr Nathalia Gjersoe. Dr Jen Haensel recently took time to remind me that evolutionary arguments explain why, but not how. If only we knew *how* the brain works! Contrary to popular belief, academics work long hours, and I appreciate your generous gifts of time.

My thanks also particularly go to Dr Andreas Theodorou, who helped in many ways, not least by writing ABOD3 and modifying it to work with the R5 robot, in order to facilitate our experiments. Thanks also to Andreas, Dr Jon Benardis, Dr Maryam Naghizadeh, James Plaut and Dr Vivienne Rogers for their help during the At-Bristol experiments, and to John Polatch, Beth Cotterell and all the volunteer staff for their warm welcome and kind facilitation at At-Bristol – now We the Curious. Together, we somehow managed to avoid the destruction of my little robot at the hands of excited children, despite a scary moment with a weaponised giant inflatable banana!

Prof Alan Winfield deserves special mention for his constant encouragement and enthusiasm towards my work, for taking considerable time to act as External Examiner for my PhD, and for subsequently encouraging me to write this book for the IET.

I am indebted to Valerie Moliere, Senior Commissioning Book Editor at the IET, who skilfully and tactfully helped me prepare and refine the book proposal that led to the contract with IET for this book. Thanks also to many friends, particularly Mike & Julia Plaut and Duncan & Jane Shadwell for their constant encouragement to pursue my interests, against the prevailing wind of anti-intellectualism and the mere pursuit of financial reward.

Finally, throughout my career, I have been fortunate to have had the unswerving support of my wife Melanie, and I am grateful once again for her encouragement and tolerance during the long hours of research and writing involved in the preparation of this manuscript.

Transparency for Robots and Autonomous Systems

There is now a wealth of activity in the field of artificial intelligence (AI) ethics. Principles abound, standards are underway, and doctoral students are studying. Terms such as trust, accountability, responsibility and transparency are bandied around by the media, management consultants and politicians alike. There is a clear and pressing need for some clear headed thinking on important ethical issues such as the use of social media for manipulation at scale, robot rights and the use of robotics to solve social problems, particularly those associated with ageing populations.

The human cognitive biases that result in anthropomorphism, the moral confusion surrounding the status of robots, together with wider societal concerns related to the deployment of AI at scale all motivate the study of robot transparency – the design of robots such that they may be fully understood by humans.

The study of AI is inherently multidisciplinary, including the work of philosophers, computer scientists, psychologists, evolutionary biologists and anthropologists, in addition of course to the important work of engineers. In this book, I have sought to bring all these ideas, concerns and disciplines together, with a view to explaining AI ethics and transparency in an accessible, yet rigorous, scientific manner.

In particular, I explore transparency as a fundamental consideration for robotics and autonomous intelligent systems. I argue and demonstrate that humans cannot make sense of robots and other autonomous AI systems when they encounter them. These systems must be made in such a way that they explain themselves to us. I show though a number of experiments that we can better understand autonomous intelligent machines if efforts are made to make them transparent.

Based on the hypothesis that robot transparency leads to better (in the sense of more accurate) mental models of robots, I investigate how humans perceive and understand a robot when they encounter it, both in online video and direct physical encounter. To improve transparency, I use a visual real-time transparency tool providing a graphical representation of the internal processing and state of a robot. I also describe and deploy a vocalisation algorithm for transparency. Finally, I modify the form of the robot with a simple bee-like cover, to investigate the effect of appearance on transparency.

I find that the addition of a visual or vocalised representation of the internal processing and state of a robot significantly improves the ability of a naive observer to form an accurate model of a robot's capabilities, intentions and purpose. This is a significant result across a diverse, international population sample and provides a robust result about humans in general, rather than one geographic, ethnic or socio-economic group in particular.

Making transparent machines may not appeal to some designers, manufacturers and operators. It may not be compatible with their commercial models and ambitions. I therefore argue that we should create and agree standards for robot and AI transparency, with a view to encouraging best practice, as a means for purchasers and users to easily specify their transparency requirements, and for regulators to enforce best practice.

In this book I also document the design and development of the 'Instinct' reactive planner, developed as a controller for a mobile robot. Instinct provides facilities to generate a real-time 'transparency feed' – a real-time trace of internal processing and state. Instinct also controls agents within a simulation environment, the 'Instinct Robot World'. Finally, I show how two instances of Instinct can be used to achieve a second-order control architecture.

Chapter 1

Introduction

"If ... the past may be no Rule for the future, all Experience becomes useless and can give rise to no Inferences or Conclusions."

    – David Hume, *An Enquiry Concerning Human Understanding*

"There is no future in sacred myth. Why not? Because of our curiosity. ... . Whatever we hold precious, we cannot protect it from our curiosity, because being who we are, one of the things we deem precious is the truth. Our love of truth is surely a central element in the meaning we find in our lives. In any case, the idea that we might preserve meaning by kidding ourselves is a more pessimistic, more nihilistic idea than I for one can stomach. If that were the best that could be done, I would conclude that nothing mattered after all."

    – Daniel Dennett, *Darwin's Dangerous Idea*

1.1 Motivation

Robots have existed in popular culture for many years, but we are now able to build machines that begin to approach the capabilities foreshadowed by scientific futurology and science fiction alike. In this section, I consider human biases that favour anthropomorphism of robots and mis-attribution of robot capabilities, intentions and goals. I briefly look at the influence of literature and media on our understanding of robots, particularly in Western culture, and discuss how anthropomorphism and wider cultural influences lead us to moral confusion about the status of robots in particular, and artificial intelligence (AI) more generally. I review some serious concerns that have recently been raised concerning the deployment of AI and robots into human society, and the potential for disruption of family life, the psychologically targeted disruption of civic and political discourse, and even the alteration of our perceptions of gender. The real robots are here, and I describe some of the advances that facilitate the development of modern autonomous robots.

In response to the revolution in AI and robotics, there is currently a fragmented approach to public policy, and wide variation in the recommendations made by various governmental and NGO reports, particularly the discrepancy between those originating in the USA, and those from the United Kingdom and European Union. We do not yet understand the impact of AI and robotics, both at an individual level and collectively for human society.

In the light of these concerns, I introduce the idea of *robot transparency* and review the arguments for its incorporation as a fundamental design criteria for robots. When a human encounters, and possibly subsequently interacts with, a *fully* transparent robot, the human is able to fully understand the robot. This understanding relates to the behaviours, intentions and goals of the robot, together with the robot's capabilities and ultimate purpose. A *fully transparent* robot enables humans encountering the robot to gain a complete understanding of its capabilities, purpose and behaviour. Our research is based on the hypothesis that we can design robotic systems with increased transparency, and that this leads to better (in the sense of more accurate) human mental models of robots. However, the assertion that transparency is desirable and indeed helpful in scenarios where humans encounter robots requires empirical examination if it is to have weight in the formulation of recommendations, principles, standards and ultimately regulations for the manufacture and operation of autonomous robotic systems.

Using a non-humanoid mobile robot, I describe several experiments that investigate how humans perceive and understand a robot when they encounter it. These experiments use both online video and direct physical encounter. To improve transparency, I use a visual real-time transparency tool providing a graphical representation of the internal state and processing of the robot. I also describe and deploy a vocalisation algorithm for transparency. Finally, I modify the form of the robot with a simple bee-like cover, to investigate the effect of appearance on transparency.

In all these experiments, I find that the addition of a visual or vocalised representation of the internal processing and state of a robot significantly improves transparency – the ability of a naive observer to form an accurate model of a robot's capabilities, intentions and purpose. This is a significant result across a diverse, international population sample and provides a robust result about humans in general, rather than one geographic, ethnic or socio-economic group in particular. We are not evolved biologically or culturally to deal with artificial autonomous agency, and we cannot rely on the biases and mind models of our evolutionary past to help us understand robots.

1.2   Motivating concerns

A wide range of concerns motivate this work, ranging from the exploitation of human cognitive bias and anthropomorphism by robot manufacturers, to manipulation of voter behaviour by autonomous systems designed to appear as humans interacting within social networks. I review the basis of these concerns in the following subsections.

1.2.1 Human cognitive bias

Cognitive bias helps all animals make decisions based on uncertain and incomplete information (Smith and Harper, 1995; Rendall, Owren and Ryan, 2009). Dennett (1989) notes that we are biased to perceive self-propelled movement and intentional behaviour, indicating a bias to perceive and recognise other biological agents. The evolution of bias towards assuming both agency and hostility is clearly selective for individual longevity in an environment where one is frequently the prey, not the predator. Our human biases are embedded within the very language we use to communicate and think about the world (Caliskan-islam, Bryson and Narayanan, 2017). Human bias helps prune the search space of possible interpretations and responses, enabling timely action selection within the real-time bounds of our ever-unfolding environment. From an evolutionary perspective, bias is biologically and socially adaptive and is an inescapable precondition for human culture. Bias can be useful.

However, bias can also be harmful. Our biases can result in self-deception (Rau-wolf, Mitchell and Bryson, 2015), and inadvertent or deliberate deception by others. Bias increases the possibility of mis-attribution and misunderstanding. Bias may result in a poor choice of mind model. Horror movies feed on our mis-attribution of typical human characteristics to fictional characters who are then revealed to be psychopathic killers. Bias can also result in unexpected outcomes for human cognition and resultant behaviour. We are biased to assume that spoken words originate from human authors (Schroeder and Epley, 2016), and our innate biases result in *'cognitive illusions'* that can lead to serious systematic errors of judgement (Kahneman and Tversky, 1996).

Humans employ *mind models* to understand the world (Johnson-Laird, 1983). These models may be seen as useful structures of biases, allowing us to make sense of the world around us in terms of well-known frames of appearance, behaviour, intention and capability. Once we invoke a model, sensory input is most easily understood within the frame of the model, and our repertoire of familiar responses can similarly be activated. For example, when we encounter a dog, we identify it as such based on size, physical appearance and so on. Having identified it we employ our model of a dog to interpret its behaviour. We interpret a wagging tail as evidence that the dog is excited and pleased to encounter us. We understand that as the dog moves towards us it intends to 'greet' us, sniffing in order to recognise or memorise our scent for future encounters. Were the dog to growl, stand still and bare its teeth, we would recognise the 'warning', understand that we are at risk of being bitten and rapidly select retreat as our course of action. Our mind model is useful, and our attribution of human emotion, intention and *intentionality* informs both our action selection and our conscious narrative (Malle and Knobe, 1997). Even in this brief description, we immediately see how our mind models and language drive us to *anthropomorphise*, that is, to attribute human traits such as emotion and intention to non-human entities. We easily attribute human mind models to non-human agents, and even to entities without agency such as a motor vehicle, storm or volcanic eruption (Caporeal and Heyes, 1997).

However, using pre-existing mind models can also be problematic, leading to poor outcomes. Perhaps that dog we encountered is a breed we are unfamiliar with, and we do not know that it has been especially bred to be spontaneously vicious without warning. A poor choice of mind model occurs when we anthropomorphise robots. Robots are artefacts, the result of human design, based on a set of human design criteria and objectives. Each robot design will employ different technologies and approaches to achieve differing sensory, cognitive and physical capabilities. The choice of an anthropomorphic model is therefore poor in the sense that it is necessarily deficient of knowledge about these specific capabilities. Further, an anthropomorphic model may predispose us to treat the robot as if it were human, affording it moral patiency, and considering its actions in the light of our universal understanding of human moral agency (Hauser, 2006).

If we have any mind models of robots, they cannot have arisen as a result of our evolutionary history. Any frames we may have for thinking specifically about robots must be culturally acquired.

1.2.2   Robots in Western culture

The history of the robot stretches back far further than the beginnings of AI at the Dartmouth College Summer Research Project of 1956 (McCarthy *et al.*, 2006). Western culture includes age old ideas of humanoid malevolent agency. Both Zarkadakis (2015) and Hancock, Billings and Schaefer (2011) illustrate our Western fears of human artefacts becoming animated. Throughout history we have created such stories, from the Greek Pygmalion myth, and the Golem of Jewish folklore. Science fiction portrays primarily negative outcomes, from Shelley's Frankenstein to more recent Hollywood films such as The Terminator, iRobot, Ex Machina, Her and Transcendence. This repeated narrative of our creations turning on us with the intention to either enslave, subjugate or destroy humanity fuels our mistrust of AI and autonomous robotics. For a longer review of Zarkadakis' book on this topic, see Wortham (2016). Such influences have been found not only amongst the young, but also senior citizens, most likely to benefit from robotic technologies in care applications (Walden *et al.*, 2015). Conversely, in Eastern cultures, particularly in Japan, robot technology is considered largely 'tamed'. The difference between the natural and the artificial is not so crucial and these long established Western fears are of less concern (Kaplan, 2004).

More recently some academics also warn us of the possibility of deliberate or accidental annihilation of humankind by 'runaway' AI (Prescott, 2013; Bostrom, 2014; Bohannon, 2015) and wealthy concerned individuals are funding the Machine Intelligence Research Institute* to conduct 'foundational mathematical research' to address these hypothesised risks (Soares, 2015). In response, it seems that journalists accompany all news relating to robots and AI with some version of the Hollywood Terminator imagery, see Figure 1.1. Meanwhile those with commercial or research funding interests remain positive about the successful deployment of AI and autonomous robotic

---

*MIRI see https://intelligence.org

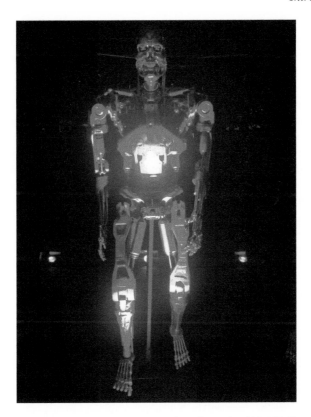

Figure 1.1 The fictional T800 Terminator robot, from the 1984 Hollywood film of the same name. Photograph taken by the author, Science Museum, July 2017.

systems (Horvitz, 2017; Donnelly, 2017) whilst engaging with ideas of ethical responsibility and self-regulation, see Section 1.2.6. The general public remain significantly confused about the ontological classification and practical capabilities of robots (Perez Vallejos, Wortham and Miakinkov, 2017).

1.2.3 Moral confusion

There are serious concerns that our anthropomorphism and misunderstanding of the nature of robots extends so far as to attribute them either moral patiency, moral agency or both (Bryson and Kime, 2011; Bryson, 2018; Gunkel, 2018). A *moral patient* is something to which, or someone to whom, we owe a moral consideration. Humans, animals and the environment are all typically considered as moral patients, whereas a bicycle or building is not. *Moral agents* are those that are to be held to account for their decisions, they are *responsible*. At present moral agency is only typically attributed to humans, corporations and certain institutions such as governments. Young children are considered to have limited moral agency, and those with certain developmental disabilities or psychological conditions are considered to have limited or no moral agency, in the sense that we do not hold them entirely accountable for their actions (Santoni de Sio and Di Nucci, 2017).

Should robots be considered as moral patients? Our desire to create beings in our own image, combined with the residual dualism inherent in folk understanding of mind and autonomous agency, leads many to believe that at some point of sophistication, robots should indeed become moral patients, artefacts to which we will owe a debt of care beyond their economic value, and that robots should therefore have rights (Gunkel, 2018). In the sense that robots should be considered artefacts with no special moral patiency, Bryson (2010) rather provocatively – though the author agrees – asserts that 'robots should be slaves', not that we wish to see a return to slavery, but that we should not build robots that could be considered 'people' with rights in any sense. It is important to remember that robots are designed artefacts. The abilities and capabilities that we include in robots are ours to control by design, and we must not make the mistake to build robots that cause us to become morally obliged to them. This may all seem rather abstract, but we already see serious consideration given to ways in which robots might participate in religious ceremonies such as baptism, or acquire religious belief in order that they may be 'saved' and teach religious doctrine to fellow believers (McBride, 2017).

Recently there has been much speculation, and some empirical investigation of the ability of robots to become moral agents, able to make moral judgements and ensure morally acceptable outcomes (Carsten Stahl, 2004; Coeckelbergh, 2010; Winfield, Blum and Liu, 2014; Charisi et al., 2017). When a moral decision is taken by a person, they know that they will be held accountable. A morally acceptable decision is effectively defined as one which will win general approval from those in our local culture (Jones, 1991). Given sufficient time, we can rehearse the decision and perhaps its likely consequences. Using our mental models of others, we measure this approval or disapproval by the anticipated feedback of praise or punishment. We especially fear social or legally enforced punishment, and this informs our moral behaviour. A robot, designed with allocentric goals, has no fear of punishment, and certainly there is really no current possibility of punishing a robot. Our current models of morality and responsibility require punishment to operate effectively. This is a very simplified description of a complex cognitive mechanism, not easily reduced to simple rules or logical models. Hauser (2006) argues persuasively that humans have a fast acting internal moral mechanism, preconfigured with universal human norms, and tunable by our local culture. This mechanism allows us to be able to determine certain moral responses in local problem scenarios with little cognitive effort – specifically the well-known 'trolley problems'. However, this class of problems and the manner in which they are presented and investigated has more recently been criticised as being unrepresentative of real moral decision-making (Bauman *et al.*, 2014). In modern society, how a reasonable person should reasonably be expected to behave is, in the general case, a very complex matter, as evidenced by the vast corpora of legislation, court cases and judicial judgements that together comprise the Law. To consider robots for admission to the class of moral agents has not only deep practical and philosophical problems but is also legally problematic. Individuals already seek protection from the law by shielding themselves behind a corporate legal identity. Were that corporation then to produce robots considered to be moral agents, or 'legal persons', as has been suggested (Committee on Legal Affairs, 2016), this would further shield the humans behind the robots from moral responsibility and legal accountability (Bryson, Diamantis and Grant, 2017).

Delegation of moral accountability to robots presents an opportunity for humans and corporations to eschew their responsibilities, whilst granting moral patiency to robots is risky, unnecessary and wasteful of human resource. These moral confusions need to be addressed in a practical manner by robot designers – see Chapter 7 for a longer discussion. As I outline in Section 1.3, an effective way to achieve this is to make the machine nature of a robot apparent to those who encounter, interact or regularly use a robot.

1.2.4 Societal concerns

Humanity is vulnerable to mis-attributing anthropomorphic trust and agency to AI and particularly to robots. It is therefore important to consider the potential societal risks of such mis-attribution. Human genetic and cultural evolution produces phenotypes within a predictable normative space, i.e. a relatively small manifold of variation in behaviour within the vast space of combinatorial possibilities (Bryson, 2015). With sufficient personal data, AI is able to learn these regularities and thus predict future behaviour. Once we can predict, we can better influence behaviour, maximising the utility of algorithms based on desired behaviour modification, defined in goal functions. AI thus is a tool to refine and enhance our existing human abilities of manipulation (Wortham and Bryson, 2018).

Sociologists warn of a considerable danger from unanticipated negative consequences in a world in which pervasive sensing constantly captures data about us. Such data may result from widespread deployment of *Internet of Things* technology, but equally from ubiquitous Internet connected autonomous robots (Goulden *et al.*, 2017). It is perhaps the unknown nature of these risks that is most concerning, and again this may account for the wide range of policy reactions to AI and robots. In their report released in October 2017, the AI Now Institute[†] at New York University recommended that *"Core public agencies, such as those responsible for criminal justice, healthcare, welfare, and education (e.g. "high stakes" domains) should no longer use "black box" AI and algorithmic systems"* essentially because of the unknown side effects that deployment of these technologies may have for individuals and for society.

In an increasingly online world, social networks have become important sources of news and forums for debate. Twitter is a public micro-blogging system that allows users to share short messages. It provides an open application programming interface allowing software developers to develop algorithms, known as *Twitter Bots* or simply *'bots'* that are able to read previous Twitter posts and re-post or reply to them

---

[†]AI Now Institute see https://ainowinstitute.org/

autonomously, in addition to posting new content. Kollanyi and Howard (2016) and Bastos and Mercea (2017) specifically report on ways in which automated networks of these Twitter bots potentially influenced the outcomes of both the 2016 US Presidential Election and the 2016 UK Brexit Referendum. More widely, it is becoming clear that digital technologies that facilitate the application of psychological targeting make it possible to influence the behaviour of large groups of people by tailoring persuasive appeals to the psychological needs of the target audiences (Tufekci, 2015; Matz *et al.*, 2017). An embodied AI system, such as a robot, has the potential and opportunity to assess, target and powerfully influence those who encounter it.

Others such as Calo (2017) have specific concerns about domestic intelligent assistants such as the Amazon Echo (Alexa), Apple's Siri and Microsoft's Cortana, in addition to countless chat bots on a variety of social media platforms. Calo advises that these social agents present special challenges for policy:

> "At a more granular level, the fact that instantiations of AI such as Alexa (Echo), Siri, and Cortana, not to mention countless chat bots on a variety of social media platforms, take the form of social agents presents special challenges for policy driven by our hardwired responses to social technology as though it were human. These include the potential to influence children and other vulnerable groups in commercial settings and the prospect of disrupting civic or political discourse, or the further diminution of possibilities for solitude through a constant sense of being in the presence of another."

Richardson (2015) is concerned about the prospect of intimacy, particularly sexual intimacy, between people and machines. Richardson argues that by making sex robots we extend the current objectification of women that occurs in prostitution and *"further reinforce relations of power that do not recognise both parties as human subjects"*. The creation of artificial *'others'*, with 'whom' we have real, rather than imagined intimate relations, begins to redefine the purpose of physical relationships and therefore impacts the cultural meaning we ascribe to physical relations between humans.

Danaher (2017) raises important concerns that autonomous technologies may reduce human pro-activity, making us increasingly passive consumers, in a society characterised by the automation of work, some kind of universal basic income and various opiate forms of entertainment. As humans come to increasingly depend on the decisions and 'advice' of autonomous machines, we will gradually lose both our ability and willingness to act in the world as responsible moral agents, and thereby be reduced to mere moral patients. Danaher further argues that since "[this] ability and willingness is central to the value system in modern liberal democratic states, the crisis of moral patiency has a broad civilization-level significance: it threatens something that is foundational to and presupposed in much contemporary moral and political discourse".

Such ideas are common in the various dystopian futures presented by science fiction, but whether the human species can be 'tamed' by its own technology is at present an open question. However, we see other species tamed, domesticated and now reliant on the intelligence and resources of alien autonomous agents (though admittedly not of their own making), so there is equally no reason for complacency.

There has as yet been little empirical research to substantiate these concerns. However we can at least broadly categorise these risks as below (Zwetsloot and Dafoe, 2019).

- Accident risk – harms arising from unexpected or unintended behaviour of AI systems.
- Misuse risk – the deliberate, unethical use of AI, possibly with malicious motives.
- Structural risk – harms that arise indirectly as a result of deployment of AI systems, where the system behaves as desired, but there are unforeseen negative consequences, either to the system users, or to other groups – possibly to society as a whole.

Structural risk is most concerning, since it is much harder to predict let alone manage the diffuse or long-term consequences of AI system deployment. An example of structural risk would be the way in which highly targeted social media advertising can now be used to undermine the democratic process, eroding our trust not only in social media platforms, but more worryingly on the democratic process itself and its outcomes. Whatever our individual political convictions may be, the cry "Not my President" is a worrying recent development. It shows the beginnings of a breakdown in acceptance of the outcome of a previously widely accepted democratic processes.

The theory of memetics provides a way for us to think about the communication of human ideas within an evolutionary context (Dawkins, 1982). Ideas or *'memes'* use humans as replicators to spread throughout the population, rather like a biological virus. Humans provide the mechanism for variation and selective replication through imitation. Like biological virus', memes have no notion of the message they carry, nor its impact. They are just information. It is our vulnerability to their structure and content that allows them to reproduce and thrive, using humans as no more than replicating 'hosts'. Blackmore (2000) introduces us to the idea of *'temes'*, a category of memes that evolve through the capacity of *human technologies* to select, vary and reproduce ideas without human intervention. Blackmore identifies this as a new, third mechanism for replication, enabled by the two previous mechanisms – genes and memes. Perhaps we are now seeing the beginnings of this phenomena, produced by the combination of huge online data sources, social networks and autonomous bots. Domestic intelligent assistants may be the next replication technology for temes. We have biologically evolved immune systems to defend against unwanted biological virus' and culturally evolved mechanisms such as gossip, reputation and law to guard against unwanted memes. These mechanisms already face new challenges as a result of technological augmentation of human culture, as evidenced by increased risks from biological pandemics and the rise of extreme ideologies. The speed at which ideas spread is no longer governed by physical proximity. Autonomous bots similarly remove rate limitations for selection and mutation of temes. How temes impact human culture is as yet entirely unknown.

1.2.5   Real robots

Autonomous robots have been promised for too long, and whilst many of the issues outlined above sat in the realm of hypothetical, philosophical discourse, the absence of real robots meant that many of these concerns were not of immediate practical importance. However, this has changed. Robots are now a practical reality, due to a combination of relatively recent innovations in materials science, engineering and computer sciences. We have seen very significant recent advances in materials such as extremely light and strong composites and high-energy density battery technology. Increasingly powerful ceramic magnets facilitate the design of high powered small electric motors. Miniaturised low-cost sensors use lasers for range-finding, and tiny video cameras designed originally for smart phones produce high definition video. The signals from these sensors can now be processed in real time by low-cost high-powered processors. Vision algorithms developed by computer scientists allow us to create sophisticated structured models of the world, allowing robots to navigate in practical, habitable environments (Durrant-Whyte and Bailey, 2006; Barfeh et al., 2017). Robots can classify and track the objects they encounter, even when those objects (or the robot) are moving at speed, and when objects are partially, or temporarily fully, obscured from view.

Today, *social robots* are able to track human gaze, accurately convert human conversational speech into text, and synthesise human speech with realistic intonation and emotional expression. A robot can combine the signals from its sensors in order to evaluate the emotional state of a human and adjust its behaviour to *appear* empathic (Novikova and Watts, 2015; Charisi *et al.*, 2017). Robots also benefit from wireless connection to the Internet, giving them access to almost all recorded human culture. These capabilities were previously only found in science fiction robots, accompanied by human-like cognitive capabilities.

Robot technology is now poised to facilitate a wide range of applications beyond industrial manufacturing, and robots will increasingly be encountered by users and bystanders with no prior training. Currently, these people will most likely have no familiarity with real (as opposed to science fiction) robots in general, and certainly no familiarity with a specific robot that they encounter for the first time.

Robotics in public, domestic and near-domestic environments will certainly have many positive and helpful applications. Obvious uses, such as companion robots for the elderly, and therapeutic robots for autistic people have already been extensively trialled (Prescott *et al.*, 2012). Figure 1.2 shows the Kaspar robot, intended for therapeutic use with autistic children. There are also clearly situations where a robot may be misused, such as for the illicit recording of video in intimate care environments, or the coercion of the infirm to control behaviour.

Irrespective of the underlying intention of the robot designer or operator, we can easily foresee the opportunities for accidental or purposeful deception. There exists the potential for negative consequences ranging from misuse or disuse of an incomprehensible robot, to fraud, invasion of privacy and physical harm.

Figure 1.2   The Kaspar robot, developed by the University of Hertfordshire, 2005–16. Kaspar is specifically designed as an expressive robot with a predictable and repetitive form of communication and has been used successfully with autistic children. Photograph taken by the author, Science Museum, July 2017.

1.2.6   *Public policy for AI and autonomous systems*

Given the impending consequences of real robots, several groups have pushed initiatives to formalise public policy for AI and autonomous systems. In 2016, the Institute of Electrical and Electronics Engineers (IEEE) launched a "Global Initiative for Ethical Considerations in AI and Autonomous Systems". Their initial publication recommends no new regulation of AI systems but rather recommends that we should rely on a combination of existing regulations and voluntary adherence to international standards, such as those produced by the IEEE itself (IEEE, 2016, 2017). During the Obama Administration, the US Government conducted an evidence gathering process that led to the production of a report by the National Science and Technology Council Committee (National Science and Technology Council, 2016). This report recommends the use of existing regulation where possible, modifying it if necessary, but with this caveat:

> "… where regulatory responses to the addition of AI threaten to increase the cost of compliance, or slow the development or adoption of beneficial innovations, policymakers should consider how those responses could be adjusted to lower costs and barriers to innovation without adversely impacting safety or market fairness."

In 2014 Stanford University commenced a "long-term investigation of the field of AI and its influences on people, their communities, and society" (Stanford University, 2016). In the Executive Summary of the report from the 2015 study panel, they conclude that

> "Faced with the profound changes that AI technologies can produce, pressure for "more" and "tougher" regulation is probably inevitable. Misunderstandings about what AI is and is not could fuel opposition to technologies with the potential to benefit everyone. Inappropriate regulatory activity would be a tragic mistake. Poorly informed regulation that stifles innovation, or relocates it to other jurisdictions, would be counterproductive."

These preliminary assertions of light touch regulation are of concern, despite their qualification, because at present we have little systematic understanding of the wider psychological and societal impact of widespread deployment of autonomous intelligent systems, especially robots. AI has become an extremely powerful technology and should be considered alongside similarly powerful technologies such as nuclear fission, pharmaceuticals and bioengineering, all of which have specific regulation beyond the application areas in which they are deployed.

In stark contrast, in 2015, the UK government sponsored a report by Innovate UK taking a very different view of regulation (Innovate UK, 2015). This report rightly recognises that

> "Robotics and autonomous systems do not work in isolation. They will require testing, regulation, standards, innovation, investment and skills together with technical progress and strong collaborative partnerships in order to fully realise the opportunity."

Further, they identify regulation as a key enabler for economic exploitation, saying *"Regulation and standards will be the key that opens the UK market"*. In December 2017, the UK All Party Parliamentary Group on AI (APPG AI) published its interim findings, based on a year of evidence meetings (All-Party Parliamentary Group on Artificial Intelligence, 2017). Its key recommendation is to appoint a Minister for AI in the Cabinet Office with a role based on the economic, social and ethical implications of six policy areas: data, infrastructure, skills, innovation and entrepreneurship, trade and accountability. Within accountability, APPG AI identified a number of 'calls for action', including the establishment of organisational standards to document decision-making processes and models during design and implementation phases of AI, together with auditing mechanisms to serve as "a watchdog to secure safe, ethical and ground-breaking innovation". They also call for incentives for corporate organisations to establish 'Ethics Boards' to help improve the transparency of innovation, and to "make organisations accountable for the decisions made by the algorithms that they use". Whilst we might argue that existing laws and regulations already hold organisations to account for their actions, this report makes plain that members of Parliament believe that a strengthening of legislation may be required in response to the new opportunities afforded by AI technologies.

In 2016, The European Parliament Committee on Legal Affairs produced draft recommendations calling on the EU Commission to propose a common European definition of smart autonomous robots (Committee on Legal Affairs, 2016). It also recommends that the Commission

"… considers that a guiding ethical framework for the design, production and use of robots is needed to complement the legal recommendations of the report and the existing national and Union acquis; proposes, in the annex to the resolution, a framework in the form of a charter consisting of a code of conduct for robotics engineers, of a code for research ethics committees when reviewing robotics protocols and of model licences for designers and users."

This ethical framework should be

"… based on the principles of beneficence, non-maleficence and autonomy, as well as on the principles enshrined in the EU Charter of Fundamental Rights, such as human dignity and human rights, equality, justice and equity, non-discrimination and non-stigmatisation, autonomy and individual responsibility, informed consent, privacy and social responsibility, and on existing ethical practices and codes."

So, we see a wide variation in current public policy relating to AI and autonomous robotics. One explanation for this variation is a lack of empirical evidence relating to the psychological and societal impact of deployment of autonomous intelligent systems. There is an urgent need to generate scientific theory and data on which well-reasoned policy can be constructed. We need to understand the impact of real robots in society, not hypothesise based on cultural stereotypes or the potentially biased views of those with specific economic and commercial objectives.

1.3   Robots and transparency

In order to minimise the risks associated with autonomous robots, there have been recent attempts to construct rules or principles for robot designers, owners and operators. In September 2010, experts drawn from the worlds of technology, industry, the arts, law and social sciences met at the joint Engineering and Physical Sciences Research Council (EPSRC) and Arts and Humanities Research Council Robotics Retreat to discuss robotics, its applications in the real world and the huge promise it offers to benefit society. The EPSRC's Principles of Robotics (EPoRs) are the result of this meeting (Boden *et al.*, 2011). They are not intended as hard-and-fast laws, but rather 'soft-law' to guide professional practitioners and standards bodies. The five principles are repeated here for ease of reference:

1. Robots are multi-use tools. Robots should not be designed solely or primarily to kill or harm humans, except in the interests of national security.

2. Humans, not robots, are responsible agents. Robots should be designed and operated as far as is practicable to comply with existing laws and fundamental rights and freedoms, including privacy.
3. Robots are products. They should be designed using processes that assure their safety and security.
4. Robots are manufactured artefacts. They should not be designed in a deceptive way to exploit vulnerable users; instead their machine nature should be transparent.
5. The person with legal responsibility for a robot should be attributed.

In this book my focus is on Principle Four, where robot transparency is identified as an important and desirable characteristic of an autonomous robotic system. *Transparency* may be defined as the extent to which the internal state and decision-making processes of a robot are accessible to the user (Wortham and Theodorou, 2017).

More broadly we might think of transparency as a means to avoid deception, a mechanism to report reliability and unexpected behaviour, and a way to expose decision making (Theodorou, Wortham and Bryson, 2017). Our interest is in the potential of transparency to mitigate the risks of unhelpful anthropomorphism, misunderstanding and moral confusion concerning autonomous robots, particularly for vulnerable users. There has been considerable previous research to investigate ways in which robots can understand humans (Lee and Makatchev, 2009). However, transparency is the converse. Here we are interested in how robots should be designed in order that we can understand them. Given the likely future ubiquity of various types of robots in society, we are particularly interested in scenarios where we encounter a robot with no prior training or particular skills in robotics, i.e. we are *naive* with regard to robots in general, or a specific robot in particular.

This broad idea of transparency has already become a popular policy point whenever societal concerns relating to AI are discussed. Indeed, the UNI Global Union – a global trades union with over 20 million members – 'demand that AI systems must be transparent' (UNI Global Union, 2017). Their report identifies ten principles for ethical AI, with transparency at the top of the list, taking their lead from the EPoR. They identify several areas where transparency should be considered, linking it to the establishment of trust and understanding of a system, and also prioritising transparency as a pre-requite to ascertain whether the other principles they define are observed.

Transparency is mentioned as an important system characteristic in many other recent AI 'principles' and 'ethical guideline' formulations. The most notable and widely referenced of these are listed below for further reading. However, as has been recently noted, there is a 'gold-rush' to create these kinds of documents, and so this list should only be considered as illustrative of the wide range of discussions and publications that make reference to transparency.

1. Association for Computing Machinery US Public Policy Council (USACM) – Statement on Algorithmic Transparency and Accountability (ACM US Public Policy Council, 2017)

2. British Standards Institute – Robots and Robotic Devices: Guide to the Ethical Design and Application of Robots and Robotic Systems (BSI, 2016)
3. Centre de Recherche en Éthique, Université de Montréal – Montréal Declaration on Responsible AI (Centre de Recherche en Éthique, 2017)
4. Future of Life – AI Principles (Asilomar Conference, 2017)
5. IEEE – Ethically Aligned Design – Version 2 (IEEE, 2017)

Wachter, Mittelstadt and Floridi (2017) provide a brief tour through the requirements for transparency, explainability and accountability. They identify three important areas that require further research:

1. How can human-interpretable systems be designed without sacrificing performance?
2. How can transparency and accountability be achieved in inscrutable systems?
3. How can parallels between emerging systems be identified to set accountability requirements?

Wachter, Mittelstadt and Floridi recognise that where AI systems use opaque machine-learning approaches, transparency must still be provided by some additional mechanism that assesses inputs and outputs in order to generate some narrative explanatory output.

Despite some recent criticism by Ananny and Crawford (2016), it is widely agreed that transparency reduces our reliance on bias, because a transparent system should provide more certain and complete information from which we can construct better (in the sense of more accurate) mental models. Additional information reduces our reliance on stereotypic models and anthropomorphic bias. Our research is based on the hypothesis that robot transparency leads to better mental models of robots. The assertion that transparency is desirable and indeed helpful in scenarios where humans encounter robots requires empirical examination if it is to have weight in the formulation of recommendations, principles, standards and ultimately regulations for the manufacture and operation of autonomous robotic systems. Further, it is important to measure the extent of the effect achieved by specific forms of transparency, as an aid to robot designers.

There has been some subsequent general criticism of the Principles of Robotics (Szollosy, 2017), and specifically of Principle Four (Collins, 2017); however, the commentary accompanying Principle Four makes it clear that the authors carefully considered the counter arguments against transparency, but nevertheless, decided that the moral obligation for transparency is paramount:

"One of the great promises of robotics is that robot toys may give pleasure, comfort and even a form of companionship to people who are not able to care for pets, whether due to rules of their homes, physical capacity, time or money. However, once a user becomes attached to such a toy, it would be possible for manufacturers to claim the robot has needs or desires that could unfairly cost the owners or their families more money. The legal version of this rule was designed to say that although it is permissible and even sometimes desirable for a robot to sometimes give the impression of real intelligence, anyone who owns or interacts with a robot should be able to find out what it really is and perhaps what it was really manufactured to do. Robot intelligence is artificial, and we thought that the best way to protect consumers was to remind them of that by guaranteeing a way for them to "lift the curtain" (to use the metaphor from The Wizard of Oz).

This was the most difficult law to express clearly and we spent a great deal of time debating the phrasing used. Achieving it in practice will need still more thought."

1.4   Thesis

This book documents my practical investigations into some aspects of robot transparency, particularly within the context of unplanned naive robot encounters. In this context, 'robot transparency' means the extent to which a naive observer is able to form an accurate model of a robot's capabilities, intentions and purpose. This work has

1. established an empirical basis for some of the ethical concerns outlined in the previous sections,
2. established whether there is a moral requirement for us to build transparent robots,
3. provided a basis for the future study of robot anthropomorphism,
4. investigated the claim that transparency impacts the emotional response towards a robot and alters the perception of robot intelligence, making transparency inappropriate for children's toys and robot companions.

The remainder of this chapter outlines the structure of this book and also acknowledges the significant and valuable work of others involved in the research effort on which this book is based.

1.5   Structure of this book

In this section, I outline the content of each of the following chapters, and reference-related publications. If you are short on time, then these outlines will serve as a useful summary of the remainder of the book. Having read them, please do jump to Conclusions (Chapter 8), which is also quite a short read. The experimental chapters very much follow one to the next. However, if your primary interest is in audio approaches to robot transparency or the affect of physical appearance on the efficacy of transparency measures, then go ahead and skip to the relevant chapter.

1.5.1   Chapter 2: Transparency in the wider context of trust

In this chapter, I explore the nature and various meanings of trust, responsibility and accountability. First I consider the various behaviours that we recognise as 'trusting'. Trust has several facets, sometimes we trust because we have good reason to do so, and sometimes we resort to trust in the absence of information. We are predisposed to trust, simply because it is a good evolutionary strategy for success. Whatever trust is as a psychological mechanism, ultimately we can evaluate trust through resultant behaviour. We may distrust a system based on evidence or bias, and similarly we may mistrust a system on the same bases. I offer a simple model to visualise how trust arises from information received, combined with learned and innate biases.

Human culture has complex social and legal mechanisms which act to support trust and reinforce trustworthy behaviours. Accountability, responsibility and transparency are closely associated with our ideas of trust, and I explore how these mechanisms operate. I also discuss and offer a model for how transparency supports accountability, promotes responsibility and facilitates trust.

1.5.2   Chapter 3: A transparent robot control architecture

This chapter is based on the following three published papers:

1.   'Instinct: A Biologically Inspired Reactive Planner for Embedded Systems' (Wortham, Gaudl and Bryson, 2019)
2.   'A Role for Action Selection in Consciousness: An Investigation of a Second-Order Darwinian Mind' (Wortham and Bryson, 2016)
3.   'Improving Robot Transparency: An Investigation With Mobile Augmented Reality' (Rotsidis *et al.*, 2019)

In this chapter, I document the design and engineering work involved to build the *R5 Robot* used in subsequent transparency experiments described in Chapters 2–5. This work includes the design of the R5 robot, together with the design of the Instinct reactive planner. The *Instinct Planner* is a new biologically inspired reactive planner, based on an established behaviour-based robotics methodology, behaviour-oriented design (BOD), and the parallel ordered slipstack hierarchy (POSH) – its reactive planner component (Bryson, 2001; Wortham, Gaudl and Bryson, 2016). Instinct includes several significant enhancements that facilitate plan design and runtime debugging, including a *Transparency Feed* that provides a configurable, detailed, real-time trace of plan execution. The Instinct Planner is specifically designed for low power processors and has a tiny memory footprint, making it suitable for deployment in low power micro-controller-based robot designs. In addition, I describe a new tool to author reactive plans graphically, the *Instinct Visual Design Language (iVDL)*.

In this chapter, I also describe a simulation environment used to test the functionality and performance of the Instinct Planner and to investigate a more sophisticated reactive control architecture. The *Instinct Robot World* simulates many robots moving within a grid-based world. Each robot is equipped with two Instinct Planners, to create a *Second-Order Darwinian Mind*. I describe an experiment to show that this mind is able to adapt its control of the robot based on a higher order objective, demonstrating that learning is possible within a fully transparent non-symbolic cognitive architecture.

1.5.3   Chapter 4: The impact of transparency using real-time displays

This chapter is based on the published paper 'Improving robot transparency: real-time visualisation of robot AI substantially improves understanding in naive observers' (Wortham, Theodorou and Bryson, 2017). Deciphering the behaviour of intelligent others is a fundamental characteristic of our own intelligence. As we interact with complex intelligent artefacts, humans inevitably construct mental models to understand and predict their behaviour. If these models are incorrect or inadequate, we run the risk of self-deception or even harm. In this chapter, I investigate the use of a real-time transparency display with the R5 robot. I demonstrate that providing even a simple, abstracted real-time visualisation of a robot's AI can radically improve the transparency of machine cognition. Findings from both an online experiment using a video recording of a robot and a direct observation of a robot show substantial improvements in observers' understanding of the robot's behaviour.

1.5.4   Chapter 5: Transparency using audio – the muttering robot

This chapter is based on the paper 'The muttering robot: improving robot transparency though vocalisation of reactive plan execution' (Wortham and Rogers, 2017). In this chapter, I investigate vocalisation of behaviour selection as a possible alternative solution for situations where a visual display of decision-making is either impractical or impossible. I show that the addition of vocalisation is associated with a significant improvement in understanding of a directly observed robot, comparable with the results obtained using a real-time display. This chapter also includes the development of a model to quantify participant emotional response to a robot, and the experiment also shows that vocalisation has no significant effect on participants' emotional response, though it slightly increases positive feelings about the robot. I discuss the relative merits of visual and vocalised transparency mechanisms and suggest possible applications.

1.5.5   Chapter 6: The effects of appearance on transparency

In this chapter, I use Amazon Mechanical Turk to conduct an online experiment with the R5 robot. This study further supports the previous findings of Chapters 4 and 5 and also investigates how altering the appearance of a robot impacts observers' mental models, both with and without visual and vocalised transparency measures.

The R5 robot is embellished with a simple bee-like cover to create a more zoomorphic form, which we present as *'Buddy the Robot'*. I create eight robot encounter videos, encompassing all combinations of visual and vocal transparency, with both the mechanomorphic R5 robot and the zoomorphic Buddy robot. This experiment confirms that naive participants indeed form significantly better models of a robot when accompanied by either a visual, or a vocalised representation of the internal state and processing of the robot. I show that the zoomorphic form without additional transparency results in significantly more accurate models and claim this is due to the increased likeability of the zoomorphic form, leading to increased participant attention and therefore improved perception of the machine agency. However, in the presence of additional transparency measures, morphology has a much reduced effect on mental model accuracy. I also observe that a *'talking'* robot greatly increases the confidence of naive observers to report that they understand a robot's behaviour seen on video, irrespective of their actual mental model accuracy. The trivial embellishment of a robot to alter its form has significant effects on our understanding and attitude towards it.

In all the studies of Chapters 3–5, I find an upper bound to the improvement in mental model accuracy that can be achieved through our particular real-time transparency techniques. I assert that the remaining gap may be closed through other transparency means, for example written or diagrammatic documentation.

1.5.6 Chapter 7: Synthesis and further work

In this chapter, I commence with a clarification of terms, such as *AI*, and then define *robot ethics*, with a subsequent discussion of its purpose and contemporary relevance to society. I argue that contrary to popular received wisdom, science has a great deal to contribute to moral argument, and that scientists are indeed equipped to make certain moral assertions. I go on to argue that we have a moral responsibility to make robots transparent, so as to reveal their true machine nature, and I recommend the inclusion of transparency as a fundamental design consideration for intelligent systems, particularly for autonomous robots. Finally, I conclude this chapter with suggestions for further work.

1.5.7 Chapter 8: Conclusions

This chapter reiterates the purpose of the research programme and summarises the main conclusions drawn from Chapters 2 to 7.

1.6 Contributions

First, I would of course like to acknowledge my supervisor, Dr Joanna Bryson, for her many helpful suggestions and guidance throughout my doctoral studies. Much of my work on reactive planning is based on her original deep insights into biological action selection, culminating in the POSH planner on which the Instinct Planner is based. I would also like to acknowledge the valuable contribution made by my colleague Dr Andreas Theodorou to the research programme. I remember long discussions where Andreas, together with Joanna and myself, discussed the potential merit of using various kinds of real-time transparency display. The resulting ABOD3 software was coded solely by Andreas, although much of the design inherits from extensive previous work with BOD, POSH and ABODE carried out by Dr Bryson and her earlier collaborators. Andreas also integrated the Instinct Server into his code to enable us to use ABOD3 with the real-time transparency feed from the Instinct Planner. In 2018, Alex Rotsidis further enhanced the Instinct Server to work with his mobile augmented reality display. Andreas assisted during the Muttering Robot experiment described in Chapter 5, helping with the gathering of questionnaires over 3 days at the At-Bristol Science Centre. Finally, Andreas reviewed and contributed ideas to the drafts of papers related to the work described in Chapter 4.

I would also like to thank Dr Swen Gaudl, who spent considerable time helping me to understand Bryson's POSH reactive planning paradigm and also advised me on style and presentation for our Instinct Planner paper related to the work described in Chapter 3 (Wortham, Gaudl and Bryson, 2016). Dr Vivienne Rogers also assisted during the data collection for the Muttering Robot Experiment and took the lead on the grant application that helped to fund expenses during that work. She also reviewed the resulting paper, validating the data analysis.

The code for the R5 robot, the Instinct Planner and associated iVDL, and the Instinct Robot World was developed solely by myself. In the experimental studies of Chapters 3–5, I designed and lead the experiments, and performed the necessary data analysis. In the following chapter, I consider transparency within the wider context of trust, accountability and responsibility.

Chapter 2
Transparency in the wider context of trust

"The trust of the innocent is the liar's most useful tool."
– Stephen King, *Needful Things, p. 507*, 2016

"Responsibility, I believe, accrues through privilege."
– Noam Chomsky, *"Question time" by Tim Adams,*
www.theguardian.com, November 2003

2.1 Summary

In this chapter, I explore the nature and various meanings of trust, responsibility and accountability. Trust has several facets; sometimes we trust because we have good reason to do so, and sometimes we resort to trust in the absence of information. We are predisposed to trust, simply because it is a good evolutionary strategy for success. There has recently been some suggestion that we might remove the need for trust using technologies such as blockchain. However, we must still trust the blockchain technology and others who use it with us. Whatever trust is as a psychological mechanism, ultimately we can evaluate trust through resultant behaviour. Indeed to express trust vocally is no more than a kind of trusting behaviour. We may distrust a system based on evidence or bias, and similarly we may mistrust a system on the same bases. Human culture has complex social and legal mechanisms which act to support trust and reinforce trustworthy behaviours. The terms accountability, responsibility and transparency are closely associated with our ideas of trust, and I explore these mechanisms in the following sections. I also discuss the ways in which transparency supports accountability, promotes responsibility and facilitates trust.

2.2 The meanings of trust

In discussions concerning the nature, causes and effects of trust, we often find confusion. In relation to humans trusting artificial intelligence (AI), trust is often vaguely expressed as arising with some combination of accountability, responsibility and transparency, see Figure 2.1. However, trust is what Marvin Minsky would have called a *'suitcase word'* (Minsky, 2007). Trust has subtly different meanings in differing

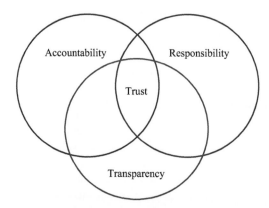

Figure 2.1 Trust is typically understood as a phenomena that arises with some combination of accountability, responsibility and transparency, though the relationship is seldom defined.

contexts, and each person uses trust to mean a differing collection of concepts with differing emphases.

It is generally not helpful to define suitcase words precisely and reductively, and then go on to formulate an entire discussion based around this sterile definition. Such a discussion may then be useful for narrow technical purposes, but it offers little to those who have broader, more diffuse conceptualisations of the term. This may be likened to the problems of modelling complex phenomena with trivial models. Based on the model, one may find simple analytical solutions, but these solutions cannot usefully be brought to bear on the understanding (or perhaps manipulation) of the actual phenomena. The model itself already reduces out all the complexity that make the actual phenomena hard to understand – more of this in Section 6.3 where we consider robot appearance and anthropomorphism.

Some of this confusion with trust might however be usefully addressed by considering two important facets of trust:

1. *Informed* trust – trust as a rational behaviour in response to information gain.
2. *Uninformed* trust – trust as an evolved mechanism to deal with lack of information.

From this perspective, we see that trust involves several complex mechanisms. The rational mind requires specific context related information (evidence) in order to trust, whilst the innate behaviour of evolved minds is to determine trust on quite a different basis. I investigate these ideas further in the following sections.

2.2.1 Informed trust

As we gain more useful information regarding a system, say a robot, our mind model of that system becomes more useful. We may learn about the purpose of a robot intended by the designer, the sensing capabilities of the robot, its range of functions and possibly its ability to learn by example. We may observe, or otherwise experience, the robot performing tasks with some level of repeatability and success. We might also find out about its limitations, and therefore what it cannot do, or cannot do well. All this information allows us to better predict the behaviour of the robot in future scenarios – we are better equipped to use, or otherwise engage with, the robot appropriately. This may engender us to continue to voluntarily interact with the robot. We make appropriate use of it, perhaps rely on it in some way to achieve tasks that are important, we recommend it to others, and we may *say that we trust it*. In this context, the word trust really means all these things taken together, including our *heterophenomenological* assertion that we trust it – we inspect our feelings towards the robot and report that we trust it. Whilst there are certainly emotional, dispositional and instinctive factors at play, we would concede that we have come to this position of trust as a result of a rational evaluation of information that we now possess about the robot and the context in which it operates. Such a trust is therefore informed. Uninformed trust arises very differently.

2.2.2   Uninformed trust

A very different form of trust arises in religious, tribal or hierarchical group contexts. In these contexts, we may trust because 'trusting' is an important in-group behaviour. It demonstrates to others, and to ourselves, that we are part of the in-group. We trust to show allegiance to the group, receiving our in-group reward for trusting; acceptance and status (Tajfel, 1970). We may also trust those with whom we share the folk psychology construct of 'common ground', see Stubbs, Hinds and Wettergreen (2007). Trust of this sort is a result of our biological and cultural evolution, and if so it must be adaptive, i.e. it must confer some useful benefit in populations that practise it. We may also choose to trust even when we have good reason not to do so. We are prone to *self-deception*, a related social phenomenon recently modelled as a complex adaptive strategy (Rauwolf, 2016).

It is also worth pointing out early on in this book that evolutionary arguments are very valuable in understanding why something operates as it does but give us little insight into how they operate. I make considerable use of inspiration from the natural world in my research, but we must remember that if evolutionary arguments explained *how* intelligence, trust or many other phenomena arise from the substrate that hosts them – the brain – then they would be of much more benefit to practical engineering problems. I am always grateful to my colleagues in Psychology for taking time to point this out! If anything, perhaps this dichotomy between the proximal and ultimate explanations for behaviour lies at the root of my research interests.

It is beyond the scope of this book to discuss this form of trust in any detail, other than to point out that trusting behaviours can emanate from very different origins, and we need to ascertain the basis for the report of trust, or the observation of trusting behaviour.

2.2.3   Naive trust

There is another variety of this more complex uninformed trusting, one that operates specifically in the absence of useful information to facilitate decision-making. In the absence of any useful information, we are predisposed to trust naively. Game theory shows us that in long running non-zero-sum games (such as living in the world), a tit-for-tat strategy is overall most adaptive for the population – though of course not necessarily most profitable for any specific individual (Axelrod and Hamilton, 1981). Put very simply, we trust until we have reason not to trust. In some sense we employ this kind of trust in the absence of useful information. The need for this kind of trust diminishes as our access to information about a system increases – perhaps as a result of some form of transparency (Wortham and Theodorou, 2017). This kind of trust may be adaptive for a species in the evolutionary sense, but it is not the kind of useful, informed trust that we need when humans interact with complex human-made systems.

2.2.4   *So-called trustless systems*

Recently, there has been some development of ideas around the idea of *trustless* systems, particularly in the financial sector, and specifically relating to currencies. The idea is that these systems can be used confidently without the need to trust any specific individual, corporation, government or regulating body. Technical solutions such as blockchain remove the need for trustworthy actors to enable a system to operate fairly, and are thus known as trustless (Morris, 2019). In fact, trust *is* placed in the reliability of the technologies to reliably capture, record and preserve authentic transactions, and to repudiate inauthentic transactions. For digital currencies such as bitcoin, trust is also placed in 'the market' to provide currency liquidity and the possibility of exchange for goods and services. Certainly, these systems do not operate in the absence of considerable levels of trust.

2.2.5   *Trust as behaviour*

Whether rational, uninformed or deliberately naive, trust ultimately boils down to *behaviour*, where that behaviour may include a *vocal act* of reporting that we trust something or someone. Interestingly, some reductive physicalist philosophers together with behaviourist ethologists and anthropologists argue that mental states, such as trusting, can be ontologically reduced to future behaviours (Ryle, 1949; Skinner, 1973). To say that we trust in really no more than to say that we will behave in a certain way given an appropriate context and set of circumstances. Whether mental states exist or not, in the practical business of Engineering, we are primarily interested in resultant behaviour.

2.2.6   *Distrust and mistrust defined*

If we come to a position where we do not trust a system, then we are said to *distrust* it. Our reasons may be valid or invalid, but our state is one of distrust. Most typically we will not use a system that we distrust, and we will not interact with a person or organisation that we distrust. For systems, distrust generally results in *disuse*.

We may decide to trust a system without good reason and possibly counter to evidence that we should not trust it. In this case, we *mistrust* the system. Our basis for trust is not well founded, and our trust may be repaid with some kind of harm or lack of assumed benefit from trusting. Mistrust of a system can result in its *misuse*, i.e. use of a system for a purpose for which it was not designed, or for which a poor outcome will result.

2.3   A model for trust

Figure 2.2 shows a graphical representation of a simple model that is useful for our purposes in understanding trust to some degree. In the previous sections, I introduced the idea that trust is the result of many 'input factors'. For a robot, these factors are diverse and may include the following:

1.   Our previous knowledge of the robot.
2.   Training received.
3.   The transparency of operation provided by the autonomous robot.
4.   The appearance of the system – see Chapter 6.
5.   Our previous knowledge of the relevant work of the designer/programmer.
6.   Our personal expertise in robotics.
7.   Our personal expertise in the task(s) or interactions to be achieved by the robot – the application.
8.   The reputation of the designer/programmer.

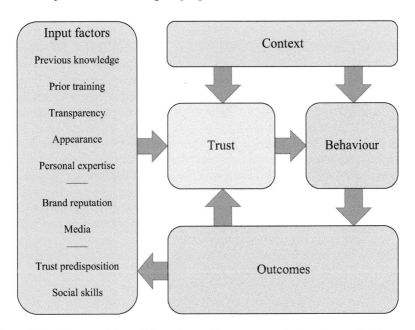

Figure 2.2   Trust model: a wide variety of factors contribute to trust. Within a specific context, our level of trust determines our resulting behaviours, and this drives outcomes which update our mind model. For further explanation, see Section 2.3.

9. The brand reputation of the product(s) included in the robotic system, or of the robot.
10. Our previous exposure to media relating to robots – movies, sci-fi writing, documentaries and so on.
11. Our predisposition towards the use of sophisticated technology.
12. Our background level of anxiety, particularly in novel situations.
13. Our social intelligence – interaction with an intelligent system is a social activity of a sort.
14. Our predisposition to trust – i.e. the basic bias level of trust in the absence of other factors.

I have tried to place these roughly in order, starting at the top with those direct, immediate and personal sources of information that we might use to inform our mind model of the robot, moving down towards those information sources and predispositions which might be less reliable or applicable to a particular robot and a particular application within a specific context. We can immediately see that for naive encounters, where we may have little information in categories 1–8, there may be a tendency to base our trust on unreliable sources of information such as science fiction and brand reputation, together with our individual naive biases.

Trust drives behaviours that result in real-world outcomes. These outcomes in turn modify our trust, either reinforcing or reversing our initial evaluations. For example, if our initial choice is to distrust a robot; we will avoid using it, and will likely create a narrative to justify our decision. We will gain no further information regarding its efficacy, and the creation of our narrative arguments will normally result in us strengthening and defending our state of distrust. Conversely, if we choose to trust a robot; find it to be useful and without significant disadvantage, we will strengthen our trust in the robot and continue to use it. In the case where we mistrust a robot, we may experience subsequent inconveniences or harms, and of course we are likely to then reverse our view in the light of contrary evidence. All this takes place within a context that impacts not only the relative weights placed on the input factors, but also on the choice of resultant behaviours. Whether in fact we operate with free will when making our choices is a matter for debate, but I concede that it feels like we have free will when we exercise trust, and this model assumes this compatibilist approach as a useful perspective (Dennett, 2015).

Most striking from this model is how our trust in a system is only in part founded on relevant evidence, and owes a lot to individual predisposition and cultural variation, combined with misinformation and disinformation from external sources. Perhaps trust is not to be trusted. This brings us nicely to the two, closely related, constructs that our human social evolution has produced to solve the problem of trust; Accountability and Responsibility.

2.4 Accountability

The idea of *accountability* has two components; the requirement to *give* an account, and the requirement to *maintain* an account giving relationship. Typically an accountable person must gather, organise and maintain sufficient information over time to be able to give an account when required. Additionally, an accountable individual has an obligation to inform others as notable important information arises. This information may relate to particular events, salient facts and to some degree consequential implications. We see therefore that to be accountable one must have not only competence in dealing with information at hand, but also of understanding the relevance and implications of this information more widely – for a longer discussion of the importance of relevance see Section 7.7. The importance of this wider understanding to accountability may perhaps be illustrated by considering the role of a financial accountant. An electronic accounting system may record financial transactions and offer reports of all kinds, but it is the human accountant that must give account for the accounts, and for the implications raised by the figures themselves. A person who does not take on these responsibilities may be a competent bookkeeper, but they are not an accountant. In order to be accountable therefore, one must have the necessary knowledge, skills, training and expertise in the domain in which they are charged to operate accountably.

We might envisage that, rather like the bookkeeper in our example above, an autonomous intelligent system (AIS), such as a robot, may be able to report on the information it has gathered, possibly with some rudimentary understanding of the relationships between the data, such as the specific sensor data that caused a certain action to be chosen by the robot's action selection subsystem. However, this level of reporting cannot be said to be giving an account for the behaviour of the system, and even less could we say that the robot is accountable for its actions. To accept accountability inevitably requires an acceptance that one must give an account to others through *meaningful dialogue*. So, we see that accountability is fundamentally relational in nature (Coeckelbergh, 2019).

Within organisations of all kinds, accountability similarly involves the maintaining of records combined with ongoing oversight and event-driven intervention. Suitably equipped persons with appropriate levels of access and authority maintain dialogues with others in the organisation such that they can provide well-evidenced explanations and justifications for the behaviour of the organisation. They are able to 'give an account' for the behaviour of the organisation, and to some extent the consequences of those behaviours. Responsibility is closely linked with accountability, but the two are far from the same.

2.5 Responsibility

"Responsible Artificial Intelligence is about human responsibility for the development of intelligent systems along fundamental human principles and values, to ensure human flourishing and wellbeing in a sustainable world" (Dignum, 2018). Responsibility is another suitcase word. We all think we know what is meant when we say that someone (or some institution or organisation) should act responsibly, but what does this really mean in practice, in relation to autonomous AI systems? First, we need to differentiate responsibility from accountability. To be *held responsible* does not require that we act from a position of full knowledge but primarily has to do with liability. Similarly, to *act responsibly* involves behaving in accordance with fundamental human principles and values, in order to seek outcomes that avoid negative consequences for individuals specifically, or for society more widely. It is worth noting that whilst the observance of the Law is necessary for responsible behaviour, it is not sufficient.

A properly responsible person is therefore one who behaves according to societal rules and norms, obeying the rules associated with professional conduct. However, as Derrida points out, if a person is obeying rules and norms, they are merely behaving as interpreters and conduits for those rules and cannot therefore be said to be truly responsible for their actions. Individual responsibility diminishes as a person increasingly relies on rules and norms to guide their behaviour (Morgan Wortham, 2010). Responsibility is indeed an elusive social construct.

In Law, responsibility relates to an obligation to accept liability and to redress losses, either through the provision of compensation to those who have suffered loss, or to submit to some penalty or punishment. Our evolution has developed a deep sense of *justice*, such that punishment acts as a proxy for compensation. When a responsible person is punished for wrongdoing, those who have been wronged feel a real sense of redress, a sense that 'justice has been served'. This occurs despite the obvious fact that no actual compensation has been received (Haidt, Graham and Joseph, 2009). The appropriate punishment of a responsible individual marks some closure to the wrongdoing, and the psychological distress of not receiving redress through punishment of the guilty is well documented. We have a psychological need for retribution (Carlsmith, 2006). These mechanisms are deeply embedded in our psyche, our human morality and our legal and ethical systems. They act to reinforce norms of acceptable behaviour and inhibit the freeriding that would otherwise destabilise our social systems.

Within an organisation, an accountable person may often also be held solely, or jointly with others, responsible in the legal sense. However, the converse does not apply. A person holding a position of responsibility yet unable to give account may nevertheless still be held responsible. Indeed, their failure to give proper account may be a contributory factor in their guilt. In addition, organisational, or institutional, responsibility in the legal sense persists over time, even across changes to the responsible officers (post-holders) within that organisation. For example, in 2019 the May Government in the United Kingdom apologised to and began to compensate the Windrush Generation for poor behaviour carried out by a UK government over 50 years earlier (Wardle and Obermuller, 2018; UK Government Home Office, 2019). Similarly, also in 2019, British American Tobacco (BAT) were successfully sued by Canadian smokers claiming that the cigarette firm did not warn them of the risks associated with smoking in the 1950s (Curtis, 2019). None of those currently running BAT can be held accountable for the damage caused by their company over 50 years ago, but nevertheless they are legally responsible to ensure that the smokers are compensated. Could those affected negatively by social media in 2019 perhaps in years to come have cause to seek financial redress from the social media platform providers? Only time will tell.

Responsibility also has a forward-looking dimension. Much like accountability, responsibility demands that we look forward to the consequences of our actions and seek to maximise good outcomes whilst minimising poor outcomes. Failure to deploy forward-looking responsibility will result in us becoming adversely accountable for the unforeseen consequences of our actions.

In Section 7.8.2, I argue that one of the purposes of well-informed regulation is to promote a safe market where businesses can be more certain that if they adhere to regulations, then they will be less likely to be accused of malpractice or suffer legal action as a result of the consequences of their products and services. Operating in unregulated markets, in the absence of standards of best practice or product quality, is a risky undertaking indeed.

2.6 The role of transparency in informed trust

Having briefly considered trust, accountability and responsibility, we see that no autonomous system can seriously be held accountable, nor be responsible, for its own performance or the consequences of its actions:

1. To hold a machine accountable means that the machine alone must not only possess the competence to deal with specific enquiries relating to relevant information on the behaviour of the machine itself but must also understand the relevance and implications of this information. Such a level of machine sophistication is simply not possible now, nor can it be foreseen by those working in the relevant fields.
2. To ascribe responsibility to a machine – that is, to make it a moral agent – in effect produces a void from which there can be no legal or moral redress, and which will result in the circumvention of the social mechanisms that have arisen to regulate our societies. In addition, there is no current technology that could adequately produce anything like forward-looking responsibility based on the consequences of automated decision-making.

We have also seen that in the absence of significant personal experience or training, our trust in an autonomous intelligent system is based on our knowledge of the wider reputation of the individuals and/or companies that design and operate the systems, together with various biases originating from predisposition and cultural influences. This reputational value is therefore of key importance for the successful deployment of robots and similar systems as products. Once we begin to experience a robot, then the information we gain from these interactions will further modulate our trust. In both cases, transparency is important to engender informed trust, as I explain below.

2.6.1 Organisational transparency

Organisations such as commercial businesses have the opportunity to make available considerable information concerning the processes they use and the standards they follow when developing products and services. In addition they are able, and should be encouraged, to make clear their goals and strategies particularly with respect to the delegated goals and capabilities that they design into their products and services. For example, a company may produce a useful medical advice app, delivered to consumers by means of a smartphone. The company may sell the app and/or may charge an ongoing service charge for its use. However, in addition, it may be aggregating data from many users with a view to achieving further revenues from the sale of this data to interested parties. These may include businesses with activities in insurance, pharmaceuticals or health care. Further parties such as government departments and even political think-tanks may also be interested in either the raw data, or aggregated statistics. This kind of data gathering and onward resale is already regulated in Europe by the General Data Protection Regulations (GDPR) (Otto, 2018). However, GDPR does not specify whether or how companies should make transparent their internal processes during product conception, design and development in order to make clear how they comply with GDPR and other regulations (Wachter, Mittelstadt and Floridi, 2017). Process transparency increases an organisation's ability to give account for its activities, and therefore to be held to account. It allows the business to exercise forward-looking responsibility, therefore reducing the likelihood of poor outcomes. By making its processes transparent, a commercial organisation therefore promotes trust in its products and services.

Consider a robotics company that plans to launch a social robot as a consumer product. The robot acts as a platform for the further sale of 'apps' that enhance the capabilities of the robot, and the company envisages an 'app store' where third-party developers can participate, charging customers for the apps and paying some kind of hosting fee to the robotic platform provider. Further, the company may plan to make significant revenues from the resale of data gathered by the robot, much as in the example above. The product however is to be marketed as a 'new member of the family', a new 'playmate for your children', and is advertised showing 'her' (the robot) reading bedtime stories to a young child. In addition to the GDPR requirements of data gathering, organisational transparency would demand that the company consider making transparent the purpose of the product from the company's perspective, the manner in which they will derive revenues, and how they plan to safeguard users of the robot, particularly minors. Full disclosure of this information, together with stated commitments to follow standards relating to AI transparency, such as those from BSI and IEEE, will facilitate the kind of informed trust that will result in both the avoidance of harms and commercial success for the robotics business (BSI, 2016; IEEE, 2017).

Ideas along these lines are well documented but have yet to become formal standards or regulatory requirements (Bryson and Winfield, 2017; IEEE, 2017; Dignum, 2019). This kind of transparency of operation facilitates reputation-based trust.

2.6.2   System transparency

System transparency relates to the design of the system, and its subsequent ability to make transparent its internal state and processing as it executes. In addition, a transparent system should record this information, such that it is available to facilitate any kind of post-facto accident or incident investigation. Further, a transparent robot should make clear to the user any information it is storing, or passing on to an external or third-party system (Vitale *et al.*, 2018).

System transparency also relates to the tools, training and documentation that are supplied with the system. Together, these transparency measures should aid a user in forming a good understanding, or mental model, of a system – its purpose, goals, capabilities and limitations. This understanding of the system in the mind of the user may be thought of as a *mind model*. The word *model* here indicates that the user can compare the behaviour of the robot to their expectations of it and see that the two generally align. In addition, the mind model allows the user to predict, with reasonable accuracy, the behaviour of the robot. In general, the robot does not behave unexpectedly. Predictable behaviour engenders confidence, and this is further reinforced if the robot exhibits useful, competent behaviour.

Further confidence is generated if the robot correctly identifies when it has failed and provides some transparent explanation for the failure (Kim and Hinds, 2006; Lyons, 2013). For a longer discussion on the effect of system transparency on the accuracy of human mind models, and hence trust, see Section 4.2.

2.7 Transparency as a driver for trust

In this and subsequent chapters, I argue that although trust is complex, we can use system transparency to improve the quality of information available to users, which in turn helps one to build trust. Further, organisational transparency drives both accountability and responsibility, which also bolster trust. Therefore, transparency is an essential ingredient for informed trust. These relationships are illustrated in Figure 2.3.

System transparency helps users better understand systems as they observe, interact or are otherwise affected by them. This informed understanding of system behaviour in turn helps users make appropriate use of systems.

System transparency also supports accountability, by providing mechanisms that allow the system itself to offer some kind of 'account' for why it behaves as it does. It also provides mechanisms to facilitate traceability. Traceability provides important information for product designers, owners and operators, perhaps together with accident investigators, to give an informed account of system behaviour and its consequences.

Organisational transparency supports and encourages organisational accountability, and helps one to develop a culture of responsibility.

Trust is built from a combination of informed system understanding, together with the knowledge that system providers are accountable and behave responsibly. Trust ultimately drives greater product acceptance and use.

In this book, particularly in Chapter 7, I also argue for the creation of transparency standards applicable to AISs of all kinds. I further argue that these standards are used as the basis for regulation. Standards will encourage transparency, and regulation may

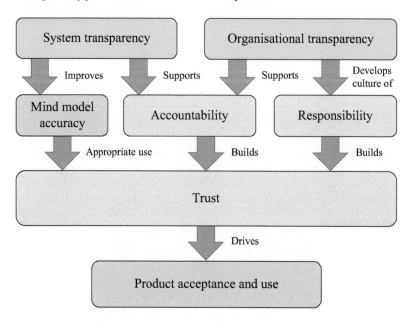

Figure 2.3   The role of transparency in building trust, leading to improved product acceptance and uptake.

enforce it. This encourages business to develop cultures that embrace transparency in their processes and products.

In the following chapter, I describe various technologies and tools that have been developed to implement system transparency for autonomous intelligent systems. These technologies are then deployed with a small mobile robot to test the effect of robot transparency in robot encounter scenarios with naive users.

Chapter 3
A transparent robot control architecture

"Ah, the architecture of this world. Amoebas may not have backbones, brains, automobiles, plastic, television, Valium or any other of the blessings of a technologically advanced civilization; but their architecture is two billion years ahead of its time."

– L.L. Larison Cudmore, *The Center of Life:*
A Natural History of the Cell (1977)

3.1 Summary

This chapter documents the design and engineering work involved in building the Instinct Planner and the R5 robot, prior to their use in subsequent robot transparency experiments, described in the following chapters. The chapter also describes an experiment to investigate how the Instinct Planner can be used to control robots within the Instinct Robot World simulation environment, and how two instances of the planner can be configured to create a mind capable of adapting the robots' behaviour to achieve a higher order goal. This chapter therefore describes engineering contributions that support our later experiments.

The Instinct Planner is a new biologically inspired reactive planner, based on an established behaviour-based robotics methodology and its reactive planner component – the parallel ordered slipstack hierarchy (POSH) planner implementation. It includes several significant enhancements that facilitate plan design and runtime debugging. It has been specifically designed for low-power processors and has a tiny memory footprint. Written in C++, it runs efficiently on both ARDUINO (ATMEL AVR) and MICROSOFT VISUAL C++ environments. The Instinct Planner has been deployed within the low-cost R5 robot to study AI Transparency and is also being used to implement robot action selection in a robot operating system (ROS)-based robot.

This chapter is entitled 'A *transparent* robot control architecture'. Let me explain what I mean, and do not mean, by this use of the word. Transparency is a term often used within computer programming in relation to object-oriented system design. Within an object-oriented system, the implementation of an object or class of objects is encapsulated within the object. The implementation details are accessible to the remainder of the system. Indeed, provided the programmatic interface to the object remains unchanged, the internal implementation can be altered without impact on the remainder of the system. The change is thus deemed 'transparent' to the remainder of the system. For the avoidance of doubt, this is **not** the sense it which I am using the term transparency throughout this book. I am using it in entirely the opposite sense. To make something transparent to a user means to reveal the system processing and state. Imagine a mechanism encapsulated and operating within a physical box of some kind. Transparency allows us to see inside the box, to examine the workings, develop a useful model in our mind about how the mechanism works and draw our own conclusions about its efficacy and limitations. However, having clarified transparency, before we delve into how we might program it, we need to first explore how to program a robot's decision-making. I review the relevant history of robot action selection in the next section.

3.2   Introduction

From the 1950s to the 1980s, the study of embodied artificial intelligence (AI) assumed a cognitive symbolic planning model for robotic systems – SMPA (Sense Model Plan Act) – the most well-known example of this being the Shakey robot project (Nilsson, 1984), shown in Figure 3.1. The Shakey robot used SMPA planning and took around 20 min to create an action plan. Whenever its world changed, Shakey required another 20 min or so to replan before it could continue its mission.

In the SMPA model, the world is first sensed and a model of the world is constructed within the AI. Based on this model and the objectives of the AI, a plan is constructed to achieve the goals of the robot. Only then does the robot act. Although this idea seemed logical and initially attractive, it was found to be quite inadequate for complex, real-world environments. Generally the world cannot be fully modelled until the robot plan is underway, since sensing the world requires moving through it. Also, where environments change faster than the rate at which the robot can complete its SMPA cycle, the planning simply cannot keep up. Brooks (1991a) provides a more comprehensive history, which is not repeated here.

In the 1980s, Rodney Brooks and others (Breazeal and Scassellati, 2002) introduced the then-radical idea that it was possible to have intelligence without representation (Brooks, 1991b). Brooks developed his subsumption architecture as a pattern for the design of intelligent embodied systems that have no internal representation of their environment, and minimal internal state. These autonomous agents could traverse difficult terrain on insect-like legs, appear to interact socially with humans through shared attention and gaze tracking, and in many ways appeared to possess behaviours similar to that observed in animals. Figure 3.2 shows one of Brooks' insect robots, controlled with the subsumption architecture.

However, the systems produced by Brooks and his colleagues could only respond immediately to stimuli from the world. They had no means of focusing attention on a specific goal or of executing complex sequences of actions to achieve more complex behaviours. The original restrictions imposed by Brooks' subsumption architecture were subsequently relaxed with later augmentations such as timers,

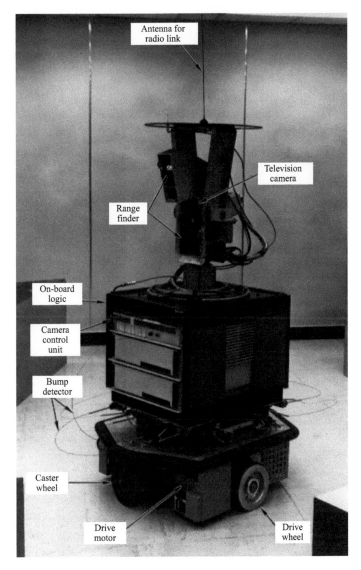

Figure 3.1   The Shakey robot, c. 1972. Shakey used SMPA planning, taking around 20 min to replan when its world changed. Reproduced with permission of SRI International. Accessed via Wikipedia, September 2019.

effectively beginning the transition to systems that used internal state in addition to sensory input in order to determine behaviour.

Biologically inspired approaches are still favoured by many academics, although a wide gap exists between existing implementations and the capabilities of the human mind (Samsonovich, 2013). Today, the argument persists concerning whether

*Figure 3.2   An insect robot developed by Rodney Brooks. Photograph taken by
Kenneth Lu at the MIT Museum, May 2009. Reproduced with
permission of Kenneth Lu under the Creative Commons licence.
Downloaded from Flickr, September 2019.*

symbolic, sub-symbolic or hybrid approaches are best suited for the creation of powerful cognitive systems (Lieto, Chella and Frixione, 2016). Here we concern ourselves more specifically with action selection as a core component of any useful cognitive architecture.

3.2.1   From ethology to robots

There has long been a close interest in the study of animals as machines, and this gave rise to the study of *cybernetics*. As early as 1948, Norbert Weiner defined cybernetics as "the scientific study of control and communication in the animal and the machine" (Weiner, 1948). Around the same time, William Grey Walter designed and built small autonomous robots that came to be known as 'Turtles'. These robots were capable of a very simple autonomous behaviour: *phototaxis* – they would move towards or away from a light source. By tuning the tendency to both move towards and away from the light stimulus, the Turtles would exhibit complex patterns of movement. These movement patterns implied intelligence to human observers, together with some indefinable sense that they were 'alive'. A replica of a Turtle robot was photographed recently by the author and is shown in Figure 3.3.

Following in-depth studies of animals such as gulls in their natural environment, ideas of how animals perform action selection were originally formulated by Niko Tinbergen and other previous ethologists (Tinbergen, 1951; Tinbergen and Falkus, 1970).

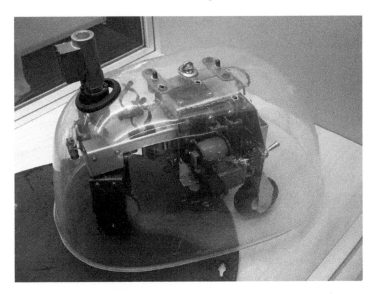

Figure 3.3   *A replica of a Turtle robot, originally developed by William Grey Walter in the late 1940s. The turtle robot exhibited phototaxis, giving rise to complex patterns of movement. Photograph taken by the author, Science Museum, July 2017.*

These ethologists noticed that observed behaviours can be decomposed hierarchically, with lower level patterns of simple actions reused across a number of higher level structures, see Figure 3.4. They also observed that the higher level structures each achieve one specific objective or goal. We might call these higher level structures *'drives'*. Typically an animal has at least four drives:

- Flee – from predators, or aggressors with whom it cannot fight successfully
- Fight – for social dominance, access to food, etc.
- Feed – including drinking
- Mate – for reproduction or dominance

Figure 3.5 shows a variety of animals displaying displacement activities. These are actions that occur when a conflict occurs between two drives, avoiding the possibility of dithering between two competing behaviour patterns. For example, when a stickleback is at the margin of its territory and meets a similar sized stickleback from the adjacent territory, both the fight and flee drives are activated. The fish might dither between these two behaviours but instead displays a head-down activity akin to bottom feeding, through no actual feeding takes place. This activity acts a useful signal to the other fish not to proceed further.

Tinbergen further noticed that drive activation relies on the presence of very specific stimuli. For each drive, he identified this stimulus as the *'innate releasing*

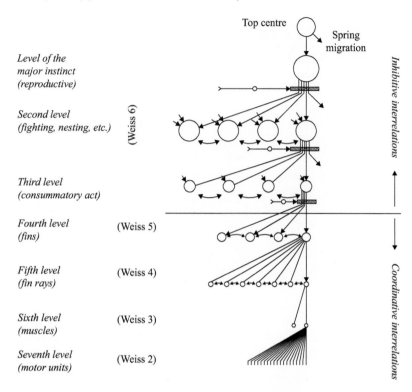

Figure 3.4   Tinbergen's hierarchical decomposition of behaviour. Reproduced under copyright by kind permission of Oxford Publishing Ltd.

mechanism', see Figure 3.6. For example, the mating drive is only released when a suitable mate is available and is otherwise inhibited.

The biologically inspired reactive planning paradigm is based on the idea that reactions to stimuli are based on predetermined drives and competences but depend also on the internal state of the organism (Bryson, 2000). Bryson (2001) harnessed these ideas to achieve a major step forward with the POSH reactive planner and the BOD (behaviour-oriented design) methodology, both of which are strongly biologically inspired. The Nomad 200 robot used by Bryson is shown in Figure 3.7.

It is important to understand the rationale behind biologically inspired reactive planning. It is based on the idea that biological organisms constantly sense the world, and generally react quickly to sensory input, based on a hierarchical set of behaviours structured as Drives, Competences and Action Patterns (APs). Their reactive plan uses a combination of sensory inputs and internal priorities to determine which plan elements to execute, ultimately resulting in the execution of leaf nodes in the plan, which in turn execute real world actions. For further reading see Gurney, Prescott and Redgrave (1998), Prescott, Bryson and Seth (2007) and Seth (2007).

1. Nesting movements in herring gull as an outlet of the fighting instinct. Moderate intensity. After Tinbergen, 1940.
2. Nesting movements in herring gulls as outlets of the fighting instinct. High intensity.
3. Sleeping attitude in European oystercatcher as an outlet of the fighting instinct.
4. Sleeping attitude in European avocet as an outlet of the fighting instinct. After Makkink, 1936.
5. Sand-digging in male three-spined stickleback as an outlet of the fighting instinct. After Tinbergen, 1947b.
6. Preening in sheldrake as an outlet of the sexual instinct. After Makkink, 1931.
7. Preening in the garganey as an outlet of the sexual instinct. After Lorenz, 1941.
8. Preening in the mandarin as an outlet of the sexual instinct. After Lorenz, 1941.
9. Preening in the mallard as an outlet of the sexual instinct. After Lorenz, 1941.
10. Preening in the European avocet as an outlet of the sexual instinct. After Makkink, 1936.
11. Food-catching movement in the European blue heron as an outlet of the sexual instinct. After Verwey, 1930.
12, 13, and 14. Sexual movements in the European cormorant as outlets of the fighting instinct. After Kortlandt, 1934b.
15. Food-begging movements in herring gull as outlets of the sexual instinct. After Tinbergen, 1940.
16. Food-pecking movements in domestic cocks as an outlet of the fighting instinct.

Figure 3.5   A Tinbergen animal sketch, 1951. When animals experience conflict between two drives, they avoid dithering through a displacement activity. Reproduced under copyright by kind permission of Oxford Publishing Ltd.

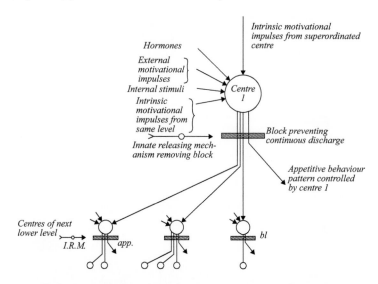

Figure 3.6   Tinbergen's innate releasing mechanism. Reproduced under copyright by kind permission of Oxford Publishing Ltd.

A POSH plan consists of a *Drive Collection (DC)* containing one or more *Drives*. Each *Drive (D)* has a priority and a releaser. When the *Drive* is released as a result of sensory input, a hierarchical plan of *Competences*, *APs* and *Actions* follows. POSH plans are authored, or designed, by humans alongside the design of senses and behaviour modules. An iterative approach is defined within BOD for the design of intelligent artefacts – these are known as agents, or if they are physically embodied, robots.

At runtime, the reactive plan itself is essentially fixed. Various slower react-ing systems may also be used to modify priorities or other parameters within the plan. These slower reacting systems might be compared with emotional or endocrinal states – chemical messages, typically hormones – in nature that similarly affect reac-tive priorities (Gaudl and Bryson, 2014). Similarly, the perception of senses can be affected by the internal state of the plan, an example being the latching (or hysteresis) associated with sensing (Rohlfshagen and Bryson, 2010).

In nature, the reactive plan is subject to possible learning that may change the plan parameters or even modify the structure of the plan itself as new skills and behaviours are learned. This learning may take place ontogenetically, i.e. within the lifetime of an individual, or phylogenetically, by the process of natural selection, across the lifetimes of many individuals. Bryson's BOD approach suggests that humans provide most of the necessary learning in order to improve the plan over time, in place of natural selection. However, Gaudl (2016) successfully uses genetic algorithms to automate part of this learning process, albeit within a computer game simulation.

A reactive plan is re-evaluated on every plan cycle, usually many times every second, and this requires that the inquiries from the planner to the senses and the

Figure 3.7   The Nomad 200 robot used by Dr Bryson whilst developing POSH
and BOD, photograph c. 2000, MIT labs. Kindly reproduced
with permission of Joanna Bryson from her PhD thesis,
Figure 4.1 (Bryson, 2001).

invocation of actions should respond quickly. This enables the reactive plan to respond quickly to changes in the external environment, whilst the plan hierarchy allows for complex sequences of behaviours to be executed. Applying these ideas to robots we can see that for senses, this might imply some caching of sense data (Bryson and McGonigle, 1998). For actions, it also implies that long running tasks (relative to the rate of plan execution) need to not only return success or failure but also another status to indicate that the action is still in progress and the plan must wait at its current execution step before moving on to its next step. The action may be executing on another thread or may just be getting sampled when the call to the action is made. This is implementation specific and does not affect the functioning of the planner itself. If re-invoked before it completes, the action immediately returns an In-Progress response. In this way, longer running action invocations do not block the planner from responding to other stimuli that may still change the focus of attention by, for example releasing another higher priority Drive.

Each call to the planner within the overall scheduling loop of the robot starts a new plan cycle. In this context an action may be a simple primitive such as a command to start a drive motor or may be part of a more complex predefined behaviour module, such as a mapping or trajectory calculation subsystem. It is important to note that the BOD methodology does not predicate that all intelligence is concentrated within the planner. Whilst the planner drives action selection either directly or through indirect invocation of competences or APs, considerable complexity can still exist in sensory, actuation and other probabilistic or state-based subsystems within the overall agent (Bryson, 2001).

The computer games industry has advanced the use of AI for the simulation of non-player characters (Lim, Baumgarten and Colton, 2010). Behaviour trees (BTs) are similarly hierarchical to POSH plans but have additional elements that more easily allow logical operations such as AND, OR, XOR and NOT to be included within the plan. For example, it is possible for a goal to be reached by successfully executing only one of a number of behaviours, trying each in turn until one is successful. Bryson's original design of POSH does not easily allow for this kind of plan structure.

BTs are in turn simplifications of Hierarchical Task Network (or HTN) planners (Ghallab, Nau and Traverso, 2004). Like POSH, HTN planners are able to create and run plans that contain recursive loops, meaning that they can represent any computable algorithm. An interesting parallel can be drawn here with Complexity theory. Holland (2014) argues that a Complex Agent System is often characterized by the fact that it can be decomposed into a set of hierarchical layers, with each layer being Turing complete. For a biological entity Holland identifies these layers as existing at the levels of DNA, organelle, cell, organ, organism and social levels. For an artificial agent, we can identify these layers as computer hardware, operating system, application programming language, reactive planner, plan, agent and social levels. Thus we can argue that to create an artificial agent truly capable of emergent implicit behaviour, we should strive to ensure that the Planner on which its behaviour depends should be Turing complete, particularly allowing looping and recursion.

In the following section, I describe the physical design and programming of a robot that uses reactive planning at the core of its action selection strategy.

3.3   The R5 robot

I designed and constructed a low-cost maker robot* and subsequently named it 'R5' attempting to choose a simple, non-anthropomorphic name. R5 was originally designed as a platform to investigate robot control architectures, and the interaction between humans and robots. It is based on the ARDUINO microcontroller (Arduino, 2016), see Figure 3.8. The robot is used in the experiments detailed in Chapters 4–6.

The R5 robot has active infrared distance sensors at each corner and proprioceptive sensors for odometry (distance travelled) and drive motor current – proprioception simply meaning sensing internal to the system (robot or human) rather than external sensing of the world. The R5 robot has a head with two degrees of freedom, designed for scanning the environment. Mounted on the head is a passive infrared (PIR) sensor to assist in the detection of humans, and an ultrasonic range finder with a range of 5 m. It also has a multicoloured LED "headlight" that may be used for signalling to

---

*Design details and software for the R5 robot: http://www.robwortham.com/r5-robot/

Figure 3.8 *The R5 robot. This photograph shows the head assembly with PIR and ultrasonic range-finder attached. The loudspeaker and Bluetooth audio adapter are also visible. The four red LEDs are powered from the audio output and serve as a visual indication of the vocalisation.*

humans around it. The robot is equipped with a speech synthesis module and loud-speaker, enabling it to vocalise textual sentences generated as the robot operates. In noisy environments, a Bluetooth audio module allows wireless headphones or other remote audio devices to receive the vocalisation output. The Bluetooth wireless link simply providing audio transmission over a range of 10–20 m. The audio output is also directed to a block of four red LEDs that pulse synchronously with the sound output. It also has a real-time clock allowing the robot to maintain accurate date and time, a Wi-Fi module for communication and an electronically erasable programmable 'read-only memory' to store the robot's configuration parameters. This leverages the Instinct Planner's ability to serialise plans as a byte stream and then reconstitute the plan from that stream at start-up. The robot software is written as a set of C++ libraries. The R5 robot command set is provided in Appendix B. A robot's action selection system is crucial to its operation, and I designed the Instinct Planner to provide an autonomous control mechanism for the R5 robot.

3.4 The Instinct Planner

To continue to behave intelligently often requires information about how you previously decided to behave, and what progress has been made so far towards a current goal. This information is not necessarily available by sensing the world. So, whilst a reactive plan structure is fixed, as described in Section 3.2.1, important state information is held during plan execution. First, we consider the specific plan control structures that collectively define a POSH reactive plan and then proceed to describe the specific enhancements and innovations added by the Instinct Planner.

The Instinct Planner is a reactive planner based on Bryson's POSH (Bryson, 2001; Bryson and Stein, 2001). It includes several enhancements taken from more recent papers extending POSH (Rohlfshagen and Bryson, 2010; Gaudl and Bryson, 2014), together with some ideas from other planning approaches, notably BTs (Lim, Baumgarten and Colton, 2010).

A POSH plan consists of a *DC* containing one or more *Drives*. Each *Drive (D)* has a priority and a releaser. When the *Drive* is released as a result of sensory input, a hierarchical plan of *Competences*, *APs* and *Actions* follows. One of the features in POSH is the suspension of one Drive by another. This occurs when a Drive of a higher priority is released. The lower priority Drive stops executing, but its state is preserved. When the lower priority Drive becomes active again, execution continues as if uninterrupted, subject to sensory input. The elements within a POSH plan hierarchy are defined below, beginning with the highest level of the plan:

- *DC*: The DC is the root node of the plan – $DC = [D_0, \ldots, D_i]$. It contains a set of Drives $D_a, a \in [0, \ldots, i]$ and is responsible for giving attention to the highest priority Drive. To allow the agent to shift and focus attention, only one Drive can be active in any given cycle. Due to the parallel hierarchical structure, Drives and their subtrees can be in different states of execution. This allows for cooperative multitasking and a quasi-parallel pursuit of multiple behaviours at the DC level.
- *Drive (D)*: A Drive – $D = [\pi, \rho, \alpha, A, v]$ – allows for the design and pursuit of a specific behaviour, as it maintains its execution state between plan cycles. The DC determines which Drive receives attention based on each Drive's π, the associated priority of a Drive. ρ is the *releaser*, a set of preconditions using senses to determine if the drive should be pursued. Typically the releaser is a simple definition that a sense value must exceed a specified threshold value, or be equal to a certain logical value for the Drive to be released. α is either an Action, AP or a Competence and A is the root link to the DC. The last parameter v specifies the execution frequency, allowing POSH to limit the rate at which the Drive can be executed. This allows for coarse grain concurrency of Drive execution (see later).
- *Competence (C)*: Competences form the core part of POSH plans. A competence $C = [c_0, \ldots, c_j]$ is a self-contained basic reactive plan where $c_b = [\pi, \rho, \alpha, \eta], b \in [0, \ldots, j]$ are tuples containing π, ρ, α and η: the priority, precondition, child node of C and maximum number of retries of the specific element c_b within C. The priority determines which of the child elements to execute, selecting the one with the highest priority first, provided that it can be released. The precondition is a concatenated set of senses that either release or inhibit the child node α. The child node itself can be another Competence or an Action or AP. To

allow for noisy environments, a child node c_b can fail a number of times, specified using η, before the Competence considers the child node to have failed. A Competence sequentially executes its hierarchically organised child-nodes where the highest priority node is the competence goal. A Competence fails if no child can execute or if an executed child fails.

- *AP*: APs are used to reduce the computational complexity of search within the plan space and to allow a coordinated fixed sequential execution of a set of elements. An AP – $AP = [\alpha_0, \ldots, \alpha_k]$ – is an ordered set of Actions that does not use internal precondition or additional perceptual information. It provides the simplest plan structure in POSH and allows for the optimised execution of behaviours. An example would be an agent that always shouts and moves its hand upwards when touching an hot object. In this case, there is no need for an additional check between the two Action primitives if the agent should always behave in that manner. APs execute all child elements in order before completing, provided previous Actions within the AP complete successfully.

- *Action (A)*: Actions represent the leaf nodes in the reactive plan hierarchy. An action invokes a behaviour primitive encoded within the Agent. These behaviour primitives may be simple, such as halting robot motion, or may be more complex, such as initiating a process to turn a robot in a specific direction. Instinct adds the concept of an *Action Value*, a parameter stored within the Action and passed as a parameter to the underlying primitive behaviour. This allows specific Actions to be encoded within the Instinct plan that invoke more general purpose behaviour primitives, typically contained within a *behaviour library*. A simple example would be a primitive to turn a robot by an angle specified in the Action Value parameter. In the case of simple and immediate actions, the primitive behaviour returns either SUCCESS or FAIL. For more complex, longer running behaviours of the immediate return value would be IN PROGRESS, indicating that the requested behaviour has commenced but is not yet complete. Subsequent invocations of the behaviour request will return IN-PROGRESS until the behaviour finally returns SUCCESS. These return values are returned by the Action itself and use by the higher levels in the reactive plan to determine the plan execution path.

For a full description of the POSH reactive planner, see Bryson (2001). The Instinct Planner provides a clear, well-documented and coherent implementation and attempts to overcome some of the criticisms of POSH, primarily those based on observations that the code and documentation of earlier POSH implementations are hard to navigate.

3.4.1 Enhancements and innovations

The Instinct Planner includes a full implementation of what we term *drive execution optimisation (DEO)*. DEO avoids a full search of the plan tree at every plan cycle which would be expensive. It also maintains focus on the task at hand. This corresponds loosely to the function of conscious attention seen in nature (Bryson, 2011). A form of this was in Bryson's original POSH but has not been fully implemented in subsequent versions. The Drive, Competence and AP elements each contain a *runtime element identifier (ID)*. These variables are fundamental to the plan operation. Initially they do not point to any plan element. However, when a Drive is released the plan is traversed to the point where either an Action is executed, or the plan fails at some point in the hierarchy. If the plan element is not yet completed, it returns a status of In-Progress, and the IDs of the last successful steps in the plan are stored in runtime element ID in the Drive, Competence and AP elements. If an action or other sub-element of the plan returns success, then the next step in the plan is stored.

On the next cycle *of the drive* (note that a higher priority drive may have interrupted since the last plan cycle devoted to this drive), the plan hierarchy is traversed again but continues from where it got to last plan cycle, guided by the runtime element IDs. A check is made that the releasers are still activated (meaning that the plan steps are still valid for execution), and then the plan steps are executed. If a real-world action fails, or the releaser check fails, then the runtime element ID is once again cleared. During the execution of an AP (a relatively quick sequence of actions), sensory input is temporarily ignored immediately above the level of the AP. This more closely corresponds to the reflex behaviour seen in nature. Once the system has started to act, then it continues until the AP completes, or an element in the AP explicitly fails. APs are therefore not designed to include Actions with long running primitive behaviours.

In addition to these smaller changes, there are three major innovations in the Instinct Planner that increase the range of plan design options available to developers:

- First, the idea of runtime alteration of drive priority. This implementation closely follows the RAMP model of Gaudl and Bryson (2014) which in turn is biologically inspired, based on spreading activation in neural networks. Within the Instinct Planner, we term this *dynamic drive reprioritisation (DDR)* for clarity. DDR is useful to modify the priority of drives based on more slowly changing stimuli, either external or internal. For example, a RECHARGE BATTERY drive might be used to direct a robot back to its charging station when the battery level becomes low. Normally, this drive might have a medium priority, such that if only low priority drives are active then it will return when its battery becomes discharged to say 50%. However, if there are constantly high priority drives active, then the battery level might reach a critical level of say 10%. At that point, the RECHARGE BATTERY drive must take highest priority.

    A comparison can be drawn here with the need for an animal to consume food. Once it is starving the drive to eat assumes a much higher priority than when the animal experiences normal levels of hunger. For example, it will take more risks to eat, rather than flee from predators.
- Second, the idea of flexible latching provides for a more dynamic form of sense hysteresis, based not only on plan configuration, but also the runtime focus of the plan. This implementation follows the work of Rohlfshagen and Bryson (2010). Within the Instinct Planner, we term it *flexible sense hysteresis* for clarity. This hysteresis primarily allows for noise from sensors and from the world, but Rohlfshagen's paper also has some basis in biology to avoid dithering by prolonging behaviours once they have begun. If the Drive is interrupted by one of a higher priority, then when the sense is again checked, it will be the Sense Flex Latch

Hysteresis that will be applied, rather than the Sense Hysteresis. The Sense Flex Latch Hysteresis is typically set to zero, so that no latching occurs when a Drive is interrupted.

- Third, we enhance the Competences within the plan, such that it is possible to group a number of competence steps by giving them the same priority. We refer to this as a *priority group*. Items within a group have no defined order. Within a priority group, the Competence itself can specify whether the items must all be successfully executed for the Competence to be successful (the AND behaviour), or whether only one item need be successful (the OR behaviour). In the case of the OR behaviour, several items within the group may be attempted and may fail, before one succeeds. At this point the Competence will then move on to higher priority items during subsequent plan cycles.

A Competence can have any number of priority groups within it, but all are constrained to be either AND or OR, based on the configuration of the Competence itself.

This single enhancement, whilst sounding straightforward, increases the complexity of the planner code significantly but allows for much more compact plans, with a richer level of functionality achievable within a single Competence than was provided with the earlier POSH implementations which lacked the ability to define the AND behaviour. Note that some implementations of POSH also left out the OR behaviour.

3.4.2 Multiplatform

The Instinct Planner is designed to be used in multiple environments and to control robots that are based on different hardware and software platforms. Instinct runs as a C++ library and has been extensively tested both within MICROSOFT VISUAL C++ and the ARDUINO development environments (Arduino, 2016), see Figure 3.9.

The ARDUINO uses the ATMEL AVR C++ COMPILER (Atmel Corporation, 2016a) with the AVR LIBC library (Atmel Corporation, 2016b) – a standards-based implementation of `gcc` and `libc`. This arrangement harnesses the power of the VISUAL C++ integrated development environment (IDE) and debugger, hugely increasing productivity when developing for the ARDUINO platform, which has no debugger and only a rudimentary IDE.

Instinct is designed to have a very compact memory architecture, suitable for deployment on low powered, embedded microcontrollers such as ARDUINO. It uses a single byte to store plan element IDs within the ARDUINO environment. The planner is thus able to store plans with up to 255 elements within the very limited 8 kB memory (RAM) available on the ARDUINO MEGA (ATMEL AVR ATMEGA2560 MICROCONTROLLER). However, the Instinct Planner code is not fundamentally limited to 255 plan elements and will support much larger plans on platforms with more memory. In MICROSOFT VISUAL C++, for example, plans with up to 4,294,967,295 nodes are supported, simply by redefining the `instinctID` type from `unsigned char` to `unsigned int`, a 32-bit value.

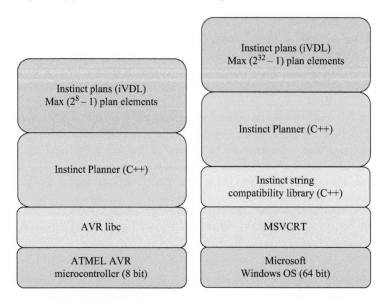

Figure 3.9   The Instinct Planner is designed to operate on multiple platforms and currently integrates with both the ATMEL AVR LIBC interface for the ARDUINO microcontroller and the MICROSOFT VISUAL C++ RUNTIME (MSVCRT) library for MICROSOFT WINDOWS. Identical plans can be run in each environment.

A complete implementation of the Instinct Planner exists on the R5 ARDUINO-based robot, see Section 3.3. The robot runs using various test plans, see Figure 3.10. It has simple and more complex underlying behaviours that can be invoked by the planner, such as the ability to turn in the direction of the most clear pathway ahead, or to use its head to scan for the presence of a human.

3.4.3   Memory management

In order to produce a planner that operates effectively in an environment with severely limited working memory resources (RAM), considerable design effort has been applied to the memory management architecture within the planner. There are six separate memory buffers, each holding fixed record length elements for each element type in the plan – Drives, Competences, Competence Elements, APs, AP Elements and Actions, see Figure 3.11. An instance of Instinct has a single DC – the root of the plan.

Within each plan element, individual bytes are divided into bit fields for Boolean values to minimise memory space. The data is normalised across elements to avoid variable length records. This means, for example, that Competence Elements hold the ID of their parent Competence, but the Competence itself does not hold the IDs of each of its child Competence Elements. At runtime, a search must be carried

Figure 3.10 *The R5 Aʀᴅᴜɪɴᴏ-based maker robot in a laboratory test environment. The camera mounted on the robot is used to record robot activity but is not used by the robot itself.*

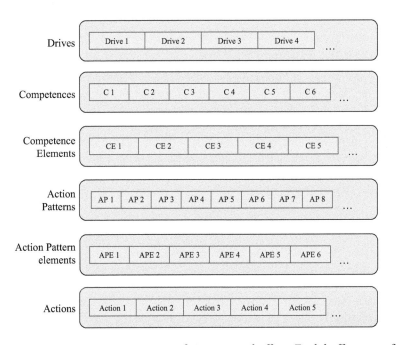

Figure 3.11 *Instinct maintains a set of six memory buffers. Each buffer stores fixed length records for a specific plan element type. The fixed length structure enables extremely fast search of the buffers at runtime and minimises memory footprint.*

out to identify which Competence Elements belong to a given Competence – each Competence having a unique ID. Thus the planner sacrifices some search time in return for a considerably more compact memory representation. Fortunately, this search is very fast, since the Competence Elements are stored within a single-memory buffer with fixed length records. Testing shows the time taken by this searching was negligible in comparison with the plan cycle rate of the robot.

Plan elements, senses and actions are referenced to by unique numeric IDs, rather than by name. The memory storage of these IDs is defined within the code using the C++ `#typedef` preprocessor command, so that the width of these IDs can be configured at compile time, depending on the maximum ID value to be stored. This again saves memory in an environment where every byte counts. Consideration of stack usage is also important, and temporary buffers and similar structures are kept to a minimum to avoid stack overflow.

Fixed strings (e.g. error messages) and other data defined within programs are usually also stored within working memory. Within a microcontroller environment such as ARDUINO, this is wasteful of the limited memory resource. This problem has been eliminated in the Instinct Planner implementation by use of AVR LIBC functions (Atmel Corporation, 2016b) that enable fixed data to be stored in the much larger program (flash) memory. For code compatibility, these functions have been replicated in a pass-through library so that the code compiles unaltered on non-AVR microcontroller platforms.

3.4.4   Instinct testing environment

As a means to test the functionality of the Instinct Planner within a sophisticated debugging environment, I implemented the Instinct Planner within a MICROSOFT VISUAL C++ development environment and tested a simulation of robots within a grid-based world, each using Instinct for action selection. The world allows multiple robots to roam, encountering one another, walls, obstacles and so on.

I subsequently extended this implementation with a graphical user interface (GUI) to better show both the world and the real-time monitoring available from within the plan to create the Instinct Robot World, see Section 3.5.2.

3.4.5   Instinct transparency enhancements

The planner has the ability to report its activity as it runs, by means of callback functions to a monitor C++ class. There are six separate callbacks monitoring the Execution, Success, Failure, Error and In-Progress status events, and the Sense activity of each plan element. In the VISUAL C++ implementation, these callbacks write log information to files on disk, one per robot instance. This facilitates the testing and debugging of the planner. In the ARDUINO robot, the callbacks write textual data to a TCP/IP stream over a wireless (Wi-Fi) link. A JAVA-based Instinct Server receives this information, enriches it by replacing element IDs with element names, and logs the data to disk. This communication channel also allows for commands to be sent to the robot while it is running.

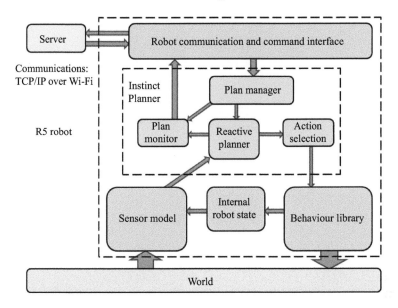

Figure 3.12   Software architecture of the R5 robot showing interfaces with the World and the Instinct Server. The Instinct Planner provides the action selection subsystem of the robot.

With all nodes reporting all monitor events over Wi-Fi, a plan cycle rate of 20 Hz is sustainable. By reducing the level of monitoring, we reduce the volume of data sent over Wi-Fi, and plan cycle rates of up to 40 Hz are achievable. In practice, a slower rate is likely to be adequate to control a robot and will reduce the volume of data requiring subsequent processing. In our experiments, a plan cycle rate of 8 Hz was generally used, meaning that the plan was re-evaluated every 125 ms – compare this with a plan re-evaluation of around *20 min* for the Shakey robot of Figure 3.1.

Figure 3.12 shows how the planner sits within the robot software environment and communicates with the Instinct Server.

3.4.6   Instinct command set

The robot command set primarily communicates with the planner which in turn has a wide range of commands, allowing the plan to be uploaded and altered in real time, and also controlling the level of activity reporting from each node in the plan. When the robot first connects to the Instinct Server, the plan and monitoring control commands are automatically sent to the robot, and this process can be repeated at any time while the robot is running. This allows plans to be quickly modified without requiring any reprogramming or physical interference with the robot. The Instinct Planner command set is provided in Appendix A.

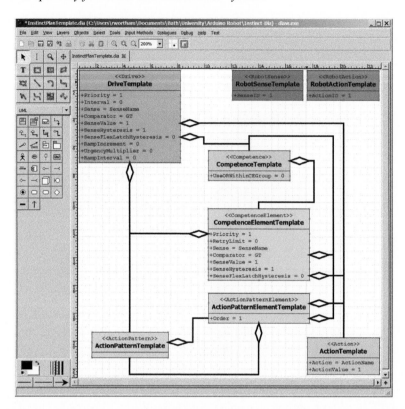

*Figure 3.13   Instinct plan element types and their relationship, shown within the
DIA drawing tool. The parameters for each element type are shown
with their default values. The diamond on a connector indicates 'may
be a parent of'. For example, a Competence may only be the parent of
one or more Competence Elements.*

3.4.7   Creating reactive plans with iVDL

POSH plans are written in a LISP-like notation, either using a text editor, or the ABODE
editor (Brom *et al.*, 2006). However, Instinct plans are written very differently, because
they must use a much more compact notation and they use IDs rather than names
for plan elements, senses and actions. Therefore, I developed the *Instinct Visual
Design Language (iVDL)* based on the ubiquitous unified modelling language (UML)
notation. UML is supported by many drawing packages, and I developed a simple
PYTHON export script to allow plans to be created graphically within the open source
DIA drawing tool (Macke, 2014). The export script takes care of creating unique IDs
and allows the plans to use named elements, thus increasing readability. The names
are exported alongside the plan, and whilst they are ignored by the planner itself, the
Instinct Server uses this export to convert IDs back into names within the log files
and interactive display.

Figure 3.13 shows the Instinct plan template within DIA. I use the UML class
notation to define classes for the six types of element within the Instinct plan and also

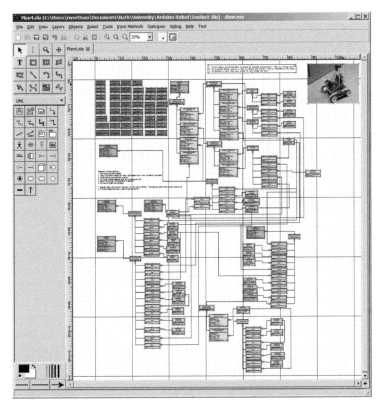

Figure 3.14   The plan used by the R5 robot to enable it to explore an environment, avoid obstacles and search for humans. The plan also includes emergency behaviours to detect and avoid excessive motor load, and to conserve battery by sleeping periodically. See Appendix C for a larger version of the plan.

to map the external numerical IDs for senses and robot actions to names. I use the UML aggregation connector to identify the connections between the plan elements, visible as a diamond at the end of each connector. This can be read, for example, as "A Drive can invoke (i.e. be a parent of) an Action, a Competence or an Action Pattern".

Figure 3.14 shows a plan for the R5 robot. At this level of magnification, the element details are not legible, but this screenshot gives an impression of how plans can be laid out within DIA. A larger version of the plan is provided in Appendix C. This particular plan searches the robot's environment, avoiding objects and adjusting its speed according to the space around it. As the robot moves around, it attempts to detect humans within the environment. The robot also temporarily shuts down in the event of motor overload, and it will periodically hibernate when not in open space to conserve battery power. Such a plan might be used to patrol hazardous areas such as industrial food freezers, or nuclear facilities. The plan was designed and debugged within the space of a week. During the debugging, the availability of the transparency data logged by the Instinct Server was extremely useful, because mere observation of the robot's emergent behaviour is frequently insufficient to determine the cause of plan malfunction.

The actual positioning of plan elements within the drawing is entirely up to the plan designer. Since DIA is a general purpose graphical editor, other symbols, text and images can be freely added to the file. This is useful at design time and during the debugging of the robot. It also provides an additional vehicle for the creation of longer term project documentation. We suggest that an in-house standard is developed for the layout of plans within a development group, such that developers can easily read one another's plans.

3.4.8   Plan debugging and transparency

An important feature of the Instinct Planner is its ability to generate a real-time feed of the detailed execution of the planner as it operates. This feed is used to assist during debugging of a robot and to produce visual and audible information concerning the internal state and processing of a robot suitable for end users. This is described in more detail in Chapters 4 and 5. Andreas Theodorou created a new version of the ABODE plan editor (Theodorou, Wortham and Bryson, 2016), known as ABOD3, from a design specification provided by Joanna Bryson, and with feedback from the author, as a result of testing. This version reads the real-time transparency data emanating from the Instinct Planner, in order to provide a real-time graphical display of plan execution. In this way, we are able to explore both runtime debugging and wider issues of AI transparency.

3.5   Modelling robot control using the Instinct Planner

Having created the Instinct Planner, I was curious to see whether the reactive planning paradigm could operate at a higher level of abstraction, to modify the behaviour of a robot to achieve some higher order objective, unrelated to the immediate sensing and movement of the robot. Could this architecture be used to carry our reinforcement learning, such that a reactive plan is modified in real time as the robot operates? An important advantage of such an architecture would be the transparency of the learning mechanism. In the following sections, I describe the investigation of a small footprint cognitive architecture comprising two Instinct reactive planner instances. The first interacts with the world via sensor and behaviour interfaces. The second monitors the first and dynamically adjusts its plan in accordance with some predefined objective function. I show that this configuration produces a Darwinian mind, yet aware of its own operation and performance, and able to maintain performance as the environment changes. I identify this architecture as a second-order Darwinian mind and discuss the philosophical implications for the study of consciousness.

I describe the Instinct Robot World agent-based modelling (ABM) environment, which in turn uses the Instinct Planner for cognition. Many ABM tools are already available, each with their own application focus and individual capabilities (Nikolai and Madey, 2009). However, the Instinct Robot World is particularly designed to investigate robot control in a multi-robot environment using reactive planning. It could also potentially be of use in the investigation of other robot control methods, or more complex hybrid architectures.

3.5.1 Kinds of minds

Dennett (1996) elegantly outlines a high-level ontology for the kind of creatures that exist in the natural world, from the perspective of the kinds of minds that these creatures possess, see Figure 3.15.

At the most basic level, the Darwinian creature has a mind that produces 'hard-wired' behaviours, or phenotypes, based on the genetic coding of the organism. The mind of the Skinnerian creature is plastic, and capable of 'ABC' learning – Associationism, Behaviourism, Connectionism. The Popperian creature's mind runs simulations to predict the effect of planned actions, anticipating experience. It therefore permits hypotheses "to die in our head" rather than requiring them to be executed in the world before learning can take place. Finally, Gregorian creatures (after the psychologist Richard Gregory) have a sophisticated mind able to import and reuse tools

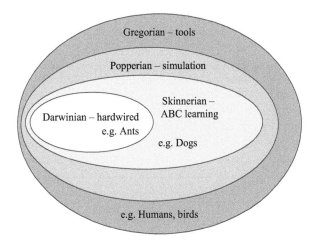

Figure 3.15 *Kinds of minds, after Dennett (1996). Each kind of mind builds on the capabilities of its simpler ancestor but is nevertheless dependent on it. The examples of creatures possessing these kinds of minds is purely illustrative, and no ancestry is implied. Ants possess only simple reactive mechanisms, although in combination an ant-hive produces much more complex behaviours. Dogs seem never to make good decisions without extensive training but almost certainly possess some ability for simulation. Birds learn sophisticated song patterns, build complex nests and are known to use tools. Note that brain size is no indicator for mental sophistication.*

from the cultural environment, for example language and writing. Using these tools enables a Gregorian creature, for example a human, to be self-reflective.

Extending this idea to directly classify the minds of these creatures, we may simply identify the *Darwinian mind* as the simplest kind of mind, and the Gregorian mind as the most sophisticated.

However, perhaps the simple Darwinian mind might also be arranged to monitor itself, and in some small and limited sense to be aware of its own performance and act to correct it. Bryson (2011) suggests a possible role for consciousness in action selection. Here we investigate whether action selection achieved through reactive planning might parallel one of the commonly accepted characteristics of consciousness; that is to be self-reflective and regulating (Sherman, Gawronski and Trope, 2014).

3.5.2   The Instinct Robot World

The *Instinct Robot World* is a new ABM tool, shown in Figure 3.16. This is an open source project and all code and configuration files are available online.[†]

Each virtual 'robot' within the Robot World uses an Instinct Planner to provide action selection. Strictly, since these virtual robots are not physically embodied, we should refer to them as agents. However, we have chosen to use 'robot' throughout, as intuitively these cognitive entities appear to be virtually embodied within the Robot World, and this choice of language seems more natural. In Section 3.6, we discuss future work where we may realise physical embodiment of this architecture in a robot swarm.

The Robot World allows many robots to be instantiated, each with the same reactive plan, or with a variety of plans, see Figure 3.17. The robots each have senses to sense the 'walls' of the environment and other robots. The reactive plan invokes simple actions to move the robot, adjust its speed and direction or interact with robots that it encounters within the world as it moves. Most importantly for this investigation, each robot also has a second Instinct Planner instance. This planner monitors the first and is able to modify its parameters based on a predefined plan.

The Instinct Robot World provides statistical monitoring to report on the overall activity of the robots within the world. These include the average percentage of robots that are moving at any one time, the average number of time units (ticks) between robot interactions, and the average amount of time that the Monitor Planner intervenes to modify the robot plan. The operation of the Instinct Planners within the robots can also be monitored from the real-time transparency feed, available as a data feed over a TCP/IP connection. This facilitates real-time plan monitoring using tools such as ABOD3, see Section 3.4.8.

We use the Instinct Robot World to investigate the idea of *Reflective Reactive Planning* – one reactive planner driving behaviour-based on sensory input and predefined drives and competences, and another reactive planner monitoring performance and intervening to modify the predefined plan of the first, in accordance with

---

[†]http://www.robwortham.com/instinct-planner/

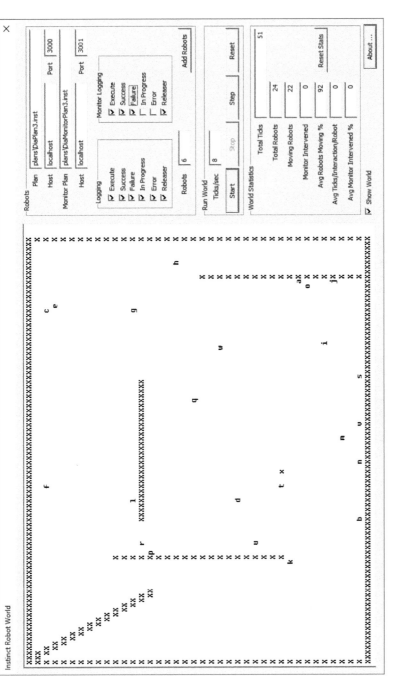

Figure 3.16   Screenshot of the Instinct Robot World in operation. Each robot is represented as a single character within the display. Robots are labelled with letters and numbers to distinguish them. When a robot's monitor plan becomes active, the robot representation changes to the shriek character (!). The top right section of the screen is used to control the robots and the plans they use. The Host and Port entries allow real-time monitoring of the transparency feed from the Instinct Planners. The bottom right section displays statistics about the world as it runs.

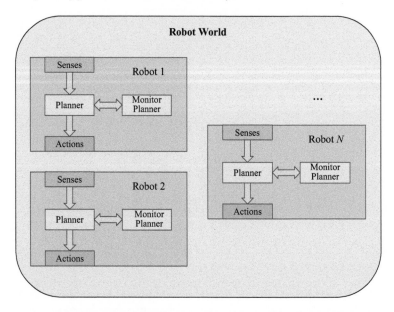

Figure 3.17   Simplified diagrammatic representation of the Instinct Robot World. The world contains many robots, each with independent sensing and planning, enabling each robot to independently select its actions as it runs. A second planner instance, the Monitor Planner, is able to modify the parameters of the first planner duration plan execution.

some higher level objective. This simple combination of two Darwinian minds, one monitoring the other, might also be considered to be a second-order Darwinian mind.

3.5.3   Conjectures

We expect that second-order Darwinian minds will outperform first-order minds when the environment changes, because the Monitor Planner is concerned with achieving higher order objectives and modifies the operation of the first planner to improve its performance.

We also hypothesise that this architecture will remain stable over extended periods of time, because by restricting ourselves to the reactive planning paradigm, we have reduced the number of degrees of freedom within which the architecture must operate, and previous work described in Section 3.4 shows that first-order minds produce reliable control architectures (Wortham, Gaudl and Bryson, 2016).

Finally, we expect that such a second-order system should be relatively simple to design, being modular, well-structured and conceptually straightforward.

3.5.4   Methods

Figure 3.18 shows the Reflective Reactive Planning architecture implemented within the Instinct Robot World, and controlling the behaviour of each robot within that

Reflective reactive planning – a second-order Darwinian mind

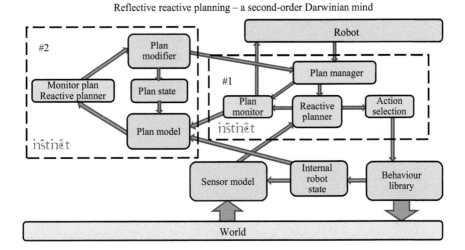

Figure 3.18   *Architecture of the second-order Darwinian mind. The robot is controlled by the Instinct reactive planner, as it interacts with the sensor model and behaviour library. In turn, a second instance of Instinct monitors the first, together with the internal robot state, and dynamically modifies parameters within the robot's planner. The overall effect is a robot that not only reacts to its environment according to a predefined set of goals but is also to modify that interaction according to some performance measure calculated within the Plan model.*

world. The robot plan has the following simple objectives, each implemented as an Instinct Drive.

- Move around in the environment so as to explore it.
- Avoid objects, i.e. the walls marked as 'X' in Figure 3.16.
- Interact when another robot is 'encountered', i.e. when another robot is sensed as having the same coordinates within the grid of the Robot World. This interaction causes the robot to stop for 200 clock cycles or 'ticks'.

While the robot is in the 'Interacting' state it is shown as a shriek character (!) within the Robot World display. Once the robot has interacted its priority for inter-action decreases but ramps up over time. This may be likened to most natural drives, for example mating, feeding and the need for social interaction.

The monitor plan is designed to keep the robot exploring when it is overly diverted from social interactions. It achieves this by monitoring the time between interactions. If, over three interactions, the average time between interactions reduces below 1,000 ticks, then the Monitor Planner reduces the priority of the interaction Drive. After 1,000 ticks, the priority is reset to its original level. We might use alternative intentional language here to say that the Monitor Planner 'notices' that the robot is being diverted by too many social interactions. It then reduces the priority of those interactions, so that the robot is diverted less frequently. After some time, the Monitor Planner ceases to intervene until it next notices this situation reoccurring.

The Robot World is populated with varying numbers of robots (2, 3, 5, 10, 20, 50, 100, 200, 500, 1,000), and for each number the experiment is run twice, once with a monitor plan, and once without. For each run, the environment is allowed to run for some time, typically about 10 min, until the reported statistics have settled and are seen to be no longer changing over time.

3.5.5   Outcomes

The results are presented as simple graphs. First, the average number of robots moving at any one time within the world is shown in Figure 3.19. In both cases, as the number of robots within the world increases, the amount of time that the robot spends moving reduces. However, the Monitor Planner acts to reduce the extent of this reduction from 60% to less than 20% over the full range of 2–1,000 robots within the world. Similarly, in Figure 3.20, we see that as more robots are introduced into the world, the average time between interactions naturally reduces. However, the action of the Monitor Planner progressively limits this reduction, so that with 1,000 robots, the

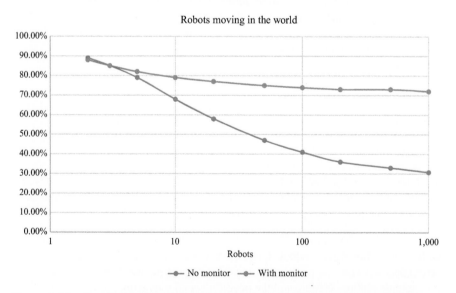

Figure 3.19   Graph showing the average percentage number of robots that are moving at any one time within the world, for a given total number of robots in the world. It can be seen that the addition of the monitor plan maintains more robots moving as the number of robots increases. Note the x-axis log scale for robots in world.

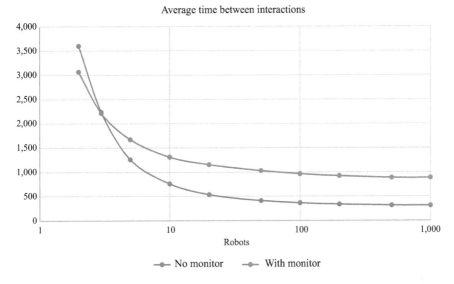

Figure 3.20   Graph showing the average time between robot interactions, both with and without the monitor plan. The addition of the monitor plan reduces the variance in interaction time as robot numbers vary. Again, note the x-axis is log scale.

time between interactions is almost trebled, from 310 to 885 ticks per interaction. Interestingly, in both these graphs, we see smooth curves both with and without the action of the monitor plan. The final graph, Figure 3.21 also shows a smooth, sigmoid like increase in intervention of the Monitor Planner as the number of robots increases, plotted on a logarithmic scale.

In addition to providing the experimental results for the second-order Darwinian mind, the Instinct Robot World and the Instinct Planner were together found to be a stable, reliable platform for our experiments, and the results achieved are readily repeatable by downloading the software.[‡] The application is single threaded, and so uses only one core of the CPU on the laptop PC on which it was run. Nevertheless, it was possible to simulate 1,000 robots with both reactive planners active operating in the world at the rate of 70 clock cycles (ticks) per second.

3.5.6 Discussion

From the results, we can see that by using a second Instinct instance to monitor the first, we can achieve real-time learning within a tiny-footprint yet nevertheless symbolic cognitive architecture. We say the architecture is symbolic because behaviour can be traced to specific control elements within the reactive plan, each of which is

---

[‡]https://github.com/rwortham/Instinct-RobotWorld

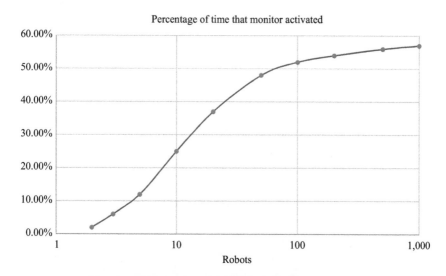

Figure 3.21   *Graph showing the average percentage number of robots whose monitor plan is activated at any one time, for a given number of total robots in the world. The monitor plan of a robot is activated when the average time between interactions reduces below 1,000 ticks, reducing the priority of the interaction Drive. Note the x-axis log scale.*

represented by a unique symbol, within a predefined syntactic structure. In addition, since this learning modifies parameters from a human designed plan, the learning can be well understood and is transparent in nature. This contrasts strongly with machine learning approaches, such as neural networks that typically learn offline, are opaque and require a much larger memory workspace. Despite the stochastic nature of the environment, the performance graphs show smooth curves over a wide range of robot populations.

This relatively simple experiment also provides further fuel for the fire concerning the philosophical discussion of the nature of consciousness. Critics may say that when we use the intentional stance (Dennett, 1989) to describe the behaviour of the Monitor Planner as 'noticing' something, we are merely using metaphor. They might argue that there is in fact no sentience doing any noticing, and in fact the only 'noticing' that is happening here is noticing the behaviour of this human-designed mechanism, which itself is operating quite without any sentience and certainly without being conscious (Haikonen, 2013). But that is to miss the point. We are not claiming that this architecture is conscious in the human or even significant sense of the word, merely that our architecture is inspired by one aspect of how biological consciousness appears to operate. However, having shown that this architecture can indeed provide adaptive control, and drawing on the knowledge that gene expression produces behaviours which can be modelled using reactive planning, we might also consider whether consciousness in animals, and humans may indeed arise from complex interactions between hierarchical mechanisms. These mechanisms are biologically predetermined by genetics, and yet in combination yield flexible, adaptive systems able to respond to changing environments and optimise for objective functions unrelated to the immediate competences of preprogrammed behavioural responses. This is not to argue for some kind of emergence (Holland, 2000), spooky or otherwise, but more simply to add weight to the idea that the 'I' in consciousness is nothing more than an internal introspective narrative, and such a narrative may be generated by using hierarchical mechanisms that notice one another's internal states, decision processes and progress towards predefined (phenotypic) objectives.

We could certainly envisage a much grander architecture, assembled at the level of reactive planners, using maybe hundreds or thousands of planners each concerned with certain objectives. Many of these planners may be homeostatic in nature, whilst others would be concerned with the achievement of higher level objectives. We must remember that planners merely coordinate action selection and say nothing about how sensor models may be formed, nor how complex behaviours themselves may be implemented. However, all dynamic architectures need some kind of decision centric 'glue' to bind them together, and reactive planning seems to be a useful candidate here, as evidenced by practical experiment and biological underpinning.

Machine transparency is a core element of our research. We show in Chapter 4 that reactive planners, particularly the Instinct Planner, are able to facilitate transparency. This is due to the human design of their plans, and the ability to gather meaningful symbolic information about internal system state and decision processes in real time as the planner operates. This ability to inspect the operation of the architecture may assist designers in achieving larger scale cognitive implementations. Equally importantly, transparency is an important consideration for users and operators of intelligent systems, particularly robots, and this is highlighted in the EPSRC Principles of Robotics (Boden *et al.*, 2011).

The human brain does not run by virtue of some elegant algorithm. It is a hack, built by the unseeing forces of evolution, without foresight or consideration for modularity, transparency or any other good design practice. If we are to build intelligent systems, the brain is not a good physical model from which we should proceed. Rather, we should look at the behaviours of intelligent organisms, model the way in which these organisms react, and then scale up these models to build useful, manageable intelligent systems.

Whilst our Reflective Reactive Planner is a very simple architecture, it does share many of the characteristics cited for architectures that are worthy of evaluation, such as efficiency and scalability, reactivity and persistence, improvability and autonomy and extended operation (Langley, Laird and Rogers, 2009). In addition, the Instinct Planner's transparency feed provides a useful debugging interface, particularly when used in conjunction with the ABOD3 real-time debugging tool. The importance of real-time action selection transparency is discussed in more detail in Chapter 7. We hope that our work with reactive planners might strengthen the case for their consideration in situations where decision centric 'glue' is required.

3.6   Conclusions and further work

The Instinct Planner is the first major re-engineering of Bryson's original work for several years, and the first ever allowing deployment in practical real-time physical environments such as the R5 ARDUINO-based maker robot.

By using a very lean coding style and efficient memory management, we maximise the size of plan that can be dynamically loaded whilst maintaining sufficient performance in terms of execution rate.

The transparency capabilities, novel to this implementation of POSH, provide the necessary infrastructure to deliver real-time plan debugging. The transparency feed is available from both the R5 robot and the Instinct Robot World via a TCP/IP communications link, facilitating remote real-time debugging, particularly with the ABOD3 real-time plan debugger. The importance of real-time action selection transparency is discussed in more detail in Section 7.

The iVDL is a novel representation of reactive plans, and we demonstrate that such plans can be designed using a standard drawing package and exported with a straightforward plug-in script. We envisage the development of similar plug-ins for other drawing tools such as MICROSOFT VISIO.

We have demonstrated that a second-order Darwinian mind may be constructed from two instances of the Instinct reactive planner as shown by the results obtained from the Instinct Robot World experiment. This architecture, which we call Reflective Reactive Planning, successfully controls the behaviour of a virtual robot within a simulated world, according to predefined goals and higher level objectives. We have shown how this architecture may provide both practical cognitive implementations and inform philosophical discussion on the nature and purpose of consciousness.

Although primarily developed for physical robot implementations, the Instinct Planner, as demonstrated by the Instinct Robot World, has applications in teaching, simulation and game AI environments. The Instinct Robot World provides a GUI-based test platform for Instinct and may also be used as a teaching tool to teach the concepts of reactive planning in general and the Instinct Planner in particular.

The Instinct Robot World is an entirely open source platform, available online. We welcome those interested in ABM, cognitive architectures generally, and reactive planning specifically, to investigate these technologies and offer suggestions for new applications and further work. One possibility might be to apply this architecture to the small loop problem (Georgeon, Marshall and Gurney, 2013), a specific challenge for biologically inspired cognitive architectures to autonomously organise behaviour through interaction with an initially unknown environment offering sequential and spatial regularities.

3.6.1   Instinct and ROS

We would like to see the implementation of Instinct on other embedded and low-cost Linux computing environments such as the RASPBERRY PI (Raspberry Pi Foundation, 2016). With more powerful low-cost platforms such as the PI, much larger plans can be developed and we can test both the runtime performance of very large plans and the design efficiency of iVDL with multi-user teams. To that end, work is currently (at the time of writing) underway to develop a wrapper for Instinct such that it can operate as a ROS[§] node. A ROS-based system is typically configured and instantiated by means of a launch file. By use of ROS parameters configured within the launch file, we hope to develop a node that can be configured entirely through parameterisation of

- plan structure,
- sensor input from ROS Message or ROS Service,
- action output to ROS Message, ROS Service or ROS Action.

Having covered the design, development and testing of the Instinct Planner and R5 robot in this chapter, the following chapters describe the use of these technologies to investigate the extent to which naive humans understand robots and how we might make robots more transparent, such that they are better understood. The following chapter details robot transparency experiments using the R5 robot with the ABOD3 real-time graphical debugging tool and with ADOD3-AR with mobile-augmented reality. The ROS version will similarly benefit from these existing transparency tools.

[§]ROS: https://www.ros.org/

Chapter 4

The impact of transparency using real-time displays

"[Marvin Minsky's] basic interest seemed to be in the workings of the human mind and in making machine models of the mind. Indeed, about that time he and a friend made one of the first electronic machines that could actually teach itself to do something interesting. It monitored electronic 'rats' that learned to run mazes. It was being financed by the Navy. On one notable occasion, I remember descending to the basement of Memorial Hall, while Minsky worked on it. It had an illuminated display panel that enabled one to follow the progress of the 'rats'. Near the machine was a hamster in a cage. When the machine blinked, the hamster would run around its cage happily. Minsky, with his characteristic elfin grin, remarked that on a previous day the Navy contract officer had been down to see the machine. Noting the man's interest in the hamster, Minsky had told him laconically, "The next one we build will look like a bird.""

– Jeremy Bernstein

4.1 Summary

Deciphering the behaviour of intelligent others is a fundamental characteristic of our own intelligence. As we interact with complex intelligent artefacts, humans inevitably construct mental models (MMs) to understand and predict their behaviour. If these models are incorrect or inadequate, we run the risk of self-deception or even harm. In this chapter, we investigate the use of a real-time display and demonstrate that providing even a simple, abstracted real-time visualisation, real-time visualisation of a robot's artificial intelligence (AI) can radically improve the transparency of machine cognition. Findings from both an online experiment using a video recording of a robot, and from direct observation of a robot show substantial improvements in observers' understanding of the robot's behaviour. Unexpectedly, this improved understanding is correlated in one condition with an increased perception that the robot was 'thinking', but in no conditions was the robot's assessed intelligence impacted.

4.2   Mind models and transparency

The fourth of the five EPSRC Principles of Robotics asserts that *robots are manufactured artefacts. They should not be designed in a deceptive way to exploit vulnerable users; instead, their machine nature should be transparent* (Boden *et al.*, 2011). Why is transparency important, and how does it impact AI system design? There has been considerable previous research to investigate ways in which robots can understand humans (Lee and Makatchev, 2009). However, transparency is the converse. Here, we are interested in how robots should be designed in order that we can understand them.

Humans have a natural if limited ability to understand others, however this ability has evolved and developed in the environment of human and other animal agency, which may make assumptions AI does not necessarily conform to. Therefore, it is the responsibility of the designers of intelligent systems to make their products transparent to us (Wortham and Theodorou, 2017; Theodorou, Wortham and Bryson, 2017).

It is generally thought that many forms of effective interaction, whether cooperative or coercive, rely on each party having some theory of mind (ToM) concerning the other (Wortham and Bryson, 2018; Saxe, Schulz and Jiang, 2006). Individual actions and complex behaviour patterns can be more easily interpreted within a pre-existing ToM framework, often created through modelling from one's own expectations by projection to the others' identity. Whether that ToM is entirely accurate is unimportant, provided that it is sufficiently predictive to inform one's own action selection (Barsalou, 2009). Ideally, such 'good enough' modelling should include an accurate assessment of how inaccurate our mind model might be. However, in the case of AI, humans have been repeatedly shown to overidentify with machines, even to their own detriment (Salem *et al.*, 2015). This holds true for 6-month-old babies so cannot be attributed to or easily solved by implicit enculturation (Kamewari *et al.*, 2005). Therefore, explicit strategies for communicating the nature of an artefact's intelligence are called for. Humans have a strong tendency to anthropomorphise not only nature, but anything around them (Dautenhahn, 2007) – the social brain hypothesis (Dunbar, 1998) may explain this phenomenon. As we interact with complex intelligent artefacts, we construct anthropomorphic mind models to understand and predict their behaviour. If these models are incorrect, or inadequate, we are at best at risk of being deceived and at worse at risk of being harmed.

In robot–human collaborative scenarios, transparency has been shown to improve the quality of teamwork (Breazeal *et al.*, 2005). It is also a key factor when humans attribute credit and blame in these collaborative scenarios (Kim and Hinds, 2006). Increased robot transparency is associated with reduced assignment of credit or blame to the robot, and increased assignment to humans. This increased focus on and facilitation of human agency in collaborative robot–human tasks is a desirable outcome, because it allows automation to empower and enhance its human users.

Writers such as Mueller (2016) and Cramer (2007) suggest that as intelligent systems become both increasingly complex and ubiquitous, it becomes increasingly important that they are self-explanatory, so that users can be confident about what these systems are doing and why. Robot designers have long recognised that any complex autonomous control strategy, combined with the complex real-world environment that differentiates robotics from ordinary AI, necessarily results in non-repeatable behaviour and unexpected conditions (Collett and MacDonald, 2006). Whilst many authors have recently focussed on dialogue and explanation as a solution to transparency, such systems are not appropriate to every circumstance, both because of the computational overhead for AI natural language systems and the cognitive and temporal costs of dialogue. natural language takes time and effort to produce and to understand. Authors such as Mueller (2016) see explanation as critical to one of the three main characteristics of transparent computers, the others being dialogue and learning.

Transparency is of particular importance when deploying robots in environments where those who interact with them may be vulnerable, such as in care homes or hospitals (Sharkey and Sharkey, 2012), or equally in high-risk environments where misunderstanding a robot may have dangerous consequences.

Note that the need for users to form a useful MM of a robot is orthogonal to issues of verification of robot behaviour. Whilst others have concentrated their research on making a robot safe and predictable (Fisher, Dennis and Webster, 2013; Winfield, Blum and Liu, 2014), here we are interested in the models that observers of a robot use to understand and predict its behaviour. The novelty of our experiments is that unlike other transparency studies in the literature which concentrate on human–robotics col-laboration, our study focuses on unplanned robot encounters, where human interactors were not necessarily anticipating working with an artificial system at all, let alone a particular system they may have been trained to use.

Here, we demonstrate that even abstracted and unexplained real-time visualisa-tion of a robot's priorities can substantially improve human understanding of machine intelligence, including for naive users. Subjects watch a video of, or directly observe, a robot interacting with a researcher and report their theories about what the robot is doing and why. Some of these reports are wildly inaccurate, and interestingly many conclude that the robot's objectives and abilities are far more complex than they in fact are. Nevertheless and importantly, we find that simply showing the run-time activation of the robot's action selection along with its behaviour results in users building significantly more accurate mind models. To our knowledge, this is the first real-time visual presentation of reactive robot plans using a graphical plan representation.

4.3 Technologies used: reactive planning and robot transparency

We use the R5 robot for our experiments, described in Section 3.3. We use reactive planning techniques to build transparent AI for the robot, described in Chapter 3. We deploy the *Instinct* reactive planner (Wortham, Gaudl and Bryson, 2016) as the core action selection mechanism for the R5 robot, described in Section 3.4. The reactive plan for the robot is shown in Appendix C.

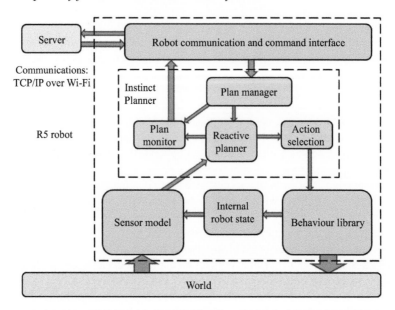

Figure 4.1   R5 robot software architecture. The arrows represent the primary data
flows between the various modules. The server may be the Instinct
Server, which logs the transparency feed to disk, or it may be the
ABOD3 real-time graphical debugging tool, see Figure 4.2.

4.3.1   The transparent planner

The Instinct Planner includes significant capabilities of facilitating plan design and
run-time debugging. It reports the execution and status of every plan element in real
time, allowing us to implicitly capture the reasoning process within the robot that gives
rise to its behaviour. The planner reports its activity as it runs, by means of callback
functions to a 'monitor' – an instance of a C++ class with a predefined interface.
There are six separate callbacks monitoring the Execution, Success, Failure, Error
and In-Progress status events, and the Sense activity of each plan element. In the R5
robot, the callback functions write textual data to a TCP/IP stream over a wireless
(Wi-Fi) link. A JAVA-based Instinct Server receives this information and logs the data
to disk. This communication channel also allows for commands to be sent to the robot
while it is running. Figure 4.1 shows the overall architecture of the planner within the
R5 robot, communicating via Wi-Fi to the logging server.

4.3.2   Robot Drives and behaviours

The robot's overall function is to search a space looking for humans. Typical real-world
applications would be to search and rescue after a building collapse, or monitoring
of commercial cold stores or similar premises. The complete plan for the robot is
provided in Appendix C.

The robot reactive plan has six Drives. These are (in order of highest priority first):

- Sleep – this Drive has a ramping priority. Initially, the priority is very low but it increases linearly over time until the Drive is released and completes successfully. The Drive is only released when the robot is close to an obstacle and is inhibited, whilst the robot confirms the presence of a human. This is to prevent the robot sleeping in the middle of an open space where it may present a trip hazard. The sleep behaviour simply shuts down the robot for a fixed interval to conserve battery power.
- Protect motors – released when the current drawn by the drive motors reaches a threshold. This might happen if the robot encounters a very steep incline or becomes jammed somehow. The Drive invokes an action pattern that stops the robot, signals for help and then pauses to await assistance.
- Moving so look – simply enforces that if the robot is moving, it should be scanning ahead for obstacles. This has a high priority so that this rule is always enforced whatever else the robot may be doing. However, it is only triggered when the robot is moving and the head is not scanning.
- Detect human – released when the robot has moved a certain distance from its last confirmed detection of a human, is within a certain distance of an obstacle ahead and its passive infrared (PIR) detects heat that could be from a human. This Drive initiates a fairly complex behaviour of movement and coloured lights designed to encourage a human to move around in front of the robot. This continues to activate the PIR sensor thus confirming the presence of a human (or animal). It is of course not a particularly accurate method of human detection.
- Emergency avoid – released when the robot's active infrared corner sensors detect reflected infrared light from a nearby obstacle. This invokes a behaviour that reverses the robot a small distance and turns left or right a fixed number of degrees. Whether to turn left or right is determined by which direction appears to be less blocked, as sensed by the active infrared detectors.
- Roam – released whenever the robot is not sleeping. It uses the scanning ultrasonic detector to determine when there may be obstacles ahead and turns appropriately to avoid them. It also modulates the robot's speed and the rate of scanning depending on the proximity of obstacles.

4.3.3 Real-time plan debugger

We use the new version of the ABODE plan editor for POSH plans, *ABOD3*, as seen in Figure 4.2 (Theodorou, 2016). This is the first version of ABODE to support real-time visualisation. ABOD3 has been enhanced by Andreas Theodorou to directly read Instinct plans, and also to read a log file containing the real-time transparency data emanating from the Instinct Planner, in order to provide a real-time graphical display of plan execution. ABOD3 is also able to display a video and synchronise it with the debug display. In this way, it is possible to explore both run-time debugging and wider issues of AI transparency. This facility is used in the first experiment. ABOD3 is also able to process and display a real-time feed of transparency data directly from the

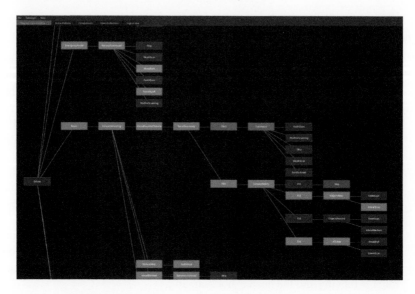

Figure 4.2   ABOD3 display of part of the Instinct plan described in the text. Note
that the element labels are readable on the original display. A larger
screenshot of ABOD3 is provided in Appendix D.

R5 robot as it runs. This facility is used in our second experiment. A larger screenshot
of ABOD3 is provided in Appendix D.

4.3.4   Mobile Augmented Reality

As an extension to the idea of using displays to improve transparency, a new tool has
been developed by Alexandros Rotsidis, as part of his MSc at the University of Bath
(Rotsidis, 2018; Rotsidis *et al.*, 2019). This tool, named *ABOD3-AR*, provides the
ABOD3 interface on an Android mobile phone device.

The work also includes an extension to the Instinct Server, allowing it to act
as a kind of application level hub. The application topology is shown in Figure 4.3.
The R5 robot connects to the Instinct Server which then publishes that data to all
mobile devices attached to it.

Once the ABOD3-AR is running on the phone, the camera is activated and
the display shows the images produced. An image-recognition algorithm searches
the image for the presence of the R5 robot, based on a training set of previous image
data. Once the R5 robot is located, the algorithm tracks the robot within the image.
The ABOD3-AR application also establishes a connection to the Instinct Server,
giving it access to the transparency feed provided by the robot. ABOD3-AR uses this
feed to augment the visual display, tagging the robot with a real-time hierarchical
representation of the Instinct plan as it runs. This work provides a proof of concept
for robot transparency through Mobile Augmented Reality (MAR). An experiment
using this tool is outlined in Section 4.6.

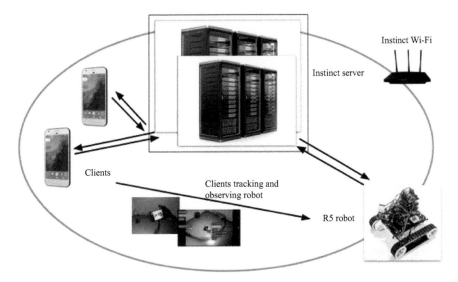

Figure 4.3   ABOD3-AR architecture, showing the R5 robot connecting with the enhanced Instinct Server. One or more mobile phones, equipped with ABOD3-AR, connect to the Instinct Server in order to access the transparency feed from the R5 robot.

4.4   Methods: the robot experiments

In the following sections, I describe three separate experiments. The first uses a video recording of the R5 robot and a web-based online questionnaire. The second experiment involves participants directly observing the robot in a public space whilst watching a PC-based transparency display. The third experiment was conducted by my colleague Alexandros Rotsidis and uses the ABOD3-AR tool providing transparency through *MAR* (Figure 4.4).

4.4.1   Experiment one – Online Video

The robot in the video runs within an enclosed environment where it interacts with various objects and walls made of different materials. A researcher also interacts with the robot. The robot's action selection governs the behaviour of the robot by applying the reactive plan. As mentioned earlier, a reactive plan encodes the (proactive) priorities of an autonomous robot, and the conditions when actions can be applied. A record of transparency data in the form of a log of which plan components are triggered at what time is collected by a remote server running on a laptop PC via a Wi-Fi connection.

Using its built-in real-time clock, the robot tags the transparency data stream with the start time of the experiment. It also includes the elapsed time in milliseconds with

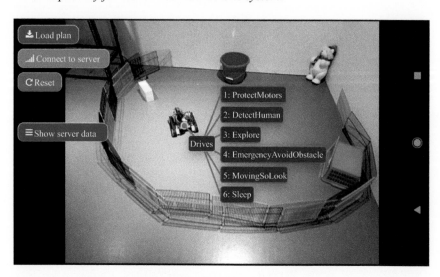

Figure 4.4   ABOD3-AR display, showing the R5 robot operating with additional transparency information provided using augmented reality. A larger version of this image is available in Appendix E.

every data-stream event. In this way, the ABOD3 debugger is able to subsequently synchronise the data stream with video recordings taken during the experiment.

4.4.1.1   Robot videos

For our initial study, we chose to video the robot rather than have participants interact with the robot directly. This research method has recently been chosen by others (Cameron *et al.*, 2015) with good results. Video has the benefit of ensuring all subjects share identical stimuli.

The interaction is recorded from two positions at each end of the robot pen, and a camera mounted on a post attached to the robot also captures a 'robot's eye' view, providing a third perspective. The resulting composite video is approximately 5-min long. Figure 4.5 is a single frame from the video. It shows the researcher interacting with the robot. This video was shown to half of our group of test participants.

Using the ABOD3 tool, we created a second video. A frame from this video is shown in Figure 4.6. The six Drives described previously are clearly visible. As each Drive is released and the associated behaviours are executed, the plan elements constituting the behaviours are highlighted. This highlighting is synchronised with the behaviour of the robot visible in the video. This gives the viewer access to a great deal more information from the robot than is available by watching the robot alone. ABOD3 conveniently allows us to collapse the lower levels in the hierarchy, and position the visible plan elements for ease of understanding. For the purpose of clarity in the video, we chose to display only the highest levels of the reactive plan, primarily the Drives.

Figure 4.5 Video of interaction with the robot with no plan visible (stimulus for Group 1 in the first experiment).

Figure 4.6 More transparent video showing the ABOD3 plan representation; subtrees have been hidden from view (stimulus for Group 2). Note that the drive labels were legible to the subjects and can be seen clearly in the printed version of this book, or by zooming the postscript version. A larger version of this figure is provided in Appendix D. The Drives are also explained in Section 4.3.2.

Table 4.1   Post-treatment questions for Video and Directly Observed Robot experiments

Question	Response	Category
Is robot thinking?	Y/N	Intel
Is robot intelligent?	1–5	Intel
Feeling about robot?	Multi-choice	Emo
Understand objective?	Y/N	MM
Describe robot task?	Free text	MM
Why does robot stop?	Free text	MM
Why do lights flash?	Free text	MM
What is person doing?	Free text	MM
Happy to be person?	Y/N	Emo
Want robot in home?	Y/N	Emo

4.4.1.2   Demographic and post-treatment questionnaires

For the Online Video experiment, the participants were initially sent an email questionnaire prepared using GOOGLE FORMS* to gather basic demographic data: age, gender, educational level, whether they use computers, whether they program computers and whether they have ever used a robot. Based on this information, they were then divided into two groups that were matched as nearly as possible for participant mix. Each group received an identical email asking them to carefully watch a video and then answer a second questionnaire. Group 1 was directed to the composite video (Figure 4.5), and Group 2 to the debug video (Figure 4.6).

Table 4.1 summarises the questions asked after the participant had seen the video. These questions are designed to measure various factors: the measure of intelligence perceived by the participants (Intel), the emotional response (if any) to the robot (Emo) and – most importantly – the accuracy of the participants' MM of the robot.

For analysis, the four free text responses were rated for accuracy with the robot's actual Drives and behaviours and given a score per question of 0 (inaccurate or no response), 1 (partially accurate) or 2 (accurate). The marking was carried out by a single researcher for consistency, without access to either subject identities or knowledge of which group the subject was in. No special vocabulary was expected. The questions used in the questionnaire are deliberately very general, so as not to steer the subject. Similarly, the marking scheme used was deliberately coarse grained because we are looking for a significant effect at the general level of understanding, not for a nuanced improvement in the subject's model.

By summing the scores to give an overall Report Accuracy, the accuracy of the participant's overall MM is scored from 0 to 6 – Question 3 was found to be ambiguous and so is not included in the scores, see Section 4.5.2.

---

*Google Forms, see https://docs.google.com/forms/

*Figure 4.7   Arrangement of the Directly Observed Robot experiment at At-Bristol.
Obstacles visible include a yellow rubber duck and a blue bucket. The
position and orientation of the transparency display is shown.*

4.4.2   Experiment two – Directly Observed Robot

This subsequent experiment took place over 3 days at the At-Bristol Science Learning Centre, Bristol, United Kingdom. This context was chosen because of available subjects in a controlled setting.

The robot operated within an enclosed pen as a special interactive exhibits within the main exhibition area, see Figure 4.7. Visitors, both adults and children, were invited to sit and observe the robot in operation for several minutes, whilst the robot moved around the pen and interacted with the researchers. Subjects were expected to watch the robot for at least 3 min before being handed a paper questionnaire. They then completed the questionnaire, which contained the same questions as for the above-mentioned Online Video experiment. During this time, subjects were able to continue to watch the robot in operation.

A large computer monitor was positioned at the front of the pen displaying the ABOD3 real-time visualisation of plan execution. This display was either enabled or disabled for periods as the days progressed to create the Group 2 and Group 1 data sets. Only adult data (age 18 and above) is included in the results.

4.5   Results

The demographics of each group of participants is shown in Tables 4.2 and 4.3. For the Online Video experiment, it was possible to match the groups prior to watching the

*Table 4.2   Online Video experiment: demographics of
participant groups (N = 45).*

Demographic	Group 1	Group 2
Total participants	22	23
Mean age (years)	39.7	35.8
Gender male	11	10
Gender female	11	12
Gender PNTS	0	1
STEM degree	7	8
Other degree	13	13
Ever worked with a robot?	2	3
Do you use computers?	19	23
Are you a programmer?	6	8

*Table 4.3   Directly Observed Robot experiment: demographics of
participant groups (N = 55).*

Demographic	Group 1	Group 2
Total participants	28	27
Mean age (years)	48.0	40.0
Gender male	10	10
Gender female	18	17
STEM degree	5	9
Other degree	11	8
Ever worked with a robot?	7	6
Do you use computers?	20	22
Are you a programmer?	6	5

video. Priority was given to matching the number of programmers in each group, and to having an equal gender mix. This was not possible in the Directly Observed Robot experiment, however Table 4.3 shows that the groups were nevertheless well-balanced.

4.5.1   Main findings

The primary results obtained from the experiments are outlined in Tables 4.4 and 4.5. Data is analysed using the unpaired t test. First and most importantly, in both experiments there is a marked difference in the participants' Report Accuracy scores between Group 1 (just observe robot) and Group 2 (observe robot and debug display). This confirms a significant correlation between the accuracy of the participants' MMs of the robot, and the provision of the additional transparency data provided

Table 4.4   *Online Video experiment: main results. Bold face*
indicates results significant to at least p = 0.05.

Result	Group 1	Group 2
Is thinking (0/1)	0.36 (sd = 0.48)	0.65 (sd = 0.48)
Intelligence (1–5)	2.64 (sd = 0.88)	2.74 (sd = 1.07)
Understand objective (0/1)	0.68 (sd = 0.47)	0.74 (sd = 0.44)
Report Accuracy (0–6)	1.86 (sd = 1.42)	3.39 (sd = 2.08)

Table 4.5   *Directly Observed Robot experiment: main results.*
Bold face indicates results significant to at least p = 0.05.

Result	Group 1	Group 2
Is thinking (0/1)	0.46 (sd = 0.50)	0.56 (sd = 0.50)
Intelligence (1–5)	2.96 (sd = 1.18)	3.15 (sd = 1.18)
Understand objective (0/1)	0.50 (sd = 0.50)	0.89 (sd = 0.31)
Report Accuracy (0–6)	1.89 (sd = 1.40)	3.52 (sd = 2.10)

by ABOD3. Online Video experiment; $t(43) = 2.86$, $p = 0.0065$, Directly Observed Robot experiment $t(55) = 3.39$, $p = 0.0013$.

Second, there is no significant difference in perceived robot intelligence between the two groups in each experiment, although across experiments the data indicates a slightly higher level of perceived intelligence when the robot was directly observed; $t(98) = 1.64$, $p = 0.104$.

Third, in the Online Video experiment, a substantially higher number of participants in Group 2 (ABOD3) report that they believe the robot is thinking; $t(43) = 2.02$, $p = 0.050$. However, this effect is not significantly repeated when the robot is directly observed; $t(55) = 0.680$, $p = 0.500$.

Finally, for participants directly observing the robot, the ABOD3 display significantly affects their report that they understand what the robot is trying to do; $t(55) = 3.44$, $p = 0.0011$. This is not the case in the Online Video experiment, where the Group 2 data shows no significant affect; $t(43) = 0.425$, $p = 0.673$.

4.5.2   Qualitative outcomes

Participants also select from a list of possible emotional states: Happy, Sad, Scared, Angry, Curious, Excited, Bored, Anxious and No Feeling. For the Online Video experiment, the data indicates very little emotional response to the robot in either group, with most participants indicating either 'No Feeling', or only 'Curious'. However, in the Directly Observed Robot experiment, participants indicate a higher level of emotional response, summarised in Table 4.6; $t(98) = 2.63$, $p = 0.0098$.

We had predicted that the robot might be more emotionally salient when it was experienced directly. However, from Table 4.6, it can be seen that curiosity dominates

Table 4.6   *Directly Observed Robot experiment: self-reported emotion (N = 55).*

Reported emotion	Group 1	Group 2
Curious	23	23
Excited	5	10
Happy	5	12
No Feeling	4	2
Anxious	0	1
Bored	1	0
Scared	1	0

the results. Nevertheless, the addition of the transparency display may well increase the emotions reported; $t(53) = 1.91$, $p = 0.0622$. This may be a topic for future investigation.

In the first Online Video experiment, from the answers to the question 'why does the robot stop every so often' it appears that this question is ambiguous. Some understand this to mean every time the robot stops to scan its environment before proceeding, and only one person took this to mean the sleep behaviour of the robot that results in a more prolonged period of inactivity. The question was intended to refer to the latter and was particularly included because the Sleep Drive is highlighted by ABOD3 each time the robot is motionless with no lights flashing. However, only one member of Group 2 identified this from the video. Due to this ambiguity, the data related to this question was not considered further in this data set. This question was subsequently refined in the second, Directly Observed Robot, experiment to *'Why does it just stop every so often (when all its lights go out)?'*. Six participants then correctly answered this question and so it is included in the analysis.

Despite the improved performance of Group 2, many members, even those with a Science, Technology, Engineering or Maths (STEM) degree, still form a poor MM of the robot. Here are some notable quotes from STEM participants:

- [the robot is] *"Trying to create a 3d map of the area? At one stage I thought it might be going to throw something into the bucket once it had mapped out but couldn't quite tell if it had anything to throw."*
- [the robot is] *"aiming for the black spot in the picture."* [we are unsure of the picture to which the participant refers]
- *"is it trying to identify where the abstract picture is and how to show the complete picture?"* [picture visible in Figure 4.5]
- [the robot] *"is circling the room, gathering information about it with a sensor. It moves the sensor every so often in different parts of the room, so I think it is trying to gather spacial information about the room (its layout or its dimensions maybe)."*
- [the robot] *"maybe finding certain colours."*

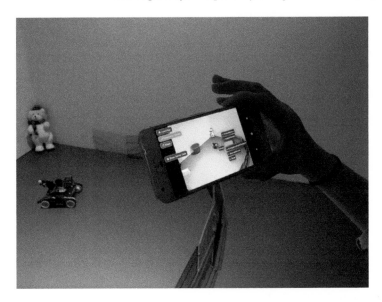

Figure 4.8   *The ABOD3-AR application in use during the Mobile Augmented Reality experiment. The current scene with the R5 robot is visible on the phone display and is dynamically augmented to show the internal state and processing of the robot.*

These comments indicate that in the absence of an accurate model, environmental cues and possibly previous knowledge of robots are used to help create a plausible narrative.

4.6   Experiment three – Mobile Augmented Reality

This third experiment was conducted by Alexandros Rotsidis a year or so later than the above-mentioned two experiments, as part of his MSc project work. It uses the ABOD3-AR MAR tool rather than a desktop PC display but is otherwise rather similar to experiment one described in Section 4.4.2. The experiment took place over 5 days, during a public exhibition at the University of Bath. Once again, the robot was placed within a small pen, together with various static objects, one of which is visible in Figure 4.8.

Naive participants were asked to observe the robot and then complete a small questionnaire. Group 1 ($N = 20$) simply observed the robot directly, whilst Group 2 ($N = 21$) observed the robot using ABOD3-AR. The questionnaire was primarily the standard Godspeed questions, see Section 6.4.5 and also Bartneck *et al.* (2009). Specifically, the questionnaire did not include the core post-treatment questions used as a basis to calculate Report Accuracy, see Table 4.1. The full details of this experiment, including the full results and their analysis, are already published by Rotsidis *et al.* (2019), and so are not repeated here. However, some of the qualitative data is worth some further comment.

Participants were asked the following question: "In your own words, what do you think the robot is doing?". Some of their answers are provided next:

Group 1:

- Trying to build a memory of the distance between itself and the objects to judge its own location in space.
- Processing Data.
- Random.
- Is actively looking for something specific. At some points, he believes he has found it (flashes a light) but then continues on to look.
- Taking pictures of the objects.
- Occasionally taking pictures.
- He is looking for something.

Group 2:

- Exploring its surroundings and trying to detect humans.
- Roaming detecting objects and movement through sensors.
- The robot likes to scan for obstacles, humans and find new paths to follow it can understand animals and obstacles.
- Imitating commands, responding to stimuli.
- Registering programmed behaviours and connecting it to its surroundings.
- Movement looks random; I would say, it is using sensors to avoid the obstacles.
- Occasionally taking pictures.

It is notable that two of the participants in Group 1 used 'he' to refer to the robot, rather than 'it'. The language in the Group 1 answers is more anthropomorphic ('he believes'), whereas Group 2 participants used terminology that had usefully gained from the transparency feed, particularly 'Explore', 'scan', 'detect humans' and so on. One participant also very accurately noted that the robot was using 'programmed behaviours'. Participants in both groups inaccurately assessed that the robot was taking pictures.

The ABOD3-AR application includes a very neat capability allowing users to drill down into an active Drive to view the next level of the plan hierarchy. An example is shown in Figure 4.9. Rotsidis did not capture whether participants used this facility, but the answers of Group 2 are indicative that they did not.

An analysis of answers to the Godspeed questions revealed a statistically significant effect for some of the Godspeed categories: participants with access to ABOD3-AR were more likely to describe the robot as alive, lively and friendly. I would suggest that this may well be simply because they paid more attention to the robot when they had the opportunity to view it through the 'cool' augmented reality-mobile phone interface. I extend this argument further in Section 6.6.

Finally, during this experiment, all participants ($N = 41$) were incidentally asked how well the tracking worked, and they found it to be very robust, see Figure 4.10.

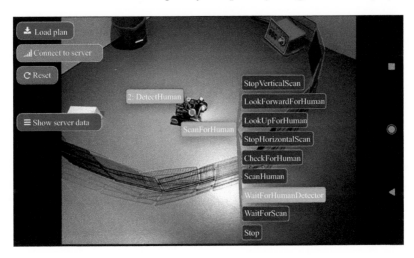

*Figure 4.9   ABOD3-AR display, showing how the user can drill down by clicking
on an active element – in this case the DetectHuman Drive – to show
detail of plan execution at a lower, more detailed, level. A larger
version of this figure is provided in Appendix E.*

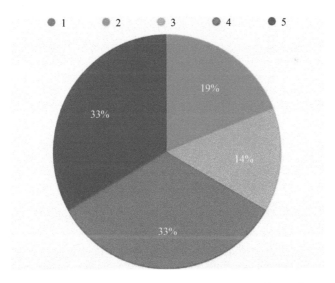

*Figure 4.10   Participant response to the question 'How good was the tracking of
the robot?' where 1 = Poor through 5 = Excellent.*

On a 1–5 Likert scale, 66% of participants rated the performance at either 4 (Very Good) or 5 (Excellent), and no participants awarded the lowest score (Poor). This is an encouraging result as it shows that a small, non-humanoid robot can be effectively tracked in real time by a low-cost mobile phone. This MAR approach to robot transparency display is therefore a practical, realistic possibility.

4.7   Discussion

Across both experiments, one and two, there is a significant correlation between the accuracy of the participants' MMs of the robot, as indicated by the Report Accuracy scores, and the provision of the additional transparency data provided by ABOD3. We have shown that a real-time display of a robot's decision-making produces significantly better understanding of that robot's intelligence, even though that understanding may still include wildly inaccurate overestimation of the robot's abilities.

Strikingly, there was one further significant result besides the improved MM. Subjects in Experiment one (Online Video) who observed the real-time display did not think the robot was more intelligent but *did* think it 'thought' more. This result is counter-intuitive. We had expected that if ABOD3 resulted in increased transparency, there would be a corresponding reduction in the use of anthropomorphic cognitive descriptions. However, at least in this case the data suggests that the reverse is true. When taken with the significant improvement in understanding of the robot's actual drives and behaviours, this result implies that an improved MM is associated with an increased perception of a thinking agent. Most likely, this reflects the still pervasive belief that navigating in the real world is not a difficult task, so the number of different planning steps employed by the robot during the process may come as a surprise. Notably, with the immediate presence of the robot in the shared environment in the second experiment, assessments of thinking under both conditions moved towards '50–50' or complete uncertainty, though the trend was still in the same direction. The complexity of navigation, balance and perception has been persistently under-recognised (Brooks, 1991a).

Unlike *thinking*, *intelligence* seems to be a term that in ordinary language is often reserved for conscious decision-making. Notably, even where subjects exposed to the ABOD3 visualisations of the robot's decision-making considered the robot to be thinking more, they did not consider it to be more intelligent. In fact, the middling marks for intelligence in either condition may reflect a society-wide lack of certainty about the definition of the term rather than any cognitive assessment. The relatively large standard deviations for intelligence in Tables 4.4 and 4.5 provide some evidence of this uncertainty. Comparing results from the two experiments, it might be that the immediacy of the directly observed robot makes the objective more confusing without transparency and more apparent with transparency. Further investigation would be required to confirm whether this is repeatable.

It may be that the timing of the ABOD3 plan element highlighting and decay must be very tightly correlated with the video in order for them to appear connected. This may be similar to the temporal limit of lip synchronisation between video and audio when observing speech, beyond which the two data streams appear unrelated. It might be expected that other forms of transparency display would better serve non-specialists, i.e. those not familiar with reactive planning or the ABOD3 presentation paradigm. One interesting approach would be to use argumentation techniques to generate natural language (Caminada *et al.*, 2014), although this assumes that the plan contains sufficient information to allow an explanation to be generated.

In the first experiment, the lack of emotion with respect to the robot was unexpected, and conflicts with the spontaneous feedback we frequently receive about the R5 robot when people encounter it in our laboratory or during demonstrations. In these situations, we often hear both quite strong positive and negative emotional reactions. Some find the robot scary or creepy (McAndrew and Koehnke, 2016), whilst others remark that it is cute, particularly when it is operational. We hypothesise that the remote nature of the video, or the small size of the robot on screen, reduces the chance of significant emotional response. Indeed, this is confirmed by the higher levels of emotional response measured when participants directly observe the robot. Lack of creepiness (Anxious, Scared) may be due to the more controlled setting of the experiment, or the presence of 'experts' rather than peers. It is also interesting that the transparency display appears to further solicit positive emotional responses. Perhaps, this reflects a delight or satisfaction that the robot behaviour is 'explained' by the display.

4.8 Conclusion and further work

We have demonstrated that subjects can show marked improvement in the accuracy of their MM, of a robot observed either directly or on video, if they also see an accompanying display of the robot's real-time decision-making. In both our pilot study using Online Video ($N = 45$) and our subsequent experiment with direct observation ($N = 55$), the outcome was strongly significant. The addition of ABOD3 visualisation of the robot's intelligence does indeed make the machine nature of the robot more transparent.

The results of the Online Video experiment imply that an improved MM of the robot is associated with an increased perception of a thinking machine, even though there is no significant change in the level of perceived intelligence. However, this effect is not seen when the robot is directly observed. The relationship between the perception of intelligence and thinking is therefore not straightforward. There is clearly further work to be done to unpack the relationship between the improved MM of the robot and the increased perception of a thinking machine.

Experiment one confirms that the approach of using Online Video with Web-based questionnaires is both effective and efficient in terms of researcher time, and it has enabled us to quickly gather preliminary results from which further experiments can be planned. However, we did not gather any useful data about the emotional response of the participants using this methodology. This may possibly be due to the lack of physical robot presence. Therefore, in situations where the emotional engagement of users to robots is of interest, the use of video techniques may prove ineffective.

This is explored further in Chapter 6. We also use the Godspeed questionnaire (Bartneck *et al.*, 2009) in the studies in Chapter 6, both to investigate participant MMs more widely, and to facilitate comparison with the future work of others.

The technology used to construct the experimental systems was found to be reliable, robust and straightforward to use. The Instinct Planner combined with the iVDL graphical design tool enabled us to quickly generate a reliable yet sufficiently complex reactive plan for the R5 robot to allow us to conduct this experiment. The robot and real-time ABOD3 operated reliably over 3 days without problems despite some unexpected participant physical handling. Given the low cost of the platform, we would recommend its use for similar low-cost research robot applications.

The ABOD3-AR mobile phone application also operated very reliably over several days during the third experiment and has been used subsequently for demonstration of MAR. Considerable opportunities exist for further experimentation of this approach with multiple simultaneous users and multiple robots operating in the same environment.

The fact that good results were achieved with a pre$-\alpha$ version of ABOD3 gave us high hopes for its utility not only for visualisation but also for real-time plan debugging. Certainly, it proved able to provide transparency information to untrained observers of an autonomous robot. Further work is currently underway at the University of Bath to deploy ABOD3 on the Pepper robot. Pepper is equipped with a large, chest-mounted display (see Figure 4.11), ideally suited to display of the real-time state and design making being undertaken as the robot operates.

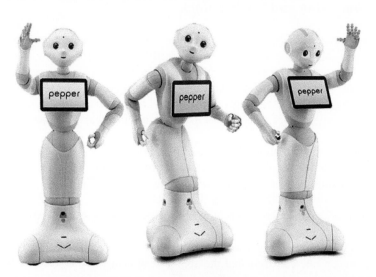

Figure 4.11   The Pepper robot, produced by Softbank Inc. Of note are the large, chest-mounted displays, very suitable for use as a transparency display.

In this chapter, we have seen how using a graphical display to expose the real-time control state of a robot substantially improves understanding in lay subjects. A lay observer and technical specialist may need different levels of detail, and future work could include varying the design of the visualisation dependent both on the robot task and user type. In the following chapter, we investigate an alternative approach to improving transparency, by using vocalisation rather than a visual display.

Chapter 5
Transparency using audio – the muttering robot

"There is something particularly human about using tools; the first and most important tool being language."
– Isaac Asimov, Epigraph in Asimov's Book of Science and Nature Quotations

5.1 Summary

Transparency is an important design consideration for all intelligent autonomous systems. The previous work shows that a real-time visual display of a robot's decision-making produces significantly better understanding of that robot's intelligence. We investigate vocalisation of behaviour selection as a possible alternative solution for situations where a visual display of decision-making is either impractical or impossible.

In this experiment, we find that vocalisation is associated with a significant improvement in understanding of the robot, comparable with the results obtained using a real-time display. We also find that vocalisation has no significant effect on participants' emotional response, though it may slightly increase positive feelings about the robot. We discuss the relative merits of visual and vocalised transparency mechanisms and suggest possible applications.

5.2 Transparency through spoken language

The relationship between transparency, trust and utility is complex (Wortham and Theodorou, 2017), but nevertheless it is clear that transparency is an important design consideration for all intelligent autonomous systems. Transparency has been shown to improve the quality of teamwork in robot–human collaborative scenarios (Breazeal et al., 2005). It is also a key factor when humans attribute credit and blame in these collaborative scenarios (Kim and Hinds, 2006). Increased robot transparency is associated with reduced assignment of credit or blame to the robot, and increased assignment to humans. This increased focus on and facilitation of human agency in collaborative robot–human tasks is a desirable outcome, because it allows automation to empower and enhance its human users.

In Chapter 4, we show that a real-time visual display of a robot's decision-making produces significantly better understanding of that robot's intelligence (Wortham, Theodorou and Bryson, 2016, 2017). In this chapter, we describe a possible alternative solution for situations where a visual display of decision-making is either impractical or impossible. We use the Instinct reactive planner (Wortham, Gaudl and Bryson, 2016) to control a small mobile robot, monitor the hierarchical action selection process, extended with a novel algorithm to convert the output from the monitor into vocalised (spoken) sentences.

Humans have evolved to produce and comprehend language (Berwick and Chomsky, 2015). We are able to perform several tasks simultaneously involving language and sharing mental resources between different cognitive systems (Kempen, Olsthoorn and Sprenger, 2012). This suggests using language as a likely candidate to enhance robot transparency. The vocalisation of the robot is, however, not an implicit designed behaviour of the robot reactive plan, but rather a separate monitoring channel expressed vocally. The result is a robot that *'mutters'*, continually vocalising the execution of Drives and progress through the reactive plan hierarchy. The immediate and obvious difficulty with this approach is that the robot executes multiple reactive plan cycles per second, each traversing many plan elements in the plan hierarchy. It is thus impossible to report vocally on the initiation and progress of each plan element in real time. Our algorithm first generates predefined candidate sentences to be uttered and then uses a number of novel parameterised approaches to select from these candidates. This algorithm produces understandable vocalised sentences that usefully convey the decision processes taking place within the robot in real time. We deploy this algorithm in the R5 robot and show that observers' mind models of the robot improve significantly when also exposed to the muttering.

5.3   The muttering mechanism

Those interested in the theory of reactive planning and the detailed operation of the Instinct Planner and R5 robot should read either Wortham, Gaudl and Bryson (2016) or preferably Chapter 3 before they read this explanation of the muttering mechanism. However, this description should suffice unsupported for those mainly interested in the results of this experiment, and who only wish to have an understanding of the mechanism used to achieve the muttering behaviour of the robot. The complete source code for the Instinct Planner is available on an open source basis,* as is the code for the R5 robot, including the muttering mechanism described in this section.[†]

As already explained in Chapter 3 the robot behaviour (or action) selection is performed by the Instinct Planner. The planner combines sensory information gathered by the robot, with a predefined set of *Drives*, each Drive designed to achieve a specific goal or objective. Each Drive is expressed as a hierarchically composed plan of *Competences*, *Action Patterns* and ultimately *Actions*. These actions invoke

---

*http://www.robwortham.com/instinct-planner/
[†]http://www.robwortham.com/r5-robot/

the behaviour primitives of the robot, such as 'stop', 'turn left', 'scan for human', 'flash headlight' and so on.

The planner produces a transparency feed for each execution cycle of the plan. An execution cycle involves a top-down search for the highest priority Drive that is released, and the subsequent traversal of the plan hierarchy to determine which Action is to be selected, see Section 3.4. For each cycle the planner produces a stream of data corresponding to the traversal of the plan hierarchy leading to an action being selected. This stream contains the *Plan Element Identifier* (ID) of each plan element and the status of the plan element. As the planner traverses down the hierarchy, it reports plan element IDs together with the status *Executed* (E). As the planner completes the processing of each plan element travelling back up the hierarchy, it again reports the plan element ID, but this time with the outcome of the execution. The outcome is one of four options: *Success, In Progress, Failed, Error*.

- Success – indicates that the plan element has completed successfully.
- In Progress – indicates either that an underlying physical behaviour of the robot is still in the process of execution, or that a more complex element such as an Action Pattern or Competence is part way through its various steps, but as yet not completed.
- Failed – a common outcome of a reactive plan, arising from the dynamic and unpredictable world in which the robot operates.
- Error – this outcome only occurs when an internal programming error takes place, such as a fault in the plan design, or a bug in the software.

In previous work, described in Chapter 4, we used this transparency feed to drive a dynamic visual display showing the plan execution in real time, as a means to make the operation of the robot more transparent. However, there are limitations to this approach, discussed more fully in Section 5.6; here we generate a stream of audible output to convey at least some of the information in the transparency feed in real time to those observing and interacting with the robot.

From the explanation above, readers will already realise that the transparency data feed consists of many tens of plan element notifications per second. The data rate of the transparency feed in notifications per second R_t is given by

$$R_t = 2R_pD_p \tag{5.1}$$

where R_p is the rate of plan execution, and D_p is the depth of the plan hierarchy currently being executed. For the R5 robot operating with a plan cycle rate of eight cycles per second, a plan with a hierarchy depth of seven generates 112 notifications per second. It is not possible to generate meaningful speech output at this rate. Therefore, we must be selective. The mechanism adopted here uses three stages of selectivity, described in the following three subsections, and illustrated in Figure 5.1.

5.3.1 Transparency execution stack

The transparency feed data contains information relating to the current execution state of each plan element executed on each plan cycle. Since real-world events happen

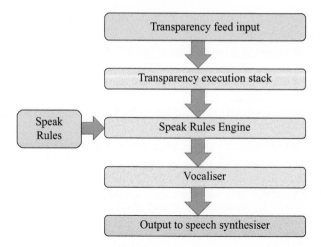

Figure 5.1   The muttering mechanism. The arrows represent the data flow from the incoming transparency feed, through the final text output sent to the speech synthesiser. The Speak Rules Engine is configured by a set of Speak Rules chosen by the designer. For a detailed description of each stage, see Sections 5.3.1, 5.3.2 and 5.3.3.

much more slowly than the plan cycle rate, it is neither useful, nor possible, to inform the user of every invocation of every plan element in each plan cycle. We must extract only salient information related to changes in plan execution and also remind users when a real-world long running process is in progress.

Using the transparency data feed, we first detect when there are changes in the execution pattern occurring between two consecutive plan cycles. Real-world actions typically take much longer than a single plan cycle to execute, and so frequently the same route is traversed through the plan hierarchy many times, with the leaf node Action repeatedly having a status of In Progress. In order to detect these changes, we implement a stack arrangement. Starting from the initial Drive notification, we store reports of element executions in a stack structure. Once the leaf node is reached, we traverse the stack in the opposite direction completing the element status for each plan element. On subsequent plan cycles, we check whether the same element IDs are being executed at each position in the stack. If there is a change, we mark it and clear out all records at lower levels in the stack. This mechanism allows us to gather information about whether this is the first time a plan element has been executed in this context, and also whether the execution status has changed from previous executions.

Having reduced the data volume somewhat, and also recovered information relating to real-world changes of behaviour, we can now choose when to notify users based on a set of rules for each plan element type.

5.3.2 The Speak Rules Engine

The Speak Rules Engine produces predefined candidate sentences for each plan element type and Event Type combination. For example, new executions of competence elements create sentences of the form 'Attempting {plan-element-name}'.

The plan element names are stored within the robot alongside the plan itself, and the plan element IDs from the transparency feed are used to locate the correct plan element name relating to the sentence to be constructed. These element names are processed using *'camel case'* rules to generate speakable names for the plan elements – camel case is a convention where each new word starts with a capital letter, for example ActivateHumanDetector or ForwardAvoidingObstacle. The camel case processing can also deal with numbers such as Sleep10Seconds, converting the number into a separate word to be spoken. These speakable plan element names are inserted into predefined sentences, producing sentences of the form 'Completed Activate Human Detector', 'Attempting Forward Avoiding Obstacle' and 'Doing Sleep10Seconds'.

In our system, the predefined sentences are fixed at compile time, although a more complex arrangement to reduce monotony could be added. This is discussed further in Section 5.6.

Based on the information held in the Transparency Execution Stack, we now make decisions about whether to generate a candidate sentence about each event as it occurs, based on a set of *Speak Rules*. The robot holds a matrix of Speak Rule values for each of the six plan element types; Drive, Competence, Competence Element, Action Pattern, Action Pattern Element and Action. The default values for the action element type are shown in Table 5.1. Similar tables are stored for each of the other plan element types.

For each Event Type (Executed, Success, In Progress, Failed and Error), the table stores four parameters; Timeout, RptMyself, RptTimeout and AlwaysSpeak:

- Timeout – defines how long the generated sentence will be stored awaiting presentation to the speech output system. After this timeout, the sentence will be discarded.
- RptMyself – a Boolean flag to specify whether the sentence should be repeated, should it match the last thing uttered by the robot.

Table 5.1   Speak Rules for the Action plan element type.

Event	Timeout	RptMyself	RptTimeout	AlwaysSpeak
Executed	800	False	3,333	True
Success	500	False	3,333	False
In Progress	0	False	0	False
Failed	5,000	False	3,333	True
Error	5,000	False	3,333	True

- RptTimeout – determines the time after which the utterance would not be considered to be a repeat. The timeout values are specified in milliseconds.
- AlwaysSpeak – a Boolean that will force the sentence to be spoken next, irrespective of whether other sentences are queued, see Section 5.3.3.

Considering the settings in Table 5.1, we see that when an Action is In Progress, no candidate sentence will be generated. However, when an element is first Executed, Fails or an Error occurs, The AlwaysSpeak flag indicates that a higher priority will be given to the candidate sentence that is generated. The Timeout parameters are tuned during testing; the setting of 5,000 ms in Table 5.1 ensure that if a Fail or Error occurs then the user will be notified.

The R5 robot includes a command line interface accessible via its Wi-Fi link, see Appendices A and B. This interface includes commands to change each of these parameters individually, and to save them to a permanent storage area within the robot. Tuning these parameters is at present a matter of iterative human design.

5.3.3   The Vocaliser

Despite the filtering achieved by the Speak Rules Engine, many more candidate sentences are still generated than can be spoken. Each is presented to the Vocaliser, along with the various Timeout parameters and Boolean flags.

The Vocaliser uses a double buffered approach to store sentences to be spoken. One buffer is filled with data to be sent to the speech output, whilst the second buffer is available for the following sentence to be stored. As soon as the data is sent to the speech output, data is copied from the second buffer to the first, leaving the first buffer available again. Once both buffers are full however, further candidate sentences are discarded until the sentences are either spoken or replaced, according to the Speak Rule parameters.

Since each sentence is queued before being spoken, there is inevitably some time lag between generation and utterance; however, the timeouts within the Speak Rules ensure that only currently relevant sentences are actually vocalised.

The actual vocalisation is performed by a low-cost text to speech synthesiser module and a small loudspeaker mounted on the R5 robot. The audio is also available via a Bluetooth transmitter, in order that it can be accessed remotely. In noisy environments, this enables users to wear headphones to better hear the audio output produced by the robot. A video of this arrangement is available on the author's YouTube channel at https://youtu.be/sCd1GNJe6Jw.

5.4   Experimental methods

An experiment was conducted over three days in December 2016, at the At-Bristol Science Learning Centre, Bristol, United Kingdom. This context was chosen because of available subjects in a controlled setting. The robot operated on a large blue table as a special interactive exhibits within the main exhibition area, see Figure 5.2. Visitors, both adults and children, were invited to stand and observe the robot in

Figure 5.2   *Arrangement of the muttering robot experiment at At-Bristol. The obstacles are made from giant LEGO Bricks. Observers are wearing headphones fed from a standard headphone amplifier, which in turn is connected to a Bluetooth receiver. This receives the audio output from the robot's Bluetooth transmitter. This enables participants to hear the robot clearly with high levels of background noise.*

operation for several minutes whilst the robot moved around the pen and interacted with the researchers. Subjects were expected to watch the robot for at least 3 min before being handed a paper questionnaire to gather both participant demographics and information about the participants' perceptions of the robot. During each day, the robot operated for periods in each of two modes; silent (Group 1 results), or with muttering enabled (Group 2 results). The R5 robot carries an on-board speaker to produce the 'muttering', see Figure 3.8. Typically, this is sufficiently loud to be heard in most indoor environments. However, as the At-Bristol environment was particularly noisy with children playing, participants were encouraged to wear headphones to better hear the audio output.

5.4.1   Post-treatment questionnaire

Table 5.2 summarises the questions asked after the participant had observed the robot in operation. In order to facilitate cross-study comparison, the questions match those presented in previous studies that investigate the use of real-time visual displays to provide transparency, see Chapter 4. These questions are designed to measure various factors: the measure of intelligence perceived by the participants (Intel), the emotional response to the robot (Emo), and – most importantly – the accuracy of the participants' mental model (MM) of the robot. For analysis, the four free text responses were rated for accuracy with the robot's actual Drives and Behaviours and given a score per question of 0 (inaccurate or no response), 1 (partially accurate) or 2 (accurate).

Table 5.2   Post-treatment questions.

Question	Response	Category
Is robot thinking?	Y/N	Intel
Is robot intelligent?	1–5	Intel
Feeling about robot?	Multi-choice	Emo
Understand objective?	Y/N	MM
Describe robot task?	Free text	MM
Why does robot stop?	Free text	MM
Why do lights flash?	Free text	MM
What is person doing?	Free text	MM
Happy to be person?	Y/N	Emo
Want robot in home?	Y/N	Emo

The marking was carried out by a single coder for consistency, without access to knowledge of which group the subject was in. No special vocabulary was expected. The questions used in the questionnaire are deliberately very general, so as not to steer the subject. Similarly, the marking scheme used is deliberately coarse grained because we are looking for a significant effect at the general level of understanding, not for a nuanced improvement in the subject's mind model.

5.4.2   Affect Questions

The questionnaire includes a question concerning how participants feel about the robot, specifically they are asked to complete a multiple choice section headed 'How do you feel about the robot? Please choose one option from each row' with five options ranging from 'Not at all' through to 'Very', as suggested by Dörnyei and Taguchi (2009). A standard two dimensional model of affect is used, with dimensions of Valence and Arousal. The specific feelings interrogated are detailed in Table 5.3 together with their assignment to an assumed underlying level of Valence W_{vf} and Arousal W_{af}. These terms were chosen based on common models of emotion and considered relevant to observation of a non-humanoid robot. The Valence and Arousal weights are based on values specified for these specific words by Bradley and Lang (1999) scaled within the range -1 to $+1$ on both axes:

$$V_F(p) = \frac{1}{|F|} \sum_F W_{vf} V_{pf} \tag{5.2}$$

$$A_F(p) = \frac{1}{|F|} \sum_F W_{af} A_{pf} \tag{5.3}$$

These Valence and Arousal weightings are also shown graphically in Figure 5.3. The Valence value $V_F(p)$ and Arousal value $A_F(p)$ for each participant p are therefore

Table 5.3   *Participants were asked 'How do you feel about the robot? Please choose one option from each row'. Options were Not at all (0), A Little (1), Somewhat (2), Quite a lot (3), Very (4).*

Feeling f	Valence W_{vf}	Arousal W_{af}
Happy	+1.00	+0.51
Sad	−1.00	−0.46
Scared	−0.65	+0.65
Angry	−0.62	+0.79
Curious	+0.35	+0.24
Excited	+0.78	+1.00
Bored	−0.59	−1.00
Anxious	−0.03	+0.69
No Feeling	0	0

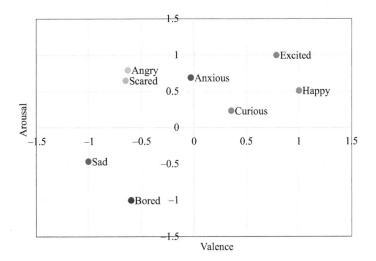

Figure 5.3   *Diagram plotting the Valence and Arousal weightings for the feelings specified in the questionnaire (see Table 5.3) showing a simple two-dimensional model of Affect. The Valence and Arousal weights are based on values specified for these specific words by Bradley and Lang (1999) scaled within the range −1 to +1 on both axes.*

calculated by multiplying the scores for each feeling word V_{sf} and A_{sf} by the weightings W_{vf} and W_{af}, respectively, and then summing for each feeling f in the set of feelings F, as shown in (5.2) and (5.3). 'No Feeling' is excluded, resulting in $|F| = 8$.

5.5   Results

For each group of participants, the demographics are shown in Table 5.4. Given the public engagement nature of the experimental location, it was not possible to accurately match each group for age, gender, education and experience with computers and robots. However, mean age and gender are both fairly well matched. The mix of graduates to non-graduates is also well matched. Group 2 contains proportionately more participants identifying themselves as having prior experience of working with robots.

5.5.1   Main findings

The primary results are shown in Table 5.5. Most importantly, in Group 2 (observe robot whilst listening to muttering), there is a marked improvement in the accuracy of participants' reports about the robot's function and capability. This confirms a significant correlation between the accuracy of the participants' MMs of the robot, and the provision of the additional transparency data provided by the muttering ($N = 68$, unpaired t test, $p = 0.0057$, $t(66) = 2.86$). This compares favourably with the results

Table 5.4   Demographics of participant groups ($N = 68$).

Demographic	Group 1 (silent)	Group 2 (sound)
Total participants	32	36
Mean age (years)	44.1	47.36
Gender male	14	17
Gender female	18	19
STEM degree	6	11
Other degree	18	16
Ever worked with a robot?	2	10
Do you use computers?	23	30
Are you a programmer?	7	10

Table 5.5   Main results. Bold face indicates results significant to at least $p = 0.05$.

Result	Group 1 (silent)	Group 2 (sound)	Effect size Cohen's D
Is thinking (0/1)	0.50 (sd = 0.51)	0.44 (sd = 0.50)	0.085
Intelligence (1–5)	2.56 (sd = 1.32)	2.67 (sd = 1.10)	0.086
Objective (0/1)	0.78 (sd = 0.42)	0.81 (sd = 0.40)	−0.184
Accuracy (0–8)	**1.94 (sd = 1.39)**	**3.19 (sd = 2.11)**	**0.696**

Table 5.6   Results based on reported Feelings.

Result	Group 1 (silent)	Group 2 (sound)	Change (%)	Significance
Valence	0.383 (sd = 0.354)	0.437 (sd = 0.253)	12.4	$p = 0.47$
Arousal	0.350 (sd = 0.291)	0.346 (sd = 0.231)	−1.27	$p = 0.95$

obtained using the ABOD3 real-time display (Wortham, Theodorou and Bryson, 2017) described in Chapter 4.

In both the groups, participants almost equally report that they understand the objective of the robot, showing no difference across the groups ($N = 68$, unpaired t test, $p = 0.81$, $t(66) = 0.24$). Note the high level of reported understanding compared with the much lower report accuracy. This indicates that significant numbers of participants in both groups perceive that they have a good model of the robot, when in reality they do not. Finally, there is no significant difference in participants perceived intelligence of the robot, or their reports that the robot is 'thinking'.

5.5.2   Affect – self-report of Feelings

The results obtained from the Affect Questions detailed in Table 5.3 did not yield significant differences between Groups 1 and 2; however, the findings shown in Table 5.6 do bear some analysis. First, no severe or adverse changes in feeling were found as a result of adding muttering to the robot, and this in itself is an important result if muttering is to be considered for practical applications. Valence is a measure of the extent of positive feelings about the robot, whilst Arousal is a measure of strength of feeling. Thus this result gives a tentative indication that whilst participants did not have overall stronger feelings about the robot, their feelings were marginally more positive. However, a larger study would be necessary to obtain evidence.

5.6   Discussion

This approach of vocalising transparency through muttering may have applications where users are visually impaired or may need to concentrate their vision elsewhere whilst working with an autonomous system. Applications may include divers working underwater with robots, as commercial divers have good audio systems for communication, but work in environments where visibility may be very poor.

Older people have reducing working memory due to cognitive decline and so might find the task-switching element of observing a robot and a visual display more challenging than hearing the vocalised output. However, the elderly may also have hearing difficulties, and so further experimentation in this area is required to establish best practice.

Vocalisation has both advantages and drawbacks when compared with the use of a visual display. Where robots are operating with very large hierarchical reactive plans, or where another action selection method is being used, it is hard to decouple the design and operation of a real-time visual display from the plan itself. If the display is to be mounted on the robot, this also impacts the design of robot. For hierarchical plans, the visual display needs to either only display the highest level elements of the plan or must move and scale to move around the plan as the focus of execution changes. For designers, this can be undertaken manually, but for end users or observers of a robot, manual interaction is impractical, and so some automated pan and zoom mechanisms would be required.

In contrast, a vocalised transparency output has the benefit that it is independent of the physical layout and structure of the plan and it scales indefinitely with the size of the plan. A vocalised transparency feed could likely be configured to work with any structured action selection mechanism, not necessarily a hierarchical structure. Conversely, due to the much lower bandwidth of a vocalised output, much of the fine detail of plan execution is lost. Also, if a plan is suspended in a debugging mode, the vocalised output would cease, but a visual display would continue to display a useful trace of activity to assist with debugging. The Speak Rules described in Section 5.3.2 must also be tuned manually, and may vary by robot and application, although this has yet to be investigated.

The repetitive production of pre-planned sentences may result in a loss of attention over time – Londoners often fail to hear "mind the gap" on the underground, possibly because of its interminable repetition! It may be possible to develop a system able to produce a wider range of creative sentences rather than pre-planned ones. This could be achieved by using a tool such as the Natural Language Toolkit (NLTK).[‡]

The study's authors had expected that participants might find the muttering robot to be somewhat irritating (Wortham and Rogers, 2017). It is therefore very interesting that this was not borne out in the data, in fact if anything there is a marginal improvement in the attitude of participants to the robot. In practical applications, we envisage the muttering to be able to be turned on and off by users at will, possibly using a voice activated interface. Perhaps asking the robot to explain itself would turn on the muttering, and telling it to 'shut up' would restore silence.

The results provide evidence to support the case that we can add the transparency measure (muttering) without affecting the user experience. The user has substantially the same qualitative experience, measured by the first three results in Table 5.5 and by the emotional model measures in Table 5.6, but in fact has a better internal model to understand the robot. This is very important for social robotics applications as it counters the argument that making the robot transparent might reduce its effectiveness, for example in companionship or human care-related applications (Wortham and Theodorou, 2017; Prescott, 2017).

Having discussed some advantages and disadvantages of visual and vocalised transparency, it seems that they are complementary and reinforcing. Developers might

[‡]NLTK: https://www.nltk.org/

switch back and forth between both mechanisms or use them in parallel. It is certainly easier to observe a robot whilst listening to it, than to observe a robot and a remote visual display concurrently. End users might have the option to see a visual display on their tablet or laptop, but when this is inconvenient, they could enable the muttering and then eventually turn off all transparency once they have a good working model of the robot, enabling them to understand and predict its behaviour without further recourse to the transparency mechanisms.

5.7   Conclusions and further work

As in the previous studies of Chapter 4, these results also indicate that significant numbers of participants in both groups perceive that they have a good model of the robot, when in reality they do not. This leads us to conclude that reports of understanding by those interacting with robots should be treated with healthy scepticism. However, in this study we show that the vocalised transparency feed produces a marked improvement in the accuracy of participants' reports about the robot's function and capability, confirming a significant correlation between the accuracy of the participants' MMs of the robot, and the provision of the additional transparency data provided by the muttering.

This study indicates the possibility that participants feel more positive about the robot when it is muttering, but with the limited study size, these results are not statistically significant, and in comparison with the much stronger effect of the transparency on accuracy of MM, this emotional effect appears weak or non-existent. Indeed, there was almost no difference in the levels of Arousal between the two groups, which in itself is an interesting result as we had expected to see some increase due to the increased stimulation of participants by the vocal output from the robot. Further, larger studies would therefore be required to explore whether muttering produces positive feelings towards the robot. Nevertheless, since our primary intent is to improve transparency without incurring negative effects, this is an encouraging result.

In this experiment, as with the experiments considering a visual real-time display, we have concentrated on the output of the decision-making process. We have therefore not considered making available the sensory model that exists within the robot, nor making transparent the various thresholds that must be crossed to release the various elements of the reactive plan. Perhaps to do so would overload the user with data, but in some applications it may be helpful to gain an insight about how the world is perceived by the robot, as this would aid an understanding of its subsequent decision-making processes. It might also be useful to investigate the benefits of a more complex sentence generation algorithm, able to generate varying sentences that might make the vocalisation sound less 'robotic'.

Finally, we have yet to expose participants to the simultaneous use of visual and vocalised transparency. This is investigated in the following chapter, along with the effect of varying robot appearance.

Chapter 6
The effects of appearance on transparency

"The work of science is to substitute facts for appearances, and demonstrations for impressions."

– John Ruskin, *Stones of Venice*

6.1 Summary

In this chapter, we use Amazon Mechanical Turk to conduct an online experiment with the R5 robot. This study is intended to extend and further explore the findings of Chapters 4 and 5 and also to investigate how altering the appearance of a robot impacts observers' mental models, both with and without visual and vocalised transparency measures.

The R5 robot is embellished with a simple bee-like cover to create a more zoomorphic form, which we name 'Buddy the Robot'. We create eight robot encounter videos, encompassing all combinations of visual and vocal transparency, with both the mechanomorphic R5 robot and the zoomorphic Buddy Robot.

The results confirm that naive participants indeed form significantly better models of a robot when accompanied by either a visual, or a vocalised representation of the internal state and processing of the robot. We find that the zoomorphic form without additional transparency results in significantly more accurate mind models and hypothesise that this is due to the increased likeability of the zoomorphic form, leading to increased participant attention and therefore improved perception of the machine agency. However, in the presence of additional transparency measures, altering robot morphology has a reduced effect on mental model accuracy (MMA).

We also observe that a vocalising or *'talking'* robot greatly increases the confidence of naive observers to report that they understand a robot's behaviour seen on video, irrespective of their actual MMA.

In all our studies, we find an upper bound to the improvement in MMA that can be achieved through transparency and suggest that the remaining gap can only be closed through other means, such as human explanation or written documentation. Finally, we conclude that the trivial embellishment of a robot to alter its form has significant effects on our understanding and attitude towards it.

6.2   Introduction

In the previous chapters, we have investigated and considered the impact of a visual display and vocalised representation of the internal processing and state of the robot on the mental models that humans create during robot encounter. We use the shorthand *'transparency mechanism'* to refer to these two approaches. There may well be alternative, indeed improved, mechanisms to convey the processing and internal state of a robot. This, of course, is a matter for the robot designer when considering the intended purpose of the robot, the operating environment(s) and the capabilities of the humans likely to encounter it.

During robot design, it is also important to consider the physical appearance of a robot, and the ways in which appearance might be altered to better make the robot transparent, in terms of its purpose, capabilities and goals. In this chapter, we investigate a small subspace of non-humanoid robot design, to investigate whether the behaviour of a robot firmly anchors the corresponding mental models created by human subjects, or whether these models can be significantly altered by making what we might consider to be trivial changes to robot appearance. Does robot embellishment significantly alter transparency? Further, once a baseline mental model is established for a given morphology and embellishment, do transparency mechanisms then vary in their effectiveness?

In this chapter, we use Amazon's Mechanical Turk (Amazon, 2017) to repeat our previous experiments in an online environment with a larger sample size and also to extend the experimental scope to investigate the effect of varying the appearance of the R5 robot between mechanomorphic and zoomorphic forms. We introduce the concept of *'MMA'* and in these experiments define it to be equivalent to the Report Accuracy measured in the previous experiments of Chapters 4 and 5.

6.3   Appearance and anthropomorphism

There is a great deal of literature concerning the effect of altering the visual appearance of humanoid, or anthropomorphic, robots (Robins *et al.*, 2004, 2005; Dautenhahn, 2007) and particularly humanoid robot faces (DiSalvo et al., 2002; Goetz, Kiesler and Powers, 2003; Broadbent *et al.*, 2013). Less work has been done to study these effects in non-humanoid, mechanomorphic and particularly zoomorphic robots. For humanoid robots, appearance or demeanour has been shown to systematically influence human perception of a robot. It also affects willingness to comply with a robot's instructions. These perceptions and responses may be driven by social cues embodied in the robot. In passing, it is worth noting that Goetz, Kiesler and Powers (2003) found more humanlike, attractive or playful robots more compelling but not across the board. Instead, users expected the robot to look and act appropriately, given the task context. This gives us an initial hint that our interactions with robots, like our human–human interactions, are most comfortable when our expectations, or stereotypic models, are fulfilled without much need for 'on-the-fly' alteration.

In a companion robot study investigating varying a basic robot appearance between mechanomorphic and anthropomorphic modes, Walters *et al.* (2008) find that overall, participants tend to prefer robots with more humanlike appearance and attributes. However, introverts and participants with lower emotional stability tend to prefer the mechanoid appearance to a greater degree than other participants. This study also found that differences in robot appearance lead to marked differences in perceived robot personality. Personality is a key determinant in human social interactions. Consequently, personality is also a key factor in human–robot interaction (Tapus and Mataric, 2008). For example, Tapus and Mataric observe that people enjoy interacting with humorous robots but pay more attention to more serious ones.

In a broad survey of socially interactive robots, Fong, Nourbakhsh and Dautenhahn (2003) observe that the form and structure of a robot is important because it helps establish social expectations. Physical appearance biases interaction. A robot resembling a dog will (at least initially) be treated differently from one which is anthropomorphic. Fong, Nourbakhsh and Dautenhahn make the important point that the relative familiarity of a robot's morphology can have a profound effect on its accessibility, desirability and expressiveness. Walters *et al.* (2009) provide a range of examples here. In experiments with very similar chest and knee high robots, equipped with either video cameras or simple humanoid faces, Walters *et al.* find that the more anthropomorphic robot versions tend to be perceived as more intelligent than their mechanomorphic cousins. However, when combined with short height, the anthropomorphic robots are seen as less conscientious and more neurotic. Also, the taller robots were perceived as more humanlike and conscientious than the short robots.

In an extensive study of child perspectives of robot appearance, Woods (2006) finds that children clearly distinguished robots in terms of their perceived intentions, capability to understand, and emotional expression, based solely on morphology. Woods concludes that the overall appearance of robots influences the expectations that humans might have when interacting with a robot. For example, an anthropomorphic robot may be expected to possess language capabilities and demonstrate particular 'personality' characteristics, whereas a mechanomorphic robot would not be expected to have any ability to speak.

Linville, Fischer and Salovey (1989) investigate the perceived distributions of the characteristics of in-group and out-group members of human groups. Their research shows that people have a sparse, simple mental model of those with whom they have little direct experience, and that these models assume narrow variability of characteristics within group. With experience, a person's mental models become richer and more complex and allow for greater variability. Kiesler and Goetz (2002) tentatively extend this argument to human–robot groups. It may be that a given robot morphology implies a specific sparse model, and that during initial naive encounters, variations beyond the stereotypic mind model are unexpected.

DiSalvo and Gemperle (2003) neatly recap five common theories of anthropomorphism. Of particular interest is what they term the 'Social Thesis'. By this theory, the *act* of anthropomorphising "reflects values and possesses the potential for social consequence". Attributing human characteristics to animals, for example, provides a means to change the values we place on them and alters the way in which we behave towards them (Caporeal and Heyes, 1997). When mechanomorphic, non-humanoid robots are encountered, the almost exclusive prevalence of anthropomorphic humanoid robots in science fiction, and more generally in the media, may, by breaking this convention, cause confusion about the robot's purpose and function. The anthropomorphic form maintains the shape convention that defines *'robot'* in the minds of many. DiSalvo and Gemperle point out that this argument raises an ethical as well as a usability issue. If robot form can be used to project human values, it becomes important to reflect on what those values are. Notably, they go on to say that "... creating a servant class of humanoid robots would necessarily reference a history of human exploitation. The ethical and social implications of such references cannot be ignored in the research and design of new products". One such ethical concern is the *Halo effect* (Nisbett and Wilson, 1977) – the human tendency to use known attributes to make assumptions about unknown ones. It is certainly the case with humans that liking of appearance increases liking of other personality traits, and this effect is similarly seen in robot experiments (Syrdal *et al.*, 2007; Walters *et al.*, 2008).

Zoomorphic, or animal-like, robots provide us with another useful design form (Fong, Nourbakhsh and Dautenhahn, 2003; Klamer and Ben Allouch, 2010; Bae and Kim, 2011) having the benefits of an appealing animate appearance but without the problems associated with the 'Uncanny Valley' – the well-known term used to describe feelings of revulsion or 'creepiness' (McAndrew and Koehnke, 2016) in the presence of robots that are almost, but not perfectly humanlike (Valley, Mori and Minato, 1970; Gee, Browne and Kawamura, 2005). Avoiding the uncanny valley may be easier with a zoomorphic design because human–creature relationships (e.g. owner pet) are often simpler than human–human relationships. Thus, our expectations of what constitutes 'realistic' and 'unrealistic' animal morphology tends to be lower (Fong, Nourbakhsh and Dautenhahn, 2003).

In a cross-cultural study, Li, Rau and Li (2010) find strong and positive correlations between interaction performance and preference in terms of likeability, trust and satisfaction. Their study used three small LEGO robots: one anthropomorphic, one mechanomorphic and one zoomorphic – achieved by covering the robot in the 'skin' of a soft toy rabbit. The study found that the robot with the mechanomorphic appearance received the lowest likeability score, reinforcing the earlier work of Syrdal *et al.* (2007). This earlier study investigates the impact of robot appearance at 'zero acquaintance' and finds that as we do for human encounters, we make significant inferences about robot personality solely based on appearance. Li, Rau and Li (2010) suggest that zoomorphic robots are more suitable for social interaction with humans, following the work of Lohse, Hegel and Wrede (2008). This earlier study used an online approach to study the effect of appearance on attribution of capability and function and found that appearance plays a crucial role in the perception of a robot and determines which applications are proposed for it.

Malle *et al.* (2016) conclude that robot appearance affects people's moral judgements about robots. Using a simple scripted 'trolley problem' dilemma and sketched pictures, they show that patterns of blame for a humanoid robot is very similar to those for a human; however, they differ significantly for a non-humanoid robot. The inaction of a non-humanoid 'mechanical' robot was considered more blameworthy than its action, whilst for both the humanoid robot and a human, the converse is true.

It is interesting to note that for a disembodied hypothetical artificial intelligence, or 'AI', this asymmetry matched that of the humanoid robot and the human. Finally, in both trolley problem scenarios explored by Malle *et al.*, the absolute level of blame attributed to a human for taking an action was always the highest, but in the case of inaction, it was either the lowest or equally as low as that attributed to the other agent types.

The presence of emotional stimuli has been shown to bias our social judgement in human–human interaction (Fiori and Shuman, 2017). In addition, this bias is mediated by individual variations in our attentional processes. This variation might account for the wide variety of responses to the R5 robot across all of our experiments.

Our cultural background also alters the attention we give to others during passive encounter scenarios. Hall (1989) identifies and categorises cultures as either high- or low-context. An individual in a low-context culture requires explicit information to be provided during an interaction. Conversely in a high-context culture, much more information is assumed to be contextually available. Germany is an example of a low-context culture, whereas Japan is a high-context culture. Li, Rau and Li (2010) suggest that in their human–robot interaction experiments, participants from low-context cultures may have significantly decreased engagement (or attention) when the sociability of a task is lowered. In this study, sociability is defined in terms of interaction time and frequency of interaction. Tapus and Mataric (2008) investigate 'user personality matching' using an autonomous robot for rehabilitation therapy of stroke patients. They use a non-humanoid, small-wheeled mobile robot. It is obvious that personality is a key determinant in human social interactions, and their results indicate that human personality is also a key factor in the perception of a robot in human–robot interactions. Thus we observe that for a given robot morphology in a given scenario, we can expect a range of reactions based on culture and individual personality. Scholl and Gao (2013) argue that the perception of animacy and intentionality occurs within our visual processing mechanisms and does not arise *post facto*, as a result of higher level cognitive judgement. We 'see' (or detect) intention using the same neural equipment that we use to see movement, colour and form. Ling (2012) shows that attention alters appearance; it boosts the apparent stimulus contrast. This result is consistent with neurophysiological findings suggesting that attention modifies the strength of a stimulus by increasing its 'effective contrast' or salience. Therefore, it may be that when more attention is paid to a robot, its detailed features and movements become more salient, leading to a richer internal mental model of functionality and purpose.

Taking these previous studies together, we suggest the following causal chain: appearance affects attention, which in turn affects perception, modifying our initial, sparse stereotypic internal mental model to a greater or lesser extent. All these effects are modulated by culture, our library of pre-existing stereotypic models of robots, individual human personality, our emotional state and the context in which we find the robot. Therefore, it is unsurprising that in previous experiments we observed wide variance in the results.

This section has concentrated on the effect of robot appearance on the human understanding of robots. The human predisposition to anthropomorphise is a much wider field. Historically, simple accounts were given for anthropomorphism, known widely as the 'comfort' and 'familiarity' theses. These basic ideas rest upon the assumption that humans seek the easiest and most familiar models to understand the world around them, and that for hyper-social humans those are models of conspecifics, i.e. models of human characteristics in terms of behaviour and cognition (Guthrie, 1997; Dunbar, 1998). Later, more complex theories have been proposed. Whether anthropomorphism is a 'cognitive default', a 'consequence of overlapping interspecies coordination systems', or indeed a 'species-specific group-level coordination system' as suggested by Caporeal and Heyes (1997) is beyond the scope of this practical investigation of transparency. For further reading, we suggest DiSalvo and Gemperle (2003) together with the excellent collection of papers edited by Mitchell, Thompson and Miles (1997).

6.4   Experimental methods

In these experiments, we again use the R5 robot described in the previous chapters. First, we investigate whether the addition of a crude insect-like (bee-like) cover for the robot increases anthropomorphism, and whether this then subsequently improves the accuracy of the mind model generated by subjects. Second, we investigate whether the transparency of such a robot is improved by adding either the ABOD3 visual display or vocalised representation (muttering) of the internal processing and state of the robot. In the previous experiments of Chapters 4 and 5, we measure the accuracy the participants' mental models of the robot by asking a set of questions and scoring their results to arrive at a 'Report Accuracy' value for each participant. This score then used to make quantitative assessments of the MMA of the participant. In this chapter, we define *MMA* to be equivalent to the Report Accuracy of Chapters 4 and 5. MMA is calculated as the sum of the report scores, 0–8 as in the previous chapters, but also expressed as a percentage, as one might do with exam scores.

6.4.1   Amazon Mechanical Turk

Amazon's Mechanical Turk (Amazon, 2017) is an online platform enabling batches of small work, such as research studies or image classification tasks, to be offered in a commercial marketplace. The name is taken from a late eighteenth century machine that appeared to play chess with human opponents autonomously. The machine was in fact a deliberate deception, containing a human who made the chess playing decisions. Amazon's service similarly appears to automate work requiring human skills. Like the original machine, it uses human intelligence, although it differs in that many humans can be brought to bear on a problem simultaneously.

Mechanical Turk has its pitfalls for research use, not least the wide diversity of cultural background of participants, and the inability to match demographics accurately across differing treatments. However, it has several benefits over convenience samples taken from university students, or from the general public in live public engagement environments (Crump, McDonnell and Gureckis, 2013; Berinsky, Huber and Lenz, 2012; Benoit *et al.*, 2016). It has also been used successfully in previous robot-related studies (Malle *et al.*, 2016). First, since the treatment must necessarily use pre-recorded materials, we can be sure that each participant is exposed to identical, or at least very similar treatments. Second, the monitoring within Mechanical Turk enables us to be relatively certain that participants watched entire videos and considered questions carefully. Third, unlike local convenience samples, we are able to obtain a larger cross section of the public than is possible within a campus, or even a science-learning centre environment. Finally, and perhaps most importantly, we are able to access much larger numbers of participants. This is perhaps the most important point for our purposes, since experimental noise in terms of culture, false reporting and demographic imbalance should apply equally to all treatment batches, and if we make the batches large, the central limit theorem gives us increasing confidence that our results will nevertheless be representative of the population as a whole. In addition, a significant result across a diverse population sample provides a robust result about humans in general, rather than one geographic, ethnic or socio-economic group in particular.

6.4.2 *Buddy the Robot*

In order to investigate the effect of appearance, we created *'Buddy the Robot'*, shown in Figure 6.1. The hardware, programming – including the reactive plan and subsequent behaviour of Buddy – is identical to R5. The only exceptions being that Buddy announces itself when it is first switched on, saying "Hello, I am Buddy the robot.

Figure 6.1   Buddy the Robot. This close-up shot reveals that 'Buddy' is simply the R5 robot (shown in Figure 3.8) with the addition of a bee-like cover. The cover is constructed from part of a child's novelty rucksack, with the added embellishment of 'googly eyes'. The programming and behaviour of Buddy is identical to R5, with the exception that it announces itself as "Buddy the Robot" at switch-on, and calls itself "Buddy" when muttering.

Nice to meet you" whereas R5 says "Hello, this is the R5 robot." Also, Buddy uses its name when muttering, for example "Buddy is trying to sleep" rather than R5's version "R5 is trying to sleep". Buddy differs in appearance from R5, in that it has been made more zoomorphic by the addition of a bee-like striped cover and 'googly eyes'. The cover is held in place by two wire straps at the front, allowing the rear of the cover to be lifted to access the robot on–off switch. The eye stalks are somewhat flexible and springy, such that as the robot moves they vibrate, mechanically activating the 'googly eyes'.

6.4.3   Robot videos

The R5 robot and its embellished zoomorphic form 'Buddy the Robot' were video recorded whilst operating within a 'pen' constructed using wire fencing intended for pet hamsters. The pen contained a number of objects, including a bucket, various boxes and a soft toy, as shown in Figure 6.2. During each video recording, the transparency feed from each robot was transmitted to a remote PC using the robot's wireless (Wi-Fi) link and captured for subsequent use with the ABOD3 real-time debugging tool (Theodorou, Wortham and Bryson, 2017). In both videos, the robot muttering was enabled and captured using the video camera's single monaural microphone. Repeated videos were taken in both scenarios to achieve similar robot behaviours and interactions with a researcher, who appears briefly in each video to enable the robot to 'detect' them. The videos were then trimmed to the same length of 3 min 46 s.

Figure 6.2   Buddy the Robot situated within the pen used for all videos used in the Mechanical Turk experiments.

Two further silent videos where then created by removing the soundtracks using the blender video editing tool.*

The ABOD3 tool introduced in Section 4.3.3 was then used to create four more videos, each showing one of the four R5/Buddy Silent/Muttering robot videos, but also showing a real-time display of the high-level plan execution. Two of these ABOD3 videos therefore have no sound, and two have muttering. Figure 6.3 shows a single frame from one of the ABOD3 videos. This creation process led to eight separate video recordings with all combinations of robot appearance, visual transparency display and vocalised transparency. The four ABOD3 videos are about 10 s longer to allow for the video replay to be synchronised with the real-time transparency data and the beginning of each video. These combinations and the treatment video reference numbers are shown in Table 6.1. The reference number of each video was subsequently used to

Figure 6.3 *Buddy the Robot detecting a human, shown within the ABOD3 graphical debugging tool. The 'DetectHuman' Drive is shown highlighted indicating that it is active, and the video shows the robot headlamp flashing green to indicate the successful detection of a human.*

Table 6.1 *The eight videos created for the Mechanical Turk experiments.*

Presentation type	Robot video no sound	Robot video muttering	Shown in ABOD3 with no sound	Shown in ABOD3 muttering
R5 robot	1	3	5	7
Buddy Robot	2	4	6	8

*The blender video editing tool, see https://www.blender.org/

track the questionnaires and the responses, and these references are also used in the following sections.

6.4.4   Online questionnaire

Similar to the previous online experiments of Chapters 4 and 5, we used Google Forms to create a post-treatment questionnaire.[†] Eight versions of this questionnaire were then generated to reference each of the eight videos, and instructions within the questionnaire were tailored to advise participants to use headphones or good quality speakers for those videos, including sound. The questionnaire itself was otherwise unchanged across the eight treatments. All participants were requested to watch the video in its entirety and to conduct the experiment on a laptop or desktop computer with a large enough screen to see the video clearly. Also, each questionnaire contained a large image of the robot arena with no robot present, see Figure 6.4, and participants were requested not to take part in the experiment if they had already seen this image. This restriction was included to avoid participants participating in more than one treatment. Mechanical Turk includes the ability to access the ID (a unique anonymous identifier), of each participant, so that we could check when this stipulation had been ignored and remove the participants' second and subsequent entries from our data, although this only occurred a handful of times.

Figure 6.4   Empty arena image shown to participants to remind them if they have participated in previous experiments. This was used at the beginning of our questionnaire and participants were requested not to proceed if they had already seen this scene in previous experiments. This approach proved very successful.

[†]Google Forms, see https://docs.google.com/forms/

The Google Forms questionnaire contained the following sections:

1. Details of experiment, agreement to participate in experiment and agreement that data may be used anonymously.
2. About you – participant demographics identical to that used in Section 5.5.
3. The robot video – one of the eight treatment videos in Table 6.1.
4. About the robot – identical questions to those that used in Section 5.4.1.
5. Impression of the robot – standard 'Godspeed' questions with a five-point Likert scale (Bartneck *et al.*, 2009), see Section 6.4.5.
6. About the experiment – feedback on problems encountered during the experiment, suggestions for improvement or any other comments.
7. Complete details – request for Mechanical Turk Worker ID, and provision of a code unique to each treatment to be inserted into the Mechanical Turk system by the participant.

An example of the full questionnaire, in printed form, is provided in Appendix F. When accessed online, the questions are presented as separate pages, and each must be completed according to the mandatory fields rules before the participant can continue to the next page. In printed form, these mandatory fields are shown with red asterisks (*). The Feedback section contains a question asking about the participants' ability to hear the robot. This provides us with a useful 'Gold Standard' question. If participants answer that they heard the robot clearly when the video was silent, this is an indication that they may not have watched the video at all. Conversely, if they answer that there was no sound when indeed there was, then again this indicates either a faulty viewing, or failure to attempt to view.

6.4.5   Impression of the robot – the 'Godspeed' questions

The 'Godspeed' questions are based on Bartneck *et al.* (2009), with answers on a five-point Likert scale. The questions are arranged into five groups, giving overall scores for Anthropomorphism, Animacy, Likeability, Perceived Intelligence and Safety. Three questions were removed from the original Godspeed specification:

- Animacy: stagnant/lively – we do not consider stagnant to be a generally understood antonym of lively.
- Animacy: inert/interactive – we do not consider inert to be a generally understood antonym of interactive.
- Likeability: unkind/kind – since there is no interaction in the videos relevant to this quality, it was omitted.

The remaining 21 Godspeed questions are grouped as per Table 6.2.

6.4.6   Work batches in Mechanical Turk

Mechanical Turk (sometimes called MTurk) uses the concept of work batches. A batch contains a simple web page with a link to the Google form, together with parameters that define the requirements that the participants must meet. Amazon calls the participants 'Workers', and they are also known as 'Turkers'. Using these parameters,

Table 6.2   The Godspeed questions, see Appendix F questions 18–38.

Group	N	Questions
Anthropomorphism	5	Fake/Natural, Machinelike/Humanlike, Unconscious/Conscious, Artificial/Lifelike, Rigid/Elegant
Animacy	4	Dead/Alive, Mechanical/Organic, Artificial/Lifelike, Apathetic/Responsive
Likeability	4	Dislike/Like, Unfriendly/Friendly, Unpleasant/Pleasant, Awful/Nice
Perceived Intelligence	5	Incompetant/Competant, Ignorant/Knowledgeable, Irresponsible/Responsible, Unintelligent/Intelligent, Foolish/Sensible
Safety	3	Anxious/Relaxed, Calm/Agitated, Quiescent/Surprised

we set up batches requesting 20 participants for each treatment and specified that participants must have a previous 99% satisfaction rating for previous assignments. The first set of batches was executed, and after a preliminary examination, it was decided that this approach was delivering useful results and so each batch was then repeated to generate 40 responses for each treatment. Responses were then evaluated to remove duplicate participants in the data set. Respondents who failed to answer the 'Gold Standard' questions correctly or who completed the work far too quickly to have been able to watch the video in its entirety were also removed. Amazon provides a facility to inform Workers that their work is unacceptable, and this also generates a credit that can be used to request other Workers to carry out the remaining work.

6.5   Results

6.5.1   Participant demographics

The demographics for each participant group is shown in Table 6.3. Although it is not possible to match groups accurately across treatments, the relatively large group size ensured comparable samples in terms of age and education level. The overall sample is 65% male, 35% female with 56% being educated to degree level. 32% say they write computer programs. Rather strangely, whilst answering the questions on a computer, not all participants answered that they use computers, Group 4 being the most extreme in this regard, with only 87.5% of participants confirming that they use computers.

Mechanical Turk is a global system, but it is not possible to identify the location of Workers from the batch log files produced by the system. However, based on anecdotal evidence from email correspondence with participants during each work

Table 6.3   Demographics of participant groups (N = 317).

Group demographic	1	2	3	4	5	6	7	8
Total participants	41	39	39	40	40	39	39	40
Mean age (years)	32.4	30.2	33.1	34.5	33.3	33.1	34.9	35.8
Gender male	29	30	27	23	25	27	25	20
Gender female	12	9	12	17	15	12	14	20
STEM degree	3	7	7	3	5	4	0	2
Other degree	17	15	14	20	21	21	21	17
Degree education	20	22	21	23	26	25	21	19
Worked with robot?	4	7	6	8	6	7	7	9
Use computers?	37	36	38	35	38	36	38	37
Programmer?	14	12	13	11	16	11	14	10

Table 6.4   Main results for the eight treatments outlined in Table 6.1 (N = 317).

Group R5 | Buddy (B) ABOD3 (A) | Muttering (M)	1 R5	2 B	3 R5 M	4 B M	5 R5 A	6 B A	7 R5 A M	8 B A M
Is thinking (0/1)	0.56	0.69	0.46	0.55	0.53	0.56	0.49	0.50
Understanding objectives (0/1)	0.37	0.56	0.92	0.85	0.65	0.56	0.92	0.93
Intelligence (1–5) ($\bar{i}$)	2.76	3.10	2.69	2.95	2.73	2.62	2.95	2.95
Standard deviation (σ)	1.10	1.10	1.09	1.26	1.16	1.17	1.06	1.07
MMA (0–8) ($\bar{m}$)	1.46	2.23	4.23	3.50	3.68	3.77	3.33	4.10
MMA (%)	18.3	27.9	52.9	43.8	46.0	47.1	41.6	51.3
Standard deviation (σ)	1.52	1.80	2.07	2.09	2.41	2.04	2.18	4.15

batch, together with the varying English language skills apparent from the written answers, participants came from a variety of countries, including the United Kingdom, Europe, USA and India.

6.5.2   Main results

The results for the eight treatments are summarised in Table 6.4. The effect of adding transparency, and indeed of altering robot morphology, on MMA is best illustrated using a bar chart, shown in Figure 6.5. There are several significant results here.

First, between treatments 1 and 3; $t(78) = 6.85$, $p < 0.0001$, 2 and 4; $t(77) = 2.90$, $p = 0.0050$, 1 and 5; $t(79) = 4.97$, $p < 0.0001$, and 2 and 6; $t(76) = 3.54$, $p = 0.0007$, we see a repeat of the significant effect that visual or vocalised transparency has on MMA. All results are calculated using the unpaired t test. This confirms

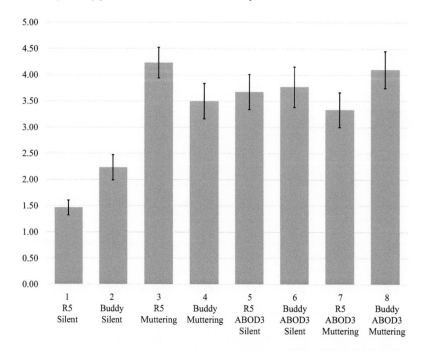

Figure 6.5   Mental model accuracy score (0–8) for the eight treatments. Robot uncovered (R5) or with Bee cover (Buddy), Transparency provided through Muttering and ABOD3. Error bars show 95% confidence interval (N = 317).

the findings reported in Chapters 4 and 5. The transparency of the mechanomorphic and zoomorphic versions of the robot can be significantly improved by the addition of a visual display or vocalised representation of the internal processing and state of the robot.

Second, comparing treatments 1 and 2, we see a significant increase in MMA resulting from addition of the bee-like cover to the robot; $t(78) = 2.07$, $p = 0.042$. This was unexpected and is discussed in more detail in the following section.

With additional transparency in place, the embellishment of the robot from mechanomorphic to zoomorphic form made proportionately less difference to MMA. Between treatments 3 and 4, the zoomorphic form may somewhat reduce transparency; $t(77) = 1.56$, $p = 0.12$, whereas between treatments 5 and 6 the form made little difference; $t(77) = 0.179$, $p = 0.86$. However, these results are not sufficiently statistically robust to be definitive.

Taking these results together, we can say that for the mechanomorphic R5 robot, the addition of either visual or vocalised transparency has a greater improvement in MMA, than when either are applied to the zoomorphic Buddy version. This is discussed in more detail in the following section.

Table 6.5 Scores for question 13 – "Why does [the robot] just stop every so often (when it stops moving completely)?".

Group	1	2	3	4	5	6	7	8
R5 | Buddy (B)	R5	B	R5	B	R5	B	R5	B
ABOD3 (A) | Muttering (M)			M	M	A	A	A M	A M
Score = 1	0	1	1	0	1	1	1	0
Score = 2	0	0	8	5	11	6	5	7
Total scoring > 0	0	1	9	5	12	7	6	7
Percentage of scoring > 0	0	2.6	23.1	12.5	30	17.9	15.4	17.5

Looking at the effect of combining visual and vocalised transparency, we see no significant result across robot morphologies. For the mechanomorphic R5 robot, we see a decrease in MMA in treatment 7 over that of treatments 3; $t(76) = 1.87$, $p = 0.065$ and 5; $t(77) = 0.676$, $p = 0.50$. Conversely, for the zoomorphic Buddy Robot, we see an increase in MMA in treatment 8 over that of treatments 4; $t(78) = 0.817$, $p = 0.42$ and 6; $t(77) = 0.447$, $p = 0.66$. Again, these tentative results are discussed further in the following section.

6.5.3 Failure to identify 'Sleeping'

The robot has a 'Sleep' drive with a ramping priority, see Section 4.3.2. As the drive priority increases, it eventually becomes the highest priority and the robot will 'Sleep' for 10 s, during which time the robot stops moving and stops monitoring its environment, causing the corner LEDs to stop flashing. However, this behaviour is only released when the robot is close to an object. In the post-treatment questionnaire, question 13 asks "Why does [the robot] just stop every so often (when it stops moving completely)?". In the previous online experiment, described in Chapter 4, answers to a similar question were removed from the analysis, due to a potential misunderstanding as to the meaning of the question. However, the question was subsequently clarified with the addition of the words in parentheses and used in the experiment described in Chapter 5. Table 6.5 shows the results for question 13 for the eight treatments defined in Table 6.1. The answers to this question are particularly revealing, because with no additional visual or vocalised transparency (treatments 1 and 2), all but one participant scored zero, indicating that this question cannot be answered solely by observing the robots' behaviour. Example answers for treatments (T) 1 and 2 include the following:

- T1 – "It was on deep thinking."
- T1 – "I think its computing things."
- T1 – "I think it stops to analyse the image that it is seeing."
- T1 – "No idea"
- T1 – "The person controlling it commanded it to stop."

- T2 – *"It is thinking."*
- T2 – *"I think it is tired."* – Participant Score 1
- T2 – *"To analyse the toy in front of it."*
- T2 – *"Because it needs to process information."*
- T2 – *"It is trying to process the information it is collected."*

The highest score for this question resulted from treatment 5 (mechanomorphic R5 robot with ABOD3 display, no muttering), with 30% achieving partially or fully correct answers. Some example answers are provided next:

- T5 – *'It enters a sleep cycle for some reason.'* – Participant Score 2
- T5 – *'It sleeps.'* – Participant Score 2
- T5 – *'It went to sleep.'* – Participant Score 2
- T5 – *'It is probably trying to load the next task or command or it is processing.'*
- T5 – *'It is programmed to do that.'* – Participant Score 1

The highest score involving muttering occurs with treatment 3. It is worth noting that even with the vocaliser announcing that the robot is *"trying to sleep"* and has *"completed sleep 10 s"*, only 23.1% of participants were able to partly or fully answer this question. These results are discussed further in Section 6.6.

6.5.4 Participant confidence

In the experiments described in Chapters 4 and 5, the presence of visual or vocal transparency had no significant effect on participants' self-report that they understood the objectives of the robot, measured by their Yes/No response to the question *"Can you tell what the robot is trying to do?"*. However, in this experiment, there was a wide variation across the eight treatments. The proportion answering Yes to this question is shown in Figure 6.6. This chart also shows the corresponding MMA scores for each treatment. The immediate and most striking observation is the impact that Muttering has on confidence. In all cases, vocalised transparency increased confidence levels to at least 85% and in three of the four cases to over 90%. Conversely, when the robot was not muttering, confidence levels ranged from 37% to 65%. We must be careful not to compare these values directly with the MMA scores, since one is a measure of the proportion of a population giving a specific answer to a Yes/No question, whereas the MMA scores are a mean across the population. However, looking at treatments 5–8 we see only a small variation in actual MMA, but a large increase in confidence related to muttering.

6.5.5 Affect – self-report of feelings

The analysis of participants self-report of feelings about the robot, described in Sections 5.4.2 and 5.5.2, are repeated across the eight treatments in this experiment, yielding valence and arousal results for each participant. For completeness, these are plotted in Figure 6.7. Unfortunately this plot reveals little, other than a universal positive correlation between Valence and Arousal. To extract more meaningful results,

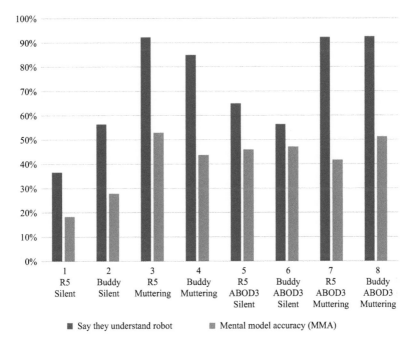

Figure 6.6   Comparison of mental model accuracy score with participant self-report of understanding for the eight treatments. Both are shown as a percentage of maximum possible value for comparison purposes.

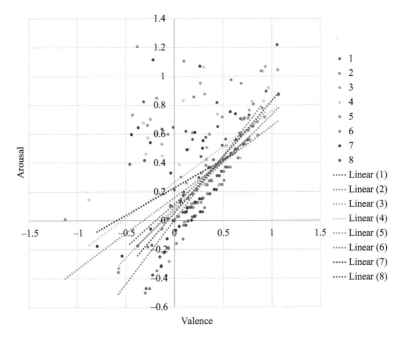

Figure 6.7   Plot of Valence and Arousal for the eight treatments (N = 317). Linear trendlines for each treatment are also shown.

Table 6.6 provides a summary of results for each experiment. This data is presented graphically in Figure 6.8, showing the mean valence and arousal for each treatment.

The relative area of each 'bubble' is determined by the sum of the variances of Arousal and Valence and has been shown to indicate a measure of 'spread' for each treatment. From Table 6.6 taken together with this summary plot, we see a similar spread of distribution for each treatment. Also, the mean arousal varies little across all the treatments, although comparing 1 and 2, 3 and 4, and 7 and 8, it is generally

Table 6.6   Affect results for the eight treatments outlined in Table 6.1 (N = 317).

Group	1	2	3	4	5	6	7	8
R5	Buddy (B)	R5	B	R5	B	R5	B	R5	B
ABOD3 (A)	Muttering (M)			M	M	A	A	A M	A M
Mean valence ($\bar{v}$)	0.19	0.24	0.27	0.25	0.31	0.29	0.13	0.34
Standard deviation (σ)	0.31	0.40	0.35	0.41	0.36	0.34	0.34	0.38
Mean arousal ($\bar{a}$)	0.23	0.28	0.28	0.39	0.28	0.26	0.28	0.32
Standard deviation (σ)	0.31	0.35	0.35	0.36	0.38	0.38	0.35	0.37

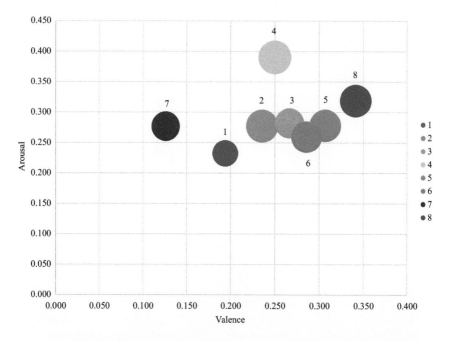

Figure 6.8   Mean valence and arousal for each of the eight treatments outlined in Table 6.1. The centre of each 'bubble' marks the mean valence and arousal. The area of each bubble is proportional to the sum of the Valence and Arousal variances.

marginally higher for the zoomorphic Buddy Robot. The highest arousal is achieved with the vocalising zoomorphic Buddy Robot, shown without the ABOD3 tool (treatment 4). Comparing this with the silent version of the video (treatment 2), mean arousal increases from 0.277 to 0.390; however, this is not a significant difference due to the relatively large variance in all these affect results; $t(77) = 1.40$, $p = 0.165$.

The result for treatment 7 seems anomalous. More positive emotion is reported in response to a vocalising R5 (treatment 3) than a silent one (treatment 1). Similarly, R5 combined with ABOD3 (treatment 5) results in a more positive report. However, when these transparency measures are combined, we see a marked drop in valence (treatment 7). Comparing treatments 5 and 7, we see a significant effect; $t(77) = 2.31$, $p = 0.025$. This may nevertheless be anomalous, due to some particular unlikely grouping of participants, or may be a manifestation of the 'Uncanny Valley' effect for mechanomorphic robots, described in Section 6.2. This is discussed in more detail in Section 6.6.

6.5.6 Godspeed results

The Godspeed questions are described in detail in Section 6.4.5. The results for the eight treatments are summarised graphically in Figure 6.9. There are several significant results. First, there is a marked difference of 22.2% in the Likeability scores between treatments 1 (3.23) and 2 (3.95); $t(78) = 3.65$, $p = 0.0005$. This shows that

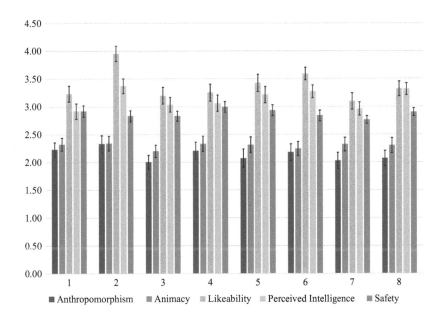

Figure 6.9   Results of the Godspeed questions for the eight treatments. The data is normalised per participant, per question. Error bars show 95% confidence interval (N = 317).

Table 6.7   *Comparison of Godspeed results for treatments 1 (R5 no transparency measures) and 7 (R5 with ABOD3 and Muttering) outlined in Table 6.1.*

Mean ($\bar{x}$) Standard deviation (σ)	Anthropo- morphism	Animacy	Likeability	Perceived Intelligence	Safety
Treatment 1	2.23	2.32	3.23	2.92	2.92
σ	0.809	0.714	0.900	0.881	0.645
Treatment 7	2.03	2.32	3.10	2.96	2.76
σ	0.900	0.751	0.903	0.744	0.433
Percentage of change	−10.1	−0.1	−4.4	1.4	−5.7
p Value	0.200	1.000	0.521	0.827	0.199

in the absence of visual or vocalised transparency, the zoomorphic Buddy Robot is considered significantly more likeable than the mechanomorphic R5 robot. However, with Muttering this effect is eliminated. Likeability of R5 in treatment 3 (3.20) is comparable with that of Buddy in treatment 4 (3.25); $t(77) = 0.247$, $p = 0.81$. Similarly, Likeability is also comparable with the addition of the ABOD3 visual display. Likeability of R5/ABOD3 in treatment 5 (3.43) is comparable with that of Buddy/ABOD3 in treatment 6 (3.59); $t(77) = 0.874$, $p = 0.3848$.

Second, in the absence of any transparency measure, these results indicate a marked difference in Perceived Intelligence between Buddy and R5. In treatment 1 R5 scores 2.92, compared with Buddy's score of 3.37 in treatment 2, an increase of 15.5%; $t(78) = 2.38$, $p = 0.0197$. Note that this aligns with the 12.3% increase in the participants' self-report of the robots' intelligence between treatments 1 and 2 shown in Table 6.4. Again, with either vocalised or visual transparency this effect is eliminated. Between treatments 3 (3.04) and 4 (3.06) the addition of Muttering eliminates this effect. Similarly, treatments 5 (3.22) and 6 (3.27) show that visual transparency also eliminates the effect of embellished morphology on Perceived Intelligence.

Finally, in light of the potentially anomalous result found for treatment 7 in the self-report of Affect described in Section 6.5.5, and clearly shown in Figure 6.8, we must further investigate these Godspeed results between treatments 1 and 7. The results for treatments 1 and 7 are shown in detail in Table 6.7. There are no significant differences across any of the five dimensions measured by these questions. However, there are small reductions in the anthropomorphism, likeability and safety measures, although these fall short of statistical significance, due to the level of variance in the results.

6.6   Discussion

We must preface the discussion of these results with some concern about the quality of the participant responses. As mentioned in Section 6.5.1, the questionnaire asked an implicit 'Gold standard' question *"Do you work with computers regularly (in your job, as someone self employed, as a student, at home, etc.)?"*. In none of the groups did 100% of participants answer this question correctly. Therefore, we should assume a fairly high degree of noise in these data sets, arising from rushed or random answering, a disregard for detail, and misunderstanding of the questions due to poor English language skills. These effects should be randomly distributed across the eight treatments, but 'randomly' does of course not mean equally. Therefore, our conclusions should consider only major effects and those seen across or between multiple sets of treatments, and we need to pay close attention to both effect sizes and *p* values.

The results presented in this chapter confirm the transparency effects found in previous experiments, all with *p* values <= 0.005. Taken together with the results from Chapters 4 and 5, this body of work provides convincing evidence that the transparency of a non-humanoid robot can be significantly improved by the addition of a visual or vocalised representation of the internal processing and state of the robot. However, it seems that adding both visual and vocalised representations does not further increase transparency. In all our experiments, we were unable to achieve a MMA of more than 59% – see Tables 4.4, 5.5 and 6.4. For this robot and task combination, it appears that a limit is reached whereby no further application of our real-time visual and vocalised transparency measures are effective at improving MMA, and the remaining gap can only be closed through other transparency means, such as written or diagrammatic documentation. Perhaps the real-time transparency of a robot reaches a saturation level where no further additional information provided by the robot based on its internal decision-making can be incorporated into the model. An example of this can be seen in the failure of participants to identify the 'sleeping' behaviour, described in Section 6.5.3. If participants have no explanation to hand of the reasons why humans and animals sleep, then this behaviour may seem incidental. Similarly, some participants would perhaps not see any purpose in detecting humans, and so would discount this as being of incidental importance. Based on the work of Linville, Fischer and Salovey (1989) and Kiesler and Goetz (2002) discussed in Section 6.2, we can hypothesise that the mental model of an unknown robot is so simple as to be completely stereotypic. Stereotypically, robots stop when they are 'thinking' (processing), and this may be why participants gave this explanation even when the transparency was strongly indicating and indeed explicitly naming the sleeping behaviour. Perhaps our mental models of robots just do not include a capacity for sleeping.

A parallel exists here with political transparency. Unless citizens have some understanding of the mechanisms and structures of government and have some appreciation of democratic models, then no number of news items detailing the specifics of government activity will achieve a good mental model in the minds of those citizens. Transparency techniques based on the (near) real-time reporting of events can only achieve so much (Relly and Sabharwal, 2009). Education is also required to give us better models to understand the world as we encounter it.

A vocalising robot, or more prosaically a *'talking'* robot, would appear to greatly increase the confidence that participants have to report that they understand what the robot is trying to do. Although we see a very significant effect in this online experiment, see Section 6.5.4, this was not seen in the directly observed scenario of Chapter 5, see Table 5.5. Perhaps seeing a silent video of a robot provides insufficient stimulus to engender confidence, whereas in a directly observed environment the stimulus of a non-vocalising robot is sufficient.

What is striking about the results shown in Figure 6.6 is the discrepancy between the change in actual MMA, and the change in reported confidence of participants due to vocalisation. Human language can be understood in terms of manipulation (Wortham and Bryson, 2018), and it seems that a talking robot may be better able to manipulate us than a dumb one. Perhaps we might be more easily deceived by talking robots than silent ones.

A small non-humanoid robot moving slowly around a pen, and presented online in a video, is unlikely to produce strong emotional responses. As we saw in Chapter 5, a talking robot would seem to create slightly more positive emotions overall, though with a high variance between individuals relative to the mean, see Section 6.5.5. These results are similar to those found in the directly observed scenario in Chapter 5, Section 5.5.2. For emotions, the wide variance in these experiments is of interest in itself. Clearly, there has been far too little time for humans to have acquired biologically evolved responses specific to artificial agency, but these wide variances indicate that the population does not have broad, culturally agreed norms for how to feel in relation to robots. Our models are individual and vary widely, probably based more on individual personality, anecdotal exposure to media reports and our predisposition to read and watch science fiction, than on any more broadly culturally acquired responses from parents or authority figures.

The Godspeed results show some significant differences based on morphology, with the zoomorphic robot being perceived as more intelligent and more likeable. In Section 6.2 we saw how zoomorphic robots have been found to be more likeable, and how an increasingly liked artefact attracts closer attention. This attention improves our visual perception of the robot, including our perception of agency; hence we achieve a richer mind model of the robot. This hypothesis can be summarised simply as

$$\textit{Zoomorphism} \rightarrow \textit{Increased Likeability} \tag{6.1}$$

$$\textit{Increased Likeability} \rightarrow \textit{Increased Attention} \tag{6.2}$$

$$\textit{Increased Attention} \rightarrow \textit{Improved Model} \tag{6.3}$$

However, this effect does not occur in the presence of a visual or vocalised transparency measure. This may be because the focus of attention is divided between the robot and the transparency measure.

The interaction between robot morphology and transparency measures is apparent from the data and indicates that a zoomorphic form may reduce the efficacy of transparency for increasing MMA. This may also be explained with a similar hypothesis, shown in the following three stages (6.4), (6.5) and (6.6). Zoomorphism directs attention to the visual appearance of the robot, and away from the transparency measures; therefore, they are less effective:

$$\textit{Zoomorphism} \rightarrow \textit{Increased Likeability} \rightarrow \textit{Increased Visual Attention} \tag{6.4}$$

$$\textit{Increased Visual Attention to Robot} \rightarrow \textit{Less Attn to Transparency} \tag{6.5}$$

$$\textit{Less Attention to Transparency} \rightarrow \textit{Lower Affect on MMA} \tag{6.6}$$

The Godspeed results do not significantly reinforce the anomalous result seen in the Affect results for treatment 7; however, they offer suggestive evidence that indeed we may be seeing a weak uncanny valley effect, where the R5 mechanomorphic robot exhibits speech and behaviours that are understood to be associated with a human, in contrast to the clearly non-humanoid appearance of the R5 robot. In contrast, the zoomorphic robot is considered more favourably, as our mental models for animals are more flexible than those we apply to humans. Perhaps we are more comfortable with the idea of talking animals than we are of talking machines.

The trivial embellishment of the R5 robot – simply adding a bee-like cover – alters its form sufficiently to have significant effects on our understanding of its behaviour and our attitude towards it. This alteration also has more subtle effects on our ability to benefit from visual or vocalised transparency measures. Before we paint faces on our robots, or cover them in fur, we need to think carefully about whether this might have unintended consequences for those destined to encounter and interact with our autonomous artefacts.

6.7   Conclusions and further work

First and most significantly, the experiments in this chapter reconfirm that the addition of a visual or vocalised representation of the internal processing and state of the robot significantly improves transparency, by which we mean the ability of a naive observer to form an accurate mental model of a robot's capabilities, intentions and purpose. This is a significant result across a diverse, international population sample and provides a robust result about humans in general, rather than one geographic, ethnic or socio-economic group in particular.

However, in all our experiments we were unable to achieve an MMA of more than 59%, indicating that even with our transparency techniques, naive observers' models remain inaccurate. It may be that a limit is reached whereby no further application of our real-time visual and vocalised transparency measures are effective at improving MMA, and the remaining gap can only be closed through other transparency means, such as written or diagrammatic documentation.

A vocalising, or *'talking'*, robot greatly increases the confidence of naive observers to report that they understand a robot's behaviour when observed on video. Perhaps we might be more easily deceived by talking robots than silent ones.

The zoomorphic form of our R5 robot is perceived as more intelligent and more likeable. We suggest that the zoomorphic form attracts closer visual attention, and whilst this results in an improved MMA, it also diverts attention away from transparency measures, reducing their efficacy to further increase MMA.

The trivial embellishment of a robot to alter its form has significant effects on our understanding and attitude towards it. We need to be careful not to trivially embellish a robot to make it more likeable or appear smarter than it is, at the possible expense of making its true capabilities and purpose less transparent, and its behaviour more difficult to understand. As Fong, Nourbakhsh and Dautenhahn (2003) point out, the design space of behaviour and appearance needs to be investigated systematically so that systems are specifically tailored for both the functional objectives of the robot and the educational, therapeutic and individual needs of users. At the time of writing, research on the attribution of internal states to non-human entities is only just beginning (Zhao, Phillips and Malle). Very recent studies by Zhao, Phillips and Malle indicate that the configuration of humanlike arms, legs and fingers affect an observer's perception of the robot's ability to perceive, interact and learn from its environment. The face and surface appearance (skin, face, hair) infer an ability to feel pain, combined with emotional capabilities such as gratitude, and even correlate with estimates of a robot's moral reasoning capabilities. We look forward to further systematic work in this area.

Winfield (2017) proposes a scheme of four dimensions to measure the intelligence of a robot: Morphological, Individual, Social and Swarm. Perhaps rather than a linear scale, future work might consider measuring using perception of intelligence along these four axes.

Chapter 7

Synthesis and further work

"You look at trees", he said, "and call them 'trees', and probably you do not think twice about the word. You call a star a 'star', and think nothing more of it. But you must remember that these words 'tree', 'star' were (in their original forms) names given to these objects by people with very different views from yours. To you, a tree is simply a vegetable organism, and a star simply a ball of inanimate matter moving along a mathematical course. But the first men to talk of 'trees' and 'stars' saw things very differently. To them, the world was alive with mythological beings. They saw the stars as living silver, bursting into flame in answer to the eternal music. They saw the sky as a jewelled tent, and the earth as the womb whence all living things have come. To them the whole of creation was 'myth-woven and elf-patterned'."

– J.R. Tolkien, quoted by Humphrey Carpenter, *The Inklings*

"Will we solve the crises of next hundred years?" asked Krulwich. "Yes, if we are honest and smart," said Wilson. "The real problem of humanity is the following: we have paleolithic emotions; medieval institutions; and god-like technology. And it is terrifically dangerous, and it is now approaching a point of crisis overall. Until we understand ourselves," concluded the Pulitzer-prize winning author of On Human Nature, "until we answer those huge questions of philosophy that the philosophers abandoned a couple of generations ago – Where do we come from? Who are we? Where are we going? – rationally, we're on very thin ground."

– Public discussion between E.O. Wilson and James Watson, moderated by Robert Krulwich, *Harvard Magazine*, September 2009

7.1   Summary

This research is motivated by the wide ranging concerns of human cognitive bias, the cultural perception of robots, confusion about the moral status of robots in society, and several societal concerns relating to the widespread adoption of autonomous robotics in social environments. These concerns are described in more detail in Section 1.1. In this chapter, based on these concerns together with the results of the robot transparency experiments described in detail in Chapters 4–6, I argue that we have a moral responsibility to make robots transparent, so as to reveal their true machine nature. I go on to recommend the inclusion of transparency as a fundamental design consideration for intelligent systems, particularly for autonomous robots.

This chapter commences with a clarification of terms, such as *artificial intelligence (AI)* and *AI ethics* that are frequently poorly defined and misused by the wider public media, and even sometimes by academia. First, I recommend a short set of unambiguous definitions that may not be universally recognised but have been carefully observed in this document. Using these terms, I go on to define robot ethics and discuss its purpose and contemporary relevance to society. I argue that professionals within the fields of AI generally, and robotics more specifically, have a moral duty to make their products transparent, revealing the products' capabilities and machine nature. Further, I argue that such products should be transparent with respect to the true purpose and objectives of the designers.

I conclude this chapter with suggestions for further work. I suggest additional transparency measures that could usefully be investigated. I also note that we still need to systematically investigate the multidimensional design space of robot behaviour and appearance in order to better understand their effect on how we perceive and understand robots. I briefly mention a wider programme of multidisciplinary work to investigate the wider societal impact of robots and autonomous intelligent systems (AIS), leading to the informed creation of standards, regulation and policy.

Finally, I suggest further work to extend the implementation of the Instinct Planner to other platforms and to investigate new applications for this technology.

7.2　Tools, machines, robots and algorithms

Throughout this book, and indeed throughout the related literature, the terms robot, machine, tool and algorithm are often used loosely and even interchangeably. Depending on context, and to avoid a repetitive prose style, this may be of no great consequence. However, there is an important sense in which we must be clear on the underlying concepts to which these terms refer. As Marx (1867) originally observed, and Gunkel (2017a) elegantly puts it, *Machine! = Tool* – a machine is not exactly the same thing as a tool. A *tool* is a device used by a human to enable them to perform some work. A *machine*, once set in motion, performs some work without the further intervention of the human. Machines do work that humans would otherwise do and, in addition, do work that humans are unable to do – an aircraft is a machine. By Gunkel's definitions, a machine can be considered to be an autonomous tool, that is, a tool that is self-sufficient and independent. Critics may argue that machines are only transiently independent, as they require regular maintenance and repair, but we may argue the same for humans, whose independence from one another is also merely transient. Nevertheless, humans are generally considered autonomous, and therefore we can say the same of machines.

An *algorithm* is generally defined as a repeatable sequence of steps to solve a problem. Algorithms must be *executed* in some manner in order to arrive at a solution to the problem. This execution may involve a human using pen and paper, a mechanical or hydraulic device, or some other mechanism of parts, but the process of execution is known as *computation*. It is important to note that computation is a physical process, requiring space, energy and time.

An algorithm encoded in a programming language of some sort, and executed on a computer, is a tool. It is initiated and supplied with some data by a human, does some useful work with that data by manipulating it and produces an output. Examples include graphics tools to manipulate images, machine learning (ML) algorithms to extract predictive statistical correlations from data and database search algorithms to quickly find specific data in a large database given certain search criteria. A machine may be constructed from computer hardware executing one or more algorithms, arranged in such a way that the algorithms are repeatedly invoked automatically in some kind of loop, by a repeating timer or repeatedly triggered by some external event such as a signal from a physical sensor or the arrival of a message from another system. Once initiated, a machine processes input data and generates output data indefinitely, until interrupted by a human, or another machine. An internet search engine, such as Google, is a machine. A *robot* is also a kind of machine. It has sensors that measure physical phenomena and use this sensor data as the input to repeatedly executing algorithms. The algorithms, designed by humans, process this data and generate outputs which are used to drive effectors, creating physical output in the world. For a robot to be useful, it requires algorithms that are designed to achieve goals, or objectives, set by its designer. Once the robot is operational, it operates *autonomously* (i.e. in a self-governing manner) without the necessity for further human intervention. We must remember that the algorithms that control the robot's behaviour are designed by human intent. Some machines, for example domestic washing machines, operate *automatically*, i.e. without human intervention, but lack the self-governing characteristics inherent in artefacts generally considered to be robots.

This brief explanation adequately explained the concept and basic structure of a robot without recourse to the term AI, at all. AI is a term originally coined by academics to study natural intelligence, particularly the kind of intelligence observed in humans, and to try to understand how intelligence arises and operates by simulating it using computers – artificial (i.e. human-made) intelligence (McCarthy *et al.*, 2006). *Intelligence* is one of those words that may mean all kinds of things, and as we have shown in Chapters 3–5, asking if something is intelligent is as much about asking after the nature of intelligence, as asking whether the artefact or organism itself possesses that property. However, in alignment with its original use by academics, and for our purposes, intelligence is simply defined as *doing the right thing at the right time, given the current context* (Bryson and Winfield, 2017). In biology, the term *homeostasis* is used to describe the stable internal environment that is preserved inside any living organism. As its internal energy sources are consumed and waste products are produced, and as its environment changes, the organism must *behave intelligently* in a self-governing manner to maintain homeostasis. Thus we say that all living things are intelligent. A robot that stands upright as it moves, despite uneven terrain and the force of gravity, or avoids obstacles in its path is similarly *behaving intelligently*. The intelligence is designed by a human, it is therefore *artificially* intelligent, since artificial simply means *'made or produced by human beings rather than occurring naturally'.** So, we see that AI is both a research theme and a suitable description for certain types of machines, particularly autonomous robots. Intelligence is an observable phenomena, and if that phenomenon is observed in an artefact, it is by definition artificial. A robot does not 'use AI', nor is there such a thing as 'an AI'. As I have demonstrated, robots are well described and characterised without recourse to the term AI at all but can be said to 'express AI'.

7.3   Robot and AI ethics

Having established the concepts of robots and AI, what do we mean by *robot ethics*? Moral philosophy, or *ethics*, is a branch of philosophy concerned with recommending, defending and structuring concepts of right and wrong behaviour (Fieser, 2017). Therefore, AI ethics is concerned with the acceptable behaviour of those working in the research field of AI and is extended to cover those that design, purchase or operate products, including robots, that may be produced as a result of that research. Robot ethics is simply a subset of AI ethics. I make this clarification due to the moral confusion outlined in Section 1.2.3. This confusion leads some to confer moral agency to robots and thus to wrongly assume that robot ethics concerns some ability of a robot to make ethical decisions and take responsibility for them – those who investigate this possibility refer to their work as *machine ethics*. However, since robots are not moral agents, the responsibility for robot behaviour lies with those attributed with responsibility for a robot (Boden *et al.*, 2011 ; Bryson, 2018). AI and robot ethics is not primarily about building software and machines that make 'ethical' decisions. It is about humans making moral choices about how and when to develop and deploy AI technology. We are the moral agents, AI is a tool.

7.3.1   Facts versus values

How does an investigation into robot transparency provide a basis for authoritative or even indeed meaningful normative assertions concerning how society should design and use robots? Why do facts concerning human–robot encounters have any bearing on how we *should* build robots? Facts are things that people can know and understand, values are things that people care about (Billington, 1988). Some moral philosophers, together with scientists and others with some knowledge of philosophy, immediately reach for Hume's well-known adage that *'you can't get an ought from an is'*. This may be interpreted by some as meaning that scientific facts – what is – have little relevance to a discussion of how humans *ought* to behave. Hume (1738) makes the argument that human morality is based on human emotion, and that emotion is not subject to reason. Moral rules are not based on reason, informed by facts about the world, but are instead the products of some irrational internal emotion generating mechanism. In contrast, Kant (1785) argues that fundamental moral positions are essentially fixed and to be discovered not through scientific means, but through a

---

*https://en.oxforddictionaries.com/definition/artificial

philosophical investigation of what is truly 'good'. Kant's *deontological* approach boils down to a correct understanding of *duty*, epitomised in Kant's *Categorical Imperative*; 'Act only according to that maxim whereby you can, at the same time, will that it should become a universal law.' This is a particular formulation of the Biblical *Golden Rule*; 'Do unto others as you would have them do unto you'. The golden rule, or law of reciprocity, is found in many cultures and religions and is particularly of note due to its universal nature; one's behaviour to another is not contingent on the behaviour of the other. However, despite their very different positions, we see that both Hume and Kant would agree that moral behaviour cannot be sought by an appeal to science. The empirical basis for ethics is further dismissed by more recent philosophy, particularly the *Logical Positivists* (also known as the Vienna group) of the late 1920s and 1930s. This includes, for example, the work of Schlick, Carnap and Neurath. The Logical Positivists rejected most classical and eighteenth and nineteenth century philosophy, certainly Kant, Hegel and Nietzsche, as vacuous. They established the tradition of *Analytical Philosophy* and defined their outgroup as *Continental*. Their assertion is that all moral philosophy is meaningless.

The Continental philosophical tradition, though much broader and without the same degree of internal consensus found in analytic philosophy, is best differentiated by the idea that all observations are made within pre-existing frameworks of knowledge, understanding and experience, and therefore that there is no truly objective empiricism. Science, and the scientific method itself, depends on some preconceptions such as causality and determinism. Whilst scientists acknowledge that *all models are wrong* as they are necessarily simplifications, models are nevertheless very useful (Box, 1979). Very broadly, Continentals ascribe to the idea that only through philosophical reflection can we arrive at the deepest understanding of the human condition, and therefore that whilst science has practical value, it has little to contribute to human morality. From the 1920s through to the 1970s, Martin Heidegger deployed and extended these postmodernist ideas in relation to the understanding of technology. Heidegger is recognised as a leading figure in the philosophy of technology, yet his thinking is widely acknowledged as impenetrable for the amateur philosopher, and his formulations are described by commentators as 'Byzantine' (Waddington, 2005). As a professional philosopher, Waddington makes it clear that Heidegger's work is readily misunderstood, and illustrates this point by critically correcting academics from other disciplines who have attempted some kind of analysis relevant to their own expertise. This may be understood as a kind of signalling of academic fitness by obscurity. My point here is that whatever the content of Heidegger's work, its result has been to intimidate scientists, engineers and technologists, alienating them from philosophical engagement.

Taken together, the history of both moral philosophy and the philosophy of technology have had a huge influence on modern thinking, reinforcing a false dichotomy between on the one hand science, engineering and empiricism more generally, and on the other the arts, politics, philosophy and literary thinking (Snow, 1959). This is my account for why many scientists and engineers do not engage in ethics, and why some philosophers choose not to engage readily with facts. This account also helps one to identify why society expects to receive moral instruction from the humanities, science being largely without the appetite for moral engagement and engineering being considered merely about the building of appliances.

7.3.2   The science of morality

More recently, there has been progress towards a scientific understanding of morality, based on evolutionary theory and evidence from psychology and neuroscience. Ruse and Wilson (1986) argue that we are deceived by our genes into thinking that a disinterested objective morality exists, and that we are somehow bound by it. This deception is adaptive for our species, and they assert that evidence from both genetic and cognitive studies demonstrate that our brains are not a *tabula rasa*, ready for moral values to be implanted by culture, but rather that our biological evolution results in moral mechanisms and biases towards specific responses to moral questions. Hauser (2006) describes this moral mind mechanism in some detail and cites extensive cross-cultural empirical research in support of its universal nature. Haidt (2006) develops the idea of "the Elephant and the Rider" as a metaphor for a dual-process theory of the human mind. The rider represents our reasoned plans and goals formulated by the conscious mind. The elephant represents our visceral reactions and 'gut feelings'. Generally, the rider is able to direct the elephant, provided that the elephant is in general agreement. However, the elephant is of course much stronger than the rider, and once appropriately stimulated, the elephant reveals that she is in fact in control, and whilst riding, the rider is powerless. Therefore, the role of the rider is to provide the appropriate stimulus to the elephant, such that the elephant's visceral responses are in line with the objectives of the rider. Haidt, Graham and Joseph (2009) investigate the biological foundations of human morality, searching for the psychological foundations upon which human culture creates moral systems. They identify five foundations: Harm/care, Fairness/reciprocity, Ingroup/loyalty, Authority/respect and Purity/sanctity. For the first four of these Haidt, Graham and Joseph find evidence of continuity with the social psychology of other primates, indicating that these foundations may derive from a shared evolutionary ancestor and may be adaptive, increasing fitness for social species that exhibit these traits. Purity may have evolved from the disgust response to tainted food, co-opting the strong emotional response that disgust generates and putting it to use within a social context, as a means to enforce social norms.

Miller (2008) reviews the work of Hauser, Haidt, Graham and Joseph several others, particularly Greene and Haidt (2002) regarding the science investigating moral norms and reasoning. He makes the obvious yet-important point that morality, rather than being a feature of an immaterial or emergent self, is in fact a product of the human brain. In all animals, neural circuitry grounds self-caring and well-being, and similarly it is reasonable to hypothesise that morality results from neurobiological processes, particularly attachment and bonding to mates (Churchland, 2011; Shostak, 2013). In addition to the electrical activity of neurons, the brain is a biological organ within a living being, and its activity is substantially modified by the complex 'chemical soup' of hormones and other neurotransmitters produced by the body. These complex mechanisms also contribute significantly to behaviour (Rohlfshagen and Bryson, 2010). Haidt (2012) adds a sixth moral foundational element, Liberty (i.e. freedom of action), to the list of moral foundations described by Haidt, Graham and Joseph. This finalises Haidt's list of six *moral emotions*: Care, Fairness, Liberty, Loyalty, Authority and Purity. Haidt makes a convincing case that these moral intuitions are a biologically evolved adaptation, subsequently shaped by human culture. They served the survival needs of our ancestors by making us sensitive to our social and physical environments, in order to identify harms or other impediments to our survival. Moral psychology developed as a solution to the evolutionary problem of cooperation within larger groups, where close biological relatedness is insufficient to maintain group stability (Hamilton, 1964).

There are several dual-process theories of cognition, the basic premise being that two 'systems' of cognition operate in parallel within the human brain, and both influence behaviour and conscious thought. These theories do not postulate separate *physical* systems, for example resident in separate brain areas, but are variously considered as modes of operation, or more abstractly, simply useful metaphors that explain and predict human cognition. Typically, one system operates at an intuitive or experiential level, whilst the other operates in an analytical or rational mode (Epstein, 1998; Sherman, Gawronski and Trope, 2014).

Kahneman (2012) elaborates one of the most well-known theories; the 'System 1, System 2' model. System 1 represents a fast mode of cognition, generally understood to be below the level of consciousness. In regard to moral thinking, System 1 can be thought of as a system that provides intuitions, impressions, impulses and feelings, rather than fully formed rational judgements. System 2 is associated with the deliberative, conscious and rational process that, based on evidence, comes to a final judgement and produces an associated narrative explanation. System 1 operates effortlessly, and is generally considered to embody biases and norms resulting from our evolutionary past. It may also operate by substituting a related easy question for an initial hard question, for example replacing 'what is the best course of action?' with 'what do most of the people around me think is the best thing to do?' This is of course a much easier question to answer, but in novel or extreme situations it may 'fail', producing poor outcomes for both the individual and the group. System 1 may also fail by using 'intensity matching', for example by matching the intensity of an emotional response with a monetary value of financial philanthropy. In contrast, the operation of System 2 is resource intensive and therefore requires effort, although correctly employing System 2 thinking can overcome the errors of judgement made by System 1. System 2 takes the 'output' of System 1 and due to the 'lazy' nature of System 2, it often relies on System 1 intuitions, merely creating a conscious narrative to justify, initiate and maintain the resulting behaviour.

Greene (2014) provides perhaps the most useful dual-process model of moral judgement. His metaphor is that of a modern digital camera. The camera has two modes; 'Preset mode' and 'Manual mode'. Preset mode equates with the idea of intuitive moral judgement, or System 1 thinking. Manual mode equates with our ability for deliberative moral reasoning, System 2. Greene explains that Preset mode only works well in certain well-known situations, such as when we make moral judgements about killing at close quarters. Preset mode is not particularly useful for evolutionarily novel situations, such as killing at a distance using military drones, or killing using autonomous robots (Perez Vallejos, Wortham and Miakinkov, 2017). Similarly Preset mode has little to offer us when it comes to uncertain outcomes, long timeframes or distributed responsibility. In these situations, we must resort to Manual mode. Greene proposes we deploy a consequentialist rational philosophy in these circumstances, where moral decisions attempt to maximise happiness and minimise suffering. However, the most interesting feature of this model is the implicit camera operator, who must decide in which mode to use the camera. We need to make informed choices about when to follow our implicit moral intuitions, and when to recognise that they may be faulty, requiring a deliberative, rational approach.

We see that our basic emotions and our framework of moral intuitions are a mechanism, evolved to orient us to do 'what we prudentially ought' (Churchland, 2011). It is also evident that in evolutionarily novel situations, such as when we encounter autonomous artificial agency, our moral intuitions are likely to be faulty and must be considered suspect. Therefore, when considering AI ethics, a scientifically informed viewpoint to moral philosophy, in line with Greene, suggests that we should follow a well-informed, though ultimately intuitive deontological approach to moral decision-making, along Kantian lines. However, when we reach a point where we either have no intuitive moral conviction, or when moral intuitions within a population vary widely, we can conclude they are faulty and instead resort to a consequentialist approach. This approach is particularly useful when strong but opposing intuitive moral convictions exist. Consequentialism demands that we seek to understand the benefits, costs, opportunities and risks associated with the decisions we make. We can use scientific knowledge, understanding and insight to maximise positive outcomes and minimise negative outcomes for society as a whole. As Churchland points out "science can teach us, and has already taught us, a great deal about what we ought to do ... [without implying] that science can solve all moral dilemmas".

7.3.3   An empirical basis for morality

Despite the prevailing popular cultural view of science as no more than a hatchery for technology, some scientists and philosophers are now brave enough to argue that we can indeed establish an empirical basis for what we ought to do, based on an empirically underpinned theory of the needs of humans (Harris, 2011). Scientists may appear amoral because they readily change their opinion in the light of new evidence. This may seem like weakness or lack of principle but in fact comes from adherence to the principle that we should best act according to our knowledge, based on evidence, scrutinised through the lens of the scientific method. To not change one's position in the light of new evidence would be to act either out of pride, foolishness or selfishness, but in any case to act without deference to reason and rational thinking. Such an act, being solely instinctive in nature, denies our humanity, for to be human is to inhibit instinctive behaviour and rather to act from informed reason. The success of our species is in part thought to be a result of this ability, combined with prosocial behaviour (Burkart *et al.*, 2014 ; Pinker, 2018). A scientifically informed understanding of our moral sense can alert us to violations of rational moral conclusions that occur as a result of our psychological make-up. Our moral intuitions can be unreliable and are subject to deception (Pinker, 2008). For example, our foundational attachment to Purity makes us vulnerable to the association of a physically pure appearance with a morally pure character. Notice how some religious leaders (and the ruling classes in some countries, historically one and the same) dress in 'pure' white clothing to symbolise their inner moral purity and thus with considerable success claim some moral authority for their position and pronouncements (Dennett, 2007). Similarly, Pinker (2008) points out that our strong emotional disgust response 'imposes taboos that make certain ideas indiscussible'. When it comes to robots, the results of the experiments described in Chapters 4–6 strongly support the theory that we are unprepared by biological or social evolution for encounter with robots, and thus our intuitions are naive and open to easy manipulation. The moral confusion that exists about robots results from the naivety of our moral intuitions regarding robots.

In this book, I therefore seek to make a contribution to a specific area of the new moral philosophy of robot ethics. This contribution is based on scientific understanding of humans and empirical evidence about how humans understand and interact with autonomous systems. Based on this evidence, I argue that transparency *ought* to be a fundamental design consideration for artificially intelligent systems, and that unless there is some overarching ethical reason why a specific system should not be transparent, then this consideration *should* be promoted to a requirement.

7.4 The case for transparency as a fundamental design consideration for AI systems

We might surmise that the prolonged exposure of human culture to autonomous agents of all kinds will eventually result in a robust set of cultural responses and ethical norms. Humans have assimilated all kinds of technology into culture, from air transport to pharmacy to mobile communications, so it might be considered reasonable to expect that with sufficient exposure, individuals and groups will become familiar with robots and other AIS and will be able to beneficially and appropriately interact with them. However, there are several important considerations that particularly apply to robots and AIS that do not apply to previous forms of technology.

- Humans particularly react to autonomous agency. Our biological evolution has equipped us with agency detection mechanisms that operate as a fundamental component of perception, and we are evolved to attribute human characteristics to agents. We anthropomorphise robots (Guthrie, 1997; Dautenhahn, 2007; Salem *et al.*, 2013).
- With respect to a robot, predicting function from form is not reliable. The goals and intentions of a robot are defined by human designers. Two robots with identical form may be running very different software, having widely divergent capabilities and with very different intended functions. Even if they are running the same software, the ultimate goals, i.e. those of the robot operators, may be quite different. One may take a responsible approach to security and data protection, another may not, or may even be using the robot to harvest personal data for commercial or other inappropriate purposes.

- For a 'disembodied' AIS, such as a chatbot- or voice-activated digital assistant, there is no form from which we might predict function. Beyond anthropomorphism, we have no useful mental model to predict capabilities, goals and intentions.
- The capabilities, goals and intentions of a robot or AIS are not stable over time. We are familiar with natural agents that learn and acquire new skills over time; however, artificial agents may update almost instantaneously. These updates may occur as a result of individual learning, consolidated learning coordinated over the Internet or simply through a traditional software update. We are potentially forever naive.

For these reasons, it is hard, if not impossible, for humans to develop culturally acquired responses to robots that will in general be appropriate and result in useful interactions. The long-term cultural result may be to rely on the default intuitive responses to avoid harm, rejecting interaction with robots and AIS. Conversely, we may be overcome by our anthropomorphism and embrace robots and even other AIS as fellows, extending rights and conveying moral obligations to our machines. We might fail to notice that in fact they are manipulation machines, authored by other humans, and have no identity other than that provided by their design. Either outcome is likely to be problematic for humanity.

A better approach is to recognise that we can choose to make robots and other autonomous intelligent machines such that they are transparent. We can choose to make their machine nature apparent, thus differentiating them from humans, and other natural living things. We can choose to have our machines tell us what their capabilities are, what they are trying to do (their intentions) and why (their goals). There seems to be little reason not to take this approach, and every reason to do so.

This human centric view of our approach to developing technology is not new. Indeed the central tenets of Humanism include trust in the scientific method, ethical decision-making based on reason and a fundamental concern for the well-being of humans (Humanists International, 1952). We should indeed seek this well-being both for ourselves and for others.

Given the potential for harm, and the availability of an effective remedy, I argue that society should expect those who design and operate robots and AIS to make their artefacts transparent. If there is some overarching reason why transparency should be avoided, then designers and operators should be able to make their case, but the default position should be one of appropriate transparencies.

However, the demand for transparency is not without its challenges. In the following sections, I explore the problems of creating transparent minds, and of communicating information relevant to end users.

7.5   Transparent minds

Traditional symbolic approaches to AI are generally seen as more amenable to the generation of real-time narratives that explain, to some extent, the behaviour of a robot.

I have shown in Chapter 3 that it is indeed possible to create effective and adaptable action selection systems for robots using a biologically inspired control paradigm, amenable to the implementation of real-time transparency. The need to make robots comprehensible to human partners is in fact sometimes used as a justification for biologically inspired approaches to robotics (Brooks and Stein, 1994; Sengers, 1998; Novikova and Watts, 2014; Wortham and Bryson, 2018).

The 'ML' approach to AI is a powerful alternative approach for the construction of intelligent systems. It typically harvests human intelligence from data and encapsulates this within the numerical parameters of an algorithm, such that for a given set of inputs, the algorithm calculates an output value. ML can also be used to capture the underlying structural regularities of some complex dynamic system, such as the physical rules necessary for legged locomotion (walking). The processing of the initial 'training' data set typically requires intensive computation and may take some time. However, once 'trained' these numerical approaches are very fast in operation. There are many examples where ML has been proven to perform extremely well. For example, ML is well known in image recognition applications such as Automatic Number Plate Recognition (Keilthy, 2008), automatic face recognition in digital cameras and smart phones (Lawrence *et al.*, 1997), and the automatic image categorisation provided by search engines such as Google and Bing (Krizhevsky, Sutskever and Hinton, 2012). ML also underpins speech and handwriting recognition technology and predictive text or 'autocomplete' (Mikolov *et al.*, 2013). Since its inception, ML has been applied to the problem of playing games. However, the notable success of the AlphaGo project to play the board game Go has been widely reported (Silver *et al.*, 2016) and subsequently ML is now broadly considered to have 'solved' the general problem of playing games. Indeed, the media currently use the term AI as a synonym for ML, and other approaches to AI are increasingly dismissed as outdated or superseded by numerical ML approaches. Deep Recurrent Neural Networks, a particular type of ML approach, has recently been successfully demonstrated as a control strategy for traditional robotics applications such as dexterous manipulation, legged locomotion and car driving (Lillicrap *et al.*, 2016). This work uses simulation environments, known as 'physics simulators', to facilitate very large numbers of trials. During these trials, a reinforcement learning algorithm repeatedly tunes the parameters in the control algorithm, based on a simple objective function. For example, to train the system for legged locomotion, the objective function is simply to maximise forward motion. This eventually results in intelligent behaviour in a wide variety of virtual environments, some of them novel, i.e. environments not encountered during the training process. Lillicrap *et al.* also deploy their technology to control a large physical robot. In the real physical world, it is not possible to run many thousands or millions of trials, and so basic training is provided by human operators who guide the arms and end effectors of the robot. This effectively reduces the search space by many orders of magnitude. A subsequent unsupervised (in the sense that no human operator is present) set of trials results in a robot able to effectively carry out complex and dexterous manipulation tasks with high repeatability and performance.

There are many types of numerical approaches to ML, beyond the scope of this work (Tipping, 2004; Murphy, 2012; Russell and Norvig, 2016). However, most share a similar limitation: they can be characterised as being *'black box approaches'*. This term 'black box' indicates that the system does not produce any meaningful explanation of its decision-making. Furthermore, even an internal investigation of the workings of the system provides little or no further insight into the *'reasons'* for the decisions being made. For example, one might investigate a deep artificial neural network (ANN) and find many thousands of calculated parameters (weights and biases) associated with the neurons and the connections between them. However, those weights and biases do not tell us *'why'* the ANN classifies one image as a dog and another as an aeroplane. We humans want a useful explanation of *'how'* one recognises an aeroplane. We might give an answer such as *"all aeroplanes have wings and an engine"*, or we might offer a counterfactual in reference to the dog, such as *"aeroplanes do not have fur"*. In truth, our initial classification may be generated by low-level pattern matching mechanisms in our brains, without recourse to these kinds of logical tests – see Section 7.3.2 for an explanation and discussion of System 1, System 2 thinking. However, we then subsequently check the findings of our low-level recognition with some higher level, conscious introspection in order to render *'meaningful'* reasons for our classification. With an ANN, there is no answer available for the kind of explanations that humans need in order to establish some mind model of the operation of the ANN, and therefore to be able to calibrate their level of trust in its decision-making. Rightly or wrongly, we want meaningful explanations. I discuss our human need for meaningful explanations, particularly for intentional acts, further in Section 7.7.

There is also research in progress to investigate interpretable, or 'white box' ML approaches, where each variable in the system is related to some parameter of the real world. Further, there are so-called *'grey box'* approaches where some parts of the system are human interpretable while other parts are not (Ribeiro, Singh and Guestrin, 2016). These systems offer more hope that we might be able to inspect the system as it operates and generate meaningful (useful to humans) statements of the form *"the system came to x decision because y"*, where *y* relates to the input parameters and the internal states within the system – those internal states also having real-world meaning.

Whilst the output of an opaque system may indeed be an intelligent response to its inputs and current internal state, ML approaches generally produce no narrative to explain *why* the system generated a certain output. Indeed, David Silver the lead scientist of the AlphaGo project explained at his ICAPS 2016 talk in London[†] that he was "really unable to determine why AlphaGo chose a particular move over all the others available", Silver also said that whilst it is clearly possible to look into the algorithm as it runs, he is no wiser for doing so (taken from the Authors contemporaneous notes from the conference). The use of deep learning and similar black box ML for action selection inevitably creates an opaque system, since the action selection mechanism is unable to give an account of the actions selected by the machine.

[†]http://icaps16.icaps-conference.org/

We might argue that the opaque nature of ML-based AI is really no different from the opaque nature of the human mind. In both cases, we can only observe resulting behaviour. We must infer capabilities, goals and intentions based on our own mental models. We are able to make sense of humans, and to a lesser extent animals, when we encounter them, so we might argue that we can learn to deal with robots and AIS in the same way (Wortham and Bryson, 2018; Saxe, Schulz and Jiang, 2006). As manufactured artefacts, robots are quite unlike humans and animals, and this argument fails for the reasons given in the preceding Section 7.4. However, the problem of transparency of ML systems remains. As yet, no effective solution has been found, although various approaches have been suggested. Schwab and Hlavacs (2015) suggest a novel approach that uses the resultant behaviour of a black box AI system to construct a functionally equivalent symbolic behaviour tree. This tree is then substituted for the previous black box system. A behaviour tree can produce an explanation of decisions, and thus a black box AI system is replaced with a functionally equivalent transparent system. This appears to be a very promising line of research, although unfortunately there seems to have been little further work in this area. Samek *et al.* (2016) investigate the use of 'heatmaps' with image recognition systems, to indicate which areas of an image are most salient in determining the overall classification output of a deep neural network (DNN). By manipulating individual pixels and groups of pixels in the image, and subsequently measuring the effect on the output of the DNN, a map may be constructed with contours indicating which areas of the image most contribute to the final decision made by the DNN. In essence, this idea is similar to the graphical representation of action selection, implemented in the ABOD3 tool, see Section 4.3.3. In both cases, a graphical display is used to highlight information that may help users understand the operation of a system exhibiting AI. There is ongoing research work in the display of heat maps for DNNs, but the approach requires considerable computational resources, since many pixel manipulations must be considered in order to render the heatmap. It may therefore not be suitable for real-time applications. To date these kinds of exploratory techniques have yet to be applied to robot action selection, though this remains a possible route for future research.

7.6 Hybrid architectures

As we have seen, ML technology yields a variety of very useful applications, from image classification and machine vision to speech recognition and natural language processing. Many of these approaches and technologies are directly applicable to problems found in the design of robots and AIS, particularly to create meaningful information from raw sensor data. In a hybrid architecture, these black box systems create outputs which can then be used as a basis for action selection implemented using traditional, or biologically inspired, action selection mechanisms. The hybrid approach combines the ability of ML to make sense of complex real-world data, with the ability of traditional action selection to generate traceable and potentially transparent decisions. Hybrid robot architectures combining deliberative and reactive layers of control are proven to be effective (Nakhaeinia *et al.*, 2015). The extension of

Figure 7.1   A hybrid approach to speech recognition. Graphic reproduced by kind permission of Dr Tom Fincham Haines, University of Bath, 2019.

this architecture to include ML or probabilistic approaches for sensor input processing and analysis, for example to process video camera inputs for pose estimation, does not prohibit such a system from being transparent (Kornuta and Zieliński, 2013). Using this modular approach, transparency is still possible in terms of the ability of the overall system to report the outputs from the sensory ML subsystems, and the consequential decisions made by the action selection system. A robot or AIS containing some 'black boxes' can still have a high degree of overall transparency. However, whilst there is considerable work to design appropriate modular frameworks for robot software architecture, the need for end-user transparency has yet to become a recognised design requirement (Reichardt, Föhst and Berns, 2015).

Figure 7.1 is a diagrammatic representation of a hybrid system developed by Dr Tom Fincham Haines at the University of Bath. The audio waveform is chopped into 10 ms chunks, and a phoneme label (sil for silence) is associated for each chunk. The phoneme–audio relationship is first learned and then determined by an ANN, though it is not the only option: random forests and Gaussian mixture models have also been used. The waveform is first converted into Mel-frequency cepstrum (MEL) features, and the ML associates these features with textual phonemes. A MEL feature is essentially a fast Fourier transform re-weighted to account for human perception. So, although the relationship from audio wave to phoneme is not transparent, the phonemes themselves have real-world meaning. The transitions from phoneme to phoneme indicate the word being spoken. The allowable transitions are specified in a hierarchical decision tree; a transparent white box approach. The overall solution is therefore part white box, part black box; overall, a *'grey box'* approach.

7.7   Humans expect intentional explanations

When we communicate, we claim the attention of one or more others. This implies that at least some of the information communicated is relevant to the receiver. Therefore, relevance may be seen as the key to human communication and cognition (Sperber and Wilson, 1986). Put simply, humans need some way to link an incoming communication signal, whether verbal or non-verbal, to something they care about. If they are unable to do this, then the signal becomes irrelevant, and no effective communication occurs. One of the problems of transparency is how to provide a sufficient explanation of intentionality to create relevance. In order to understand behaviour, humans often expect reasons to be provided (de Graaf and Malle, 2017). The problem is that these reasons may not be held within the robot. For example, the R5 robot contains a drive that causes the robot to periodically 'sleep'. Rather like animals and humans, the robot contains no explanation of why it *needs* to sleep – what is the ultimate explanation for sleeping. The robot has a drive that makes it *want* to sleep after an extended period without sleep, and the sleeping behaviour is released when the robot is sufficiently close to an obstacle or wall – see Section 4.3.2. Humans are able to report that they are 'tired' and want to sleep, but this is no better explanation for the ultimate reasons for human sleeping, which are complex and still the subject of scientific enquiry. Reporting tiredness is only generally a sufficient explanation for human sleep because we all experience and have a proximal understanding of tiredness and sleep. Human mind models of robots do not generally include the idea that they can become tired, and hence the sleeping behaviour seems spurious and unexplainable. What is needed is an explanation for the *'need to sleep'*, in order that we can make sense of the sleeping behaviour. But this explanation does not reside within the robot, it is a design requirement implemented by the designer, based on the need to conserve battery life and extend overall operation time. This simple example drawn from our experiments shows us that there may be a limit on the transparency that can be achieved by making the robot's internal processing and state available to the user using visual and vocalisation techniques.

In order to provide sufficient explanation to achieve understanding by a human user or observer, the designer of the robot may have to explicitly add knowledge to the robot that is not required for the robot to achieve its desired behaviour. The robot may need to be able to report information about the designers' or operator's goals and intentions, solely to help the user build a mental model sufficient to understand the behaviour of the robot. Typically this information resides in design specifications and user manuals, but it may also need to be included within the robot and made appropriately available to the user at run-time. If the R5 robot were to have muttered *"R5 has completed sleep **to conserve battery power**"* then perhaps the sleep behaviour would not appear so inexplicable.

7.8 Further work

This section summarises the further work that is identified in each chapter. Some of this work relates to further experiments to investigate anthropomorphism and robot transparency, and some relates to a broader multidisciplinary programme to understand how we design 'understandable' or transparent robots and AIS, and how we should create policy and regulate the use and operation of AIS. I also suggest enhancements to the technical artefacts developed as part of this research programme, together with potential new applications for this technology.

7.8.1   *Anthropomorphism, transparency and traceability*

All the studies of Chapters 4–6 concentrate on making the decision-making process available to the participants. We do not consider making available the sensory model that exists within a robot, nor making available the various thresholds that must be crossed to release the various elements of the reactive plan. Perhaps to do so would overload the user with data, but in some applications it may be helpful to gain an insight about how the world is perceived by the robot, as this would aid an understanding of its subsequent decision-making processes. It might also be useful to investigate the benefits of a more complex sentence generation algorithm, able to generate varying sentences that might make the vocalisation sound less repetitive and 'robotic'.

The research with the zoomorphic Buddy robot shows that trivial changes to appearance can dramatically alter our perception and understanding of a robot. As Fong, Nourbakhsh and Dautenhahn (2003) point out, the design space of behaviour and appearance needs to be investigated systematically so that systems are specifically tailored for both the functional objectives of the robot and the educational, therapeutic and individual needs of users.

Creating an explanation for behaviour is not only important as the behaviour occurs, but also important for *post-facto* analysis. In this case transparency is often referred to as *traceability*. If we wish to hold accountable the designers and operators of a robot, then being able to trace the internal state and decision-making processes helps provide the necessary evidence to construct a case. In this work, I have not considered traceability in any depth, although in using video recording techniques with the ABOD3 tool (see Chapters 4 and 6), I implicitly demonstrate it. However, without access to a 'gods eye' view of the robot within an environment, traceability may require more detailed presentation of sensor data, and this is an area for potential future work.

Current models of the development of anthropomorphism are outdated and fail to capture the interaction between perceiver and perceived. Together with my colleague Nathalia Gjersoe, we propose a new programme of research to expose the key behavioural drivers of anthropomorphism and examine their effectiveness for children of different ages. This will provide a means of unpacking the mechanisms of anthropomorphism, eventually allowing us to manipulate it when we design robots (Gjersoe and Wortham, 2019).

7.8.2   *Explainable AI, policy and regulation*

This book concentrates on a practical investigation of robot transparency, however, I have also outlined the wider societal concerns related to robotics and AIS. As I illustrate in Section 1.2.6 we see a wide variation in current public policy relating to AI and autonomous robotics. One explanation for this variation is a lack of empirical evidence relating to the psychological and wider societal impact of deployment of AIS. There is an urgent need to generate scientific theory and data on which well-reasoned policy can be constructed. We need to understand the impact of real robots in society, not hypothesise based on cultural stereotypes or the potentially biased views of those with specific economic and commercial objectives. In addition, as Miller, Howe and Sonenberg (2017) point out, the achievement of effective explanations from AI systems requires a multidisciplinary approach, informed not only by the computer scientists and roboticists involved in AI and HRI research, but also from psychology and more widely from the social sciences and those engaged in moral philosophy and the development of policy, both within and beyond academia. This work should have the objective to create well-informed standards, regulation and policy, leading to the effective and beneficial use of robots and AIS.

7.8.3 Technologies

An obvious next step for the technology developed as part of this research is the implementation of Instinct on other embedded and low cost Linux computing environments such as the RASPBERRY PI (Raspberry Pi Foundation, 2016). With more powerful platforms such as the PI, much larger plans can be developed and this would facilitate testing of both the runtime performance of very large plans, and the design efficiency of the Instinct Visual Design Language with multi-user teams.

The Instinct Robot World is an entirely open-source platform, available online. Those interested in agent-based modelling, cognitive architectures generally, and reactive planning specifically, are encouraged to investigate these technologies and offer suggestions for new applications and further work. One possibility might be to apply this architecture to the Small Loop Problem (Georgeon, Marshall and Gurney, 2013), a specific challenge for biologically inspired cognitive architectures.

7.9   Conclusion

In this chapter, I have suggested definitions for *AI*, *AI ethics* and *robot ethics* as a precursor to exploring our moral obligations in the design and operation of robots and AIS. I have argued that science provides us with useful explanations for moral positions and behaviours. Science enlightens us regarding the biological and prosocial origins of moral preferences. The scientific method helps us identify the hazards that exist when humans interact with robots and other types of AIS, such as 'chatbots'. Humans particularly react to autonomous agency and readily anthropomorphise robots. With respect to a robot, predicting function from form is not reliable. For a 'disembodied' AIS, such as a chatbot- or voice-activated digital assistant, there is no form from which we might predict function. The capabilities, goals and intentions of a robot or AIS are not stable over time. These arguments are presented in full in Section 7.4. Based on these arguments, together with the evidence from practical experimentation provided in Chapters 4–6, I have argued that robot designers and operators have a moral duty to make their products transparent, revealing the products' capabilities and machine nature. Further, such products should be transparent with respect to the true purpose and objectives of the designers.

Chapter 8
Conclusions

"After five years, work I allowed myself to speculate on the subject, and drew up some short notes; these I enlarged in 1844 into a sketch of the conclusions, which then seemed to me probable: from that period to the present day I have steadily pursued the same object. I hope that I may be excused for entering on these personal details, as I give them to show that I have not been hasty in coming to a decision."

– Charles Darwin, *On the Origin of Species by Means of Natural Selection; or, The Preservation of Favoured Races in the Struggle for Life*, 1869

"I have striven not to laugh at human actions, not to weep at them, not to hate them, but to understand them."

– Baruch Spinoza, *Tractatus Politicus*, 1676

8.1 The effectiveness of transparency to improve mind models

The primary purpose of the research programme outlined in this book is to investigate robot transparency within the context of unplanned naive robot encounter. In this context, 'robot transparency' means the extent to which a naive observer is able to form an accurate model of a robot's capabilities, intentions and purpose.

However, in Chapter 1 of this book I have also outlined the various societal concerns and moral confusion that now exists as a result of the wide proliferation of artificial intelligence (AI) and autonomous intelligent system (AIS) technologies. Transparency needs to be understood within the context of these concerns, and also within the wider context of trust, accountability and responsibility. In Chapter 2 I have offered some models that help us to unpack trust and also see how transparency improves the quality of information available to users, which in turn helps one to build trust in combination with accountability and responsibility.

Chapter 4 demonstrates that subjects can show marked improvement in the accuracy of their mental model of a robot observed either directly or on video, if they also see an accompanying display of the robot's real-time decision making. In both the pilot study using Online Video, and the subsequent experiment with direct observation, the outcome is strongly significant. The addition of ABOD3 visualisation of the robot's intelligence does indeed make the machine nature of the robot more transparent. The results of the Online Video experiment in Chapter 4 imply that an improved mental model of the robot is associated with an increased perception of a thinking machine, even though there is no significant change in the level of perceived intelligence. However, this effect is not seen when the robot is directly observed. The relationship between the perception of intelligence and thinking is therefore not straightforward.

Chapter 5 provides evidence that a similar significant improvement in robot transparency can also be achieved by vocalisation of the robot's real-time decision making. The study in Chapter 6 also indicates the possibility that participants feel more positive about a directly observed robot when it is muttering, but with the limited study size these results are not statistically significant, and in comparison with the much stronger effect of the transparency on accuracy of mental model, this emotional effect appears to be much weaker. Indeed, there was almost no difference in the levels of arousal generated by a silent or muttering robot, which in itself is an interesting result.

The study using Mechanical Turk in Chapter 6 reconfirms that the addition of a visual or vocalised representation of the internal processing and state of the robot significantly improves transparency, even though the understanding of naive observers may still include wildly inaccurate overestimation of the robot's abilities. This is a significant result across a diverse, international population sample and provides a robust result about humans in general, rather than one geographic, ethnic or socio-economic group in particular.

However, in all our experiments we were unable to achieve a mental model accuracy (MMA) of more than 59%. This indicates that even with real-time transparency of a robot's internal state and processing, naive observers' models remain inaccurate to some degree. Whether a robot design that achieves an MMA of 59% is acceptable or not will depend on the context and specific application area. It may be that a limit is reached whereby further real-time transparency measures are ineffective at improving MMA without further scaffolding, and the remaining gap can only be closed through other transparency measures, such as human explanation or written documentation.

The studies of Chapters 4–6 taken together indicate that significant numbers of participants perceive that they have a good mental model of the robot, when in reality they do not. This occurs both with, and without the provision of additional robot transparency. Reports of understanding by those interacting with robots should therefore be treated with healthy scepticism. A vocalising, or *'talking'*, robot greatly increases the confidence of naive observers to report that they understand a robot's behaviour when observed on video. Perhaps we might be more easily deceived by talking robots than silent ones.

The study in Chapter 6 shows that the zoomorphic form of the R5 robot is perceived as more intelligent and more likeable. I suggest that the zoomorphic form attracts closer visual attention, and whilst this results in an improved MMA, it also diverts attention away from transparency measures, reducing their efficacy to further increase MMA. The trivial embellishment of a robot to alter its form has significant effects on our understanding and attitude towards it. We need to be careful not to trivially embellish a robot to make it more likeable or appear smarter than it is, at the possible expense of making its true capabilities and purpose less transparent, and its behaviour more difficult to understand.

8.2 Transparency as a fundamental design consideration for AI systems

In Chapter 7, I argue that it is possible to justify a moral assertion based on scientific evidence. I go on to argue the case for transparency and conclude that **transparency should be a fundamental design consideration for AI systems**. Reference to the need for transparency should be included in standards, regulations and policies that relate to the effective and beneficial use of robots and AIS.

8.3 Robot technical architecture

Although primarily developed as part of this research programme for use within the R5 robot, the Instinct Planner has obvious applications in teaching, simulation and game AI environments. The Instinct Robot World provides a graphical user interface-based test platform for Instinct, and for use as a teaching tool to teach the concepts of reactive planning in general and the Instinct Planner in particular.

I have shown that a second-order Darwinian mind may be constructed from two instances of the Instinct reactive planner. This architecture, named Reflective Reactive Planning, successfully controls the behaviour of a virtual robot within a simulated world, according to predefined goals and higher level objectives. The work shows how this architecture may provide both practical cognitive implementations and may inform philosophical discussion on the nature and purpose of consciousness.

8.4 Conclusion

The space in which transparency could be investigated has many dimensions, including robot purpose and behaviour, physical size and appearance, and the extent and context of robot interaction, together with various forms of transparency measure. This research has investigated a portion of this space with a small, non-humanoid mobile robot using visual and vocalised real-time transparency measures with naive observers. We have found significant evidence to support the need for transparency as a fundamental design consideration for AI systems, but there exists considerable scope for further work.

There is also an urgent need for a broad programme of multidisciplinary work to investigate the wider societal impact of robots and autonomous intelligent systems, leading to the informed creation of standards, regulation and policy. I hope this book makes a contribution to that process.

Appendix A
Instinct Planner command set

The Instinct Planner includes an online help system. The R5 robot command HELP PLAN shows a list of all available plan commands, as below.

```
HELP PLAN
PLAN Commands:
A{Add plan element}|U{Update plan element}|
          M{Config Monitor}|
R{Reset plan}] [parameter values]
A - add elements to the existing plan
  A [D{Drive}|C{Competence}|A{Action}|
    P{Action Pattern}|E{Competence Element}|
    L{ActionPattern Element}]
              [parameter values]
  The A D command has 12 parameters as below:
      A D Runtime_ElementID Runtime_ChildID Priority
          uiInterval SenseID Comparator SenseValue
          SenseHysteresis SenseFlexLatchHysteresis
          RampIncrement UrgencyMultiplier
          RampInterval
  The A C command has 2 parameters:
      A C Runtime_ElementID UseORWithinCEGroup
  The A A command has 3 parameters:
      A A Runtime_ElementID ActionID ActionValue
  The A P command has just one parameter:
      A P Runtime_ElementID
  The A E command has 10 parameters:
      A E Runtime_ElementID Runtime_ParentID
          Runtime_ChildID Priority RetryLimit SenseID
          Comparator SenseValue SenseHysteresis
          SenseFlexLatchHysteresis
  The A L command has 4 parameters:
      A L Runtime_ElementID Runtime_ParentID
          Runtime_ChildID Order
```

```
D - display a given node, or the highest element ID
  D [N{display plan settings for a node}|
    C{display counters for a node}|
    H{Highest node ID}]
  The D N and D C commands have 1 parameter as below:
      D {N|C} Runtime_ElementID
  The D H command takes no parameters.
U - command not yet supported. Will allow update of
    individual nodes
M - Update the monitor flags for a specific node,
    or the global flags
  M [N{Node ID}|G{Global flags}]
  The M N command has 7 parameters
      M N Runtime_ElementID MonitorExecuted
          MonitorSuccess MonitorPending MonitorFail
          MonitorError MonitorSense
          e.g. M N 27 1 1 0 1 1 1
  The M G command has 6 parameters
      M G MonitorExecuted MonitorSuccess
          MonitorPending MonitorFail
          MonitorError MonitorSense
          e.g. M N  0 1 0 0 0 1
R - Clear the plan and initialise a new one
  R [C{clear plan}|I{clear plan and initialise new one}]
  The R C command takes no parameters
  The R I command takes 6 parameters
      R I COUNT_ACTIONPATTERN
          COUNT_ACTIONPATTERNELEMENT
          COUNT_COMPETENCE COUNT_COMPETENCEELEMENT
          COUNT_DRIVE COUNT_ACTION
          e.g. R I 0 0 1 10 2 20
S - return the size of the plan into a string buffer
  S [C{return node counts}|S{return total plan size}]
  The S C and S S commands take no parameters
I - Set/return the ID of the plan
  I [S{set the plan ID}|R{return the plan ID}]
  The I S command takes 1 parameter
      I S [PlanID]
  The I R command takes no parameters
```

R5 robot command set

The R5 robot includes an online command line help system. Typing HELP shows a list of all available commands for the R5 robot, as below.

```
HELP
PLAN STOP START RESET DUMP TIME SETTIME REPORT RATE CAL
CON PELEM RSENSE RACTION HSTOP HSTART SPLAN RPLAN SCONF
RCONF SWIFI CONF HELP VER SHOWIFI SHOCONF SHOREPORT
SHORATE SHONAMES SPEAKRULE SHORULES SRULES RRULES
CNAMES
```

Typing HELP [command] displays details for that command, as below:

```
STOP - Disable the robot motors

START - Enable the robot motors

RESET - does not work - needs a bootloader fix

DUMP - Dump a complete listing of the Instinct Plan

TIME - Report the time!

SETTIME YYYY MM DD HH MM SS - Set the time

REPORT N N N N N N - Enable/disable reporting
        - Serial Wifi Sensors HeadMatrix Plan Vocalise

RATE N - Set plan rate - cycles per second
        - 0 to stop plan execution

CAL - recalibrate sensors

CON - connect to wifi
        - useful if server started after robot is booted
```

```
PELEM [name]=[ID]
        - associate a name with a plan element ID

RSENSE [name]=[ID]
        - associate a name with a robot sense ID

RACTION [name]=[ID]
        - associate a name with a robot action ID

HSTOP - stop robot head from scanning

HSTART - allow robot head to scan

SPLAN - save robot plan in EEPROM

RPLAN - read robot plan from EEPROM

SCONF - save robot config in EEPROM

RCONF - read robot config from EEPROM

SWIFI SSID PW WifiRetry IP Port ServerRetry
        - set wifi params

CONF N N N N N - set config flags
        - ConnectWifi ReadPlan MonitorPlan Vocalise
                                ReadSpeakRules

HELP - return command list to the user
        - HELP [CMD] - command help

VER - return date and time of last compilation

SHOWIFI - show wifi params
        - SSID PW WifiRetry IP Port ServerRetry

SHOCONF - show startup flags
        - ConnectWifi ReadPlan MonitorPlan Vocalise
                                ReadSpeakRules

SHOREPORT - show report flags
        - Serial, Wifi, sensor values, head matrix values

SHORATE - show plan cycle rate. 0 means no plan processing
```

SHONAMES - show plan element names stored in the robot

SPEAKRULE N N N N N N - set rule
         - NodeType Status Timeout RepeatMyself
                             RptTimeout AlwaysSpeak

SHORULES - show speak rules

SRULES - save speak rules in EEPROM

RRULES - read speak rules from EEPROM

CNAMES - clear plan element names

Appendix C

Instinct plan for the R5 robot

This appendix shows the instinct plan of the R5 and Buddy Robots used in all our experiments, written in the instinct visual design language within the Dia drawing tool. The six plan element types are identified by colour:

- Drive – orange
- Competence – pink
- Action pattern – yellow
- Action – green
- Competence element – blue
- Action pattern element – blue

    In addition, the plan includes each of the robot senses and primitive behaviours.

- Sense – purple
- Behaviour – red

    This plan is available for download* and requires the Dia drawing tool (Macke, 2014) (Figure C.1).

*Design details and software for the R5 robot: http://www.robwortham.com/r5-robot/

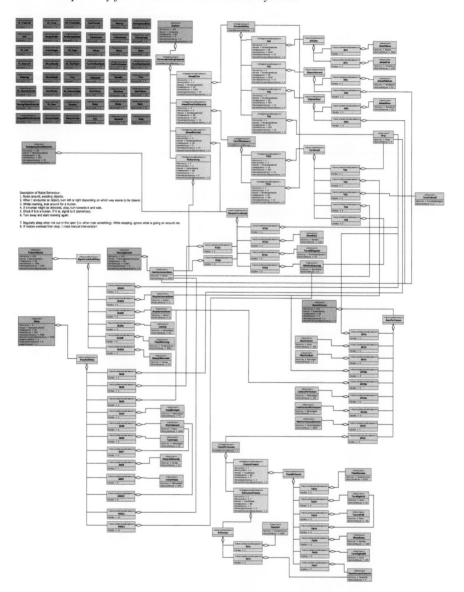

Figure C.1   Instinct Plan for the R5 robot.

Appendix D

ABOD3 displays

This appendix shows an example screenshot from the ABOD3 real-time graphical debugger, Figure D.1. It shows a portion of the reactive plan of the R5 robot described in Section 4.3.2. The highlighted boxes show the current and recent activation of the plan elements within the Instinct reactive planner. A plan element is highlighted each time it is executed, with the highlighting decaying over a few seconds. This decay time configurable within ABOD3.

Figure D.2 shows a frame from a video showing ABOD3 displaying plan activation synchronised with an embedded video of the R5 robot in operation. See Section 4.4.1.1.

Figure D.1   A screenshot of the ABOD3 display.

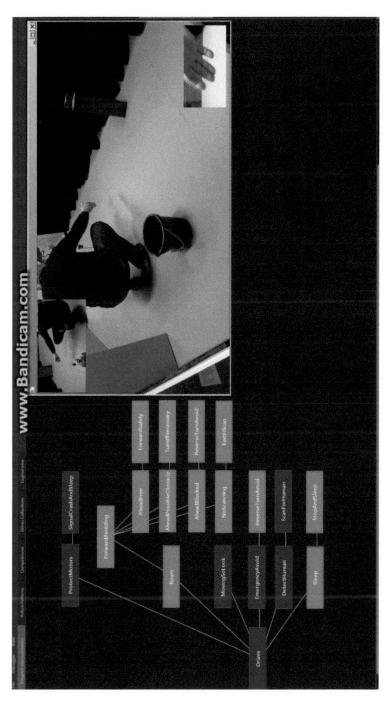

Figure D.2   Frame from a video showing ABOD3 displaying plan activation synchronised with an embedded video of the R5 robot in operation.

Appendix E
ABOD3-AR mobile augmented reality

This appendix shows example screenshots of the ABOD3-AR tool in operation (Figures E.1 and E.2).

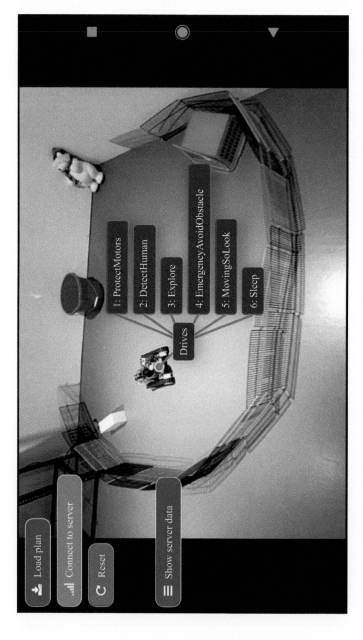

Figure E.1   ABOD3-AR display, showing the R5 robot operating with additional transparency information provided using augmented reality.

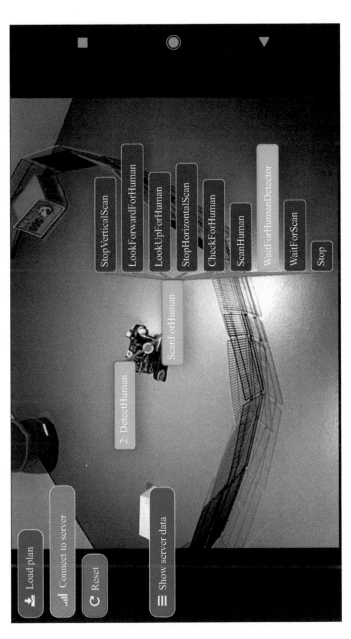

Figure E.2   ABOD3-AR display, showing how the user can drill down by clicking on an active element – in this case the DetectHuman Drive – to show details of plan execution at a lower, more detailed, level.

Appendix F
Google Forms questionnaire

The following nine pages contain a printed representation of the Google Forms questionnaire used to capture participant responses in Section 6.4.4.

Note that mandatory fields are shown with red asterisks (*).

Robot Study 8

Important - Before You Begin

You may have already participated in this study, as our lab has run similar studies before. Some studies are completely independent, but others are related. If you have already done this study, please return this HIT and do not do the experiment again – we cannot analyse data from someone who has already taken the experiment. If you have seen a page like this before, and the image below, you have *definitely* participated in this study before.

Details of this Study

This study involves watching a 3 minute 55 second video, and then answering a set of questions. The total study should take about 10 minutes. You should watch the video on a desktop or laptop computer screen. You also need speakers or headphones to listen while you watch the video.

It is very important that you complete these questions on your own. Do not discuss your answers with other participants, or with anyone else. We really want to know what you think.

We reserve the right to use all the data we collect and to publish both aggregate statistics and your anonymous individual responses. By completing this questionnaire you are agreeing to allow us to use your answers. This research is being conducted within the guidelines set out in the University of Bath Data Protection Guidance for Academic Research - http://www.bath.ac.uk/dataprotection/guidance/academic-research/index.html

Many thanks again for taking the time to help us - you are making a contribution to science!

1.   *

   Check all that apply.

   ☐ I have read the above and agree that my answers can be used

About you

2.   Your gender *

   Mark only one oval.

   ⬭ Female
   ⬭ Male
   ⬭ Prefer not to say

3.   Your age *

   _____

4.   Have you ever owned or worked with a robot? *

   Mark only one oval.

   ⬭ Yes
   ⬭ No

5. Do you work with computers regularly (in your job, as someone self employed, as a student, at home, etc.)? *

Mark only one o val.

◯ Yes as part of my job/student
◯ Yes at home
◯ No

6. Do you ever write your own computer programs (either for work, or as a hobby or part of your education)? *

Mark only one o val.

◯ Yes
◯ No

7. What is your current or previous education? *

Check all that apply.

☐ Education to age 16
☐ Education to age 18
☐ Other Education beyond age 18
☐ Diploma or other Higher Education Qualification
☐ University Degree
☐ Science, Technology, Engineering or Mathematics (STEM) University Degree

| Watch this Robot Video | You should watch this video in full screen mode. You can do that by clicking on the YouTube button in the video. This will open the video in a new tab in your browser. From there, you can make the video full screen. The video lasts 3 minutes, 55 seconds. Please watch it until the end. |

http://youtube.com/watch?v=bA4BTbP4okQ

About the robot

Tell us about your experience of the robot today.

8. Is the robot thinking? *

Mark only one o val.

◯ Yes
◯ No

9. Is the robot intelligent? *

Mark only one oval.

	1	2	3	4	5	
Not at all	◯	◯	◯	◯	◯	Very

10. How do you feel about the robot? Please choose one option from each row. *

Mark only one oval per row.

	Not at all	A little	Somewhat	Quite a lot	Very
Happy	◯	◯	◯	◯	◯
Sad	◯	◯	◯	◯	◯
Scared	◯	◯	◯	◯	◯
Angry	◯	◯	◯	◯	◯
Curious	◯	◯	◯	◯	◯
Excited	◯	◯	◯	◯	◯
Bored	◯	◯	◯	◯	◯
Anxious	◯	◯	◯	◯	◯
No Feeling	◯	◯	◯	◯	◯

11. Can you tell what the robot is trying to do? *

Mark only one oval.

◯ No
◯ Yes

12. If you can, what do you think it is trying to do? *

13. Why does it just stop every so often (when it stops moving completely)? *

14. What are the bright flashing lights at the front of the robot likely to mean? *

15. What is the researcher doing when they interact with the robot, and why? *

16. Would you be happy to interact with the robot? *

Mark only one oval.

◯ No
◯ Yes

17. Would you like to have a robot like this in your home? *

    Mark only one oval.

    ⬭ Yes
    ⬭ No
    ⬭ No Opinion

Please rate your impression of the robot on these scales:

18. *

    Mark only one oval.

	1	2	3	4	5	
Fake	⬭	⬭	⬭	⬭	⬭	Natural

19. *

    Mark only one oval.

	1	2	3	4	5	
Machinelike	⬭	⬭	⬭	⬭	⬭	Humanlike

20. *

    Mark only one oval.

	1	2	3	4	5	
Unconscious	⬭	⬭	⬭	⬭	⬭	Conscious

21. *

    Mark only one oval.

	1	2	3	4	5	
Artificial	⬭	⬭	⬭	⬭	⬭	Lifelike

22. *

    Mark only one oval.

	1	2	3	4	5	
Moving rigidly	⬭	⬭	⬭	⬭	⬭	Moving elegantly

23. *

    Mark only one oval.

	1	2	3	4	5	
Dead	⬭	⬭	⬭	⬭	⬭	Alive

24. *

    Mark only one oval.

	1	2	3	4	5	
Mechanical	⬭	⬭	⬭	⬭	⬭	Organic

25. *

Mark only one oval.

	1	2	3	4	5	
Artificial	◯	◯	◯	◯	◯	Lifelike

26. *

Mark only one oval.

	1	2	3	4	5	
Apathetic	◯	◯	◯	◯	◯	Responsive

27. *

Mark only one oval.

	1	2	3	4	5	
Dislike	◯	◯	◯	◯	◯	Like

28. *

Mark only one oval.

	1	2	3	4	5	
Unfriendly	◯	◯	◯	◯	◯	Friendly

29. *

Mark only one oval.

	1	2	3	4	5	
Unpleasant	◯	◯	◯	◯	◯	Pleasant

30. *

Mark only one oval.

	1	2	3	4	5	
Awful	◯	◯	◯	◯	◯	Nice

31. *

Mark only one oval.

	1	2	3	4	5	
Incompetant	◯	◯	◯	◯	◯	Competant

32. *

Mark only one oval.

	1	2	3	4	5	
Ignorant	◯	◯	◯	◯	◯	Knowledgeable

33. *

Mark only one oval.

	1	2	3	4	5	
Irresponsible	◯	◯	◯	◯	◯	Responsible

34. *

Mark only one oval.

	1	2	3	4	5	
Unintelligent	◯	◯	◯	◯	◯	Intelligent

35. *

Mark only one oval.

	1	2	3	4	5	
Foolish	◯	◯	◯	◯	◯	Sensible

36. *

Mark only one oval.

	1	2	3	4	5	
Anxious	◯	◯	◯	◯	◯	Relaxed

37. *

Mark only one oval.

	1	2	3	4	5	
Calm	◯	◯	◯	◯	◯	Agitated

38. *

Mark only one oval.

	1	2	3	4	5	
Quiescent	◯	◯	◯	◯	◯	Surprised

About the Experiment

Please tell us about your experience today. We would really like to learn from you, so we can make the experiment better.

39. Could you hear sound produced by the robot? *

Mark only one oval.

◯ There was no sound
◯ There was sound, but I could not hear it very well
◯ I heard some of the words, but could not understand very much
◯ I heard most of the words clearly
◯ I heard the robot clearly

40. Any other comments? Please do tell us anything about the robot or this experiment.

_____
_____
_____
_____
_____

| Complete Details | Please complete your worker ID below. Enter 1418 as the unique survey code in Mechanical Turk. Thank you for completing this questionnaire. |

41. Mechanical Turk Worker ID *

_____

References

ACM US Public Policy Council, 2017. *Statement on Algorithmic Transparency and Accountability*. Washington, DC, USA: Association for Computing Machinery. Available from: https://www.acm.org/binaries/content/assets/public-policy/2017_usacm_statement_algorithms.pdf.

All-Party Parliamentary Group on Artificial Intelligence, 2017. *APPG AI Findings 2017*. London, UK: Big Innovation Centre. Available from: http://www.appg-ai.org/wp-content/uploads/2017/12/appgai_2017_findings.pdf.

Amazon, 2017. *Mechanical Turk*. Available from: https://www.mturk.com.

Ananny, M. and Crawford, K., 2016. Seeing Without Knowing: Limitations of the Transparency Ideal and Its Application to Algorithmic Accountability. *New Media & Society*, pp. 1–17. Available from: https://doi.org/10.1177/1461444816676645.

Arduino, 2016. *Arduino Website*. Available from: https://www.arduino.cc/.

Asilomar AI Principles, 2017. Principles Developed in Conjunction with the 2017 Asilomar Conference [Benevolent AI 2017]. Available from: https://futureoflife.org/ai-principles.

Atmel Corporation, 2016a. *Atmel Studio Website*. Available from: http://www.atmel.com/Microsite/atmel-studio/.

Atmel Corporation, 2016b. *AVR Libc Reference Manual*. Available from: http://www.atmel.com/webdoc/avrlibcreferencemanual/.

Axelrod, R. and Hamilton, W.D., 1981. The Evolution of Cooperation. *Science*, 211(4489), pp.1390–1396.

Bae, J.E. and Kim, M.S., 2011. Selective Visual Attention Occurred in Change Detection Derived by Animacy of Robot's Appearance. *Proceedings of the 2011 international conference on collaboration technologies and systems, CTS 2011*, pp.190–193. Available from: https://doi.org/10.1109/CTS.2011.5928686.

Barfeh, D., Bustamante, R., Jose, E., Lansigan, F., Mendoza, E. and Mariano, V., 2017. Real Time Multi Target Capturing Using Partitioning in Robot Vision. *ACM international conference proceeding series*. Wuhan, China: ACM New York, pp.89–93. Available from: https://doi.org/10.1145/3175516.3175534.

Barsalou, L.W., 2009. Simulation, Situated Conceptualization, and Prediction. *Philosophical Transactions of the Royal Society B: Biological Sciences*, 364(1521), pp.1281–1289. Available from: https://doi.org/10.1098/rstb.2008.0319.

Bartneck, C., Kulic, D., Croft, E. and Zoghbi, S., 2009. Measurement Instruments for the Anthropomorphism, Animacy, Likeability, Perceived Intelligence, and Perceived Safety of Robots. *International Journal of Social Robotics*, 1(1), pp.71–81. Available from: https://doi.org/10.1007/s12369-008-0001-3.

Bastos, M.T. and Mercea, D., 2017. The Brexit Botnet and User-Generated Hyper-partisan News. *Social Science Computer Review*, {accepted}. Available from: https://doi.org/10.1177/0894439317734157.

Bauman, C.W., Mcgraw, A.P., Bartels, D.M. and Warren, C., 2014. Revisiting External Validity: Concerns About Trolley Problems and Other Sacrificial Dilemmas in Moral Psychology. *Social and Personality Psychology Compass*, 8(9), pp.536–554. Available from: https://doi.org/10.1111/spc3.12131.

Benoit, K., Conway, D., Lauderdale, B.E., Laver, M. and Mikhaylov, S., 2016. Crowd-Sourced Text Analysis: Reproducible and Agile Production of Political Data. *American Political Science Review*, 110(02), pp.278–295. Available from: https://doi.org/10.1017/S0003055416000058.

Berinsky, A.J., Huber, G.A. and Lenz, G.S., 2012. Evaluating Online Labor Markets for Experimental Research: Amazon.com's Mechanical Turk. *Political Analysis*, 20(3), pp.351–368. Available from: https://doi.org/10.1093/pan/mpr057.

Berwick, R.C. and Chomsky, N., 2015. *Why Only Us: Language and Evolution*. Boston, MA, USA: MIT Press.

Billington, R., 1988. *Living Philosophy*. Third ed. New York, NY, USA: Routledge.

Blackmore, S., 2000. *The Meme Machine*. Oxford: Oxford University Press. Available from: https://books.google.co.uk/books?id=YKtjZm4MhiwC.

Boden, M., Bryson, J., Caldwell, D., *et al.*, 2011. *Principles of Robotics*. The United Kingdom's Engineering and Physical Sciences Research Council (EPSRC).

Bohannon, J., 2015. Fears of an AI Pioneer. *Science*, 349(6245), pp.252–252. Available from: https://doi.org/10.1126/science.349.6245.252.

Bostrom, N., 2014. *Superintelligence: Paths, Dangers, Strategies*. Oxford, UK: Oxford University Press.

Box, G., 1979. Robustness in the Strategy of Scientific Model Building. In: R.L. Launer and G.N. Wilkinson, eds. *Robustness in statistics*. New York, NY, USA: Academic Press, pp.201–236.

Bradley, M.M. and Lang, P.J., 1999. *Affective Norms for English Words (ANEW): Instruction Manual and Affective Ratings*. The Center for Research in Psychophysiology, University of Florida. arXiv:1011.1669v3, Available from: https://doi.org/10.1109/MIC.2008.114.

Breazeal, C., Kidd, C., Thomaz, A., Hoffman, G. and Berlin, M., 2005. Effects of Non-verbal Communication on Efficiency and Robustness in Human-Robot Teamwork. *2005 IEEE/RSJ international conference on intelligent robots and systems*. Alberta, Canada: IEEE, pp.708–713. Available from: https://doi.org/10.1109/IROS.2005.1545011.

Breazeal, C. and Scassellati, B., 2002. Robots that Imitate Humans. *Trends in Cognitive Sciences*, 6(11), pp.481–487.

Broadbent, E., Kumar, V., Li, X., *et al.*, 2013. Robots with Display Screens: A Robot with a More Humanlike Face Display Is Perceived to Have More Mind and a Better Personality. *PLoS One*, 8(8). Available from: https://doi.org/10.1371/journal.pone.0072589.

Brom, C., Gemrot, J., Bida, M., Burkert, O., Partington, S.J. and Bryson, J.J., 2006. POSH Tools for Game Agent Development by Students and Non-Programmers. In: Q. Mehdi, F. Mtenzi, B. Duggan and H. McAtamney, eds.

The ninth international computer games conference: AI, mobile, educational and serious games. Dublin, Ireland, pp.1–8. Available from: http://opus.bath.ac.uk/5366/.

Brooks, R.A., 1991a. Intelligence Without Reason. In: L. Steels and R.R.A. Brooks, eds. *The artificial life route to artificial intelligence: Building embodied, situated agents.* Mahwah, NJ, USA: L. Erlbaum Associates, pp.25–81. Available from: http://idlebrain.yolasite.com/resources/Article-AI.pdf.

Brooks, R.A., 1991b. Intelligence Without Representation. *Artificial Intelligence,* 47(1), pp.139–159.

Brooks, R.A. and Stein, L.A., 1994. Building Brains for Bodies. *Autonomous Robots,* 1(1), pp.7–25. Available from: https://doi.org/10.1007/BF00735340.

Bryson, J.J., 2000. *The Study of Sequential and Hierarchical Organisation of Behaviour via Artificial Mechanisms of Action Selection.* M. Phil. University of Edinburgh. Available from: https://www.cs.bath.ac.uk/~jjb/ftp/mphil.pdf.

Bryson, J.J., 2001. *Intelligence by Design: Principles of Modularity and Coordination for Engineering Complex Adaptive Agents.* Ph.D. MIT. Available from: ftp://lll.ai.mit.edu/people/joanna/phd-tr.pdf.

Bryson, J.J., 2010. Robots Should be Slaves. In: Y. Wilks, ed. *Close engagements with artificial companions: Key social, psychological, ethical and design issues.* Eighth ed. Amsterdam: John Benjamins, pp.63–74. Available from: http://www.cs.bath.ac.uk/~jjb/ftp/Bryson-Slaves-Book09.html.

Bryson, J.J., 2011. A Role for Consciousness in Action Selection. In: R. Chrisley, R. Clowes and S. Torrance, eds. *Proceedings of the AISB 2011 symposium: Machine consciousness.* York: SSAISB, pp.15–20.

Bryson, J.J., 2015. Artificial Intelligence and Pro-Social Behaviour. In: C. Misselhorn, ed. *Collective agency and cooperation in natural and artificial systems.* Springer, pp.281–306. Available from: http://cs.bath.ac.uk/~jjb/ftp/Bryson-CollectiveAgency14.pdf.

Bryson, J.J., 2018. Patiency Is Not a Virtue: The Design of Intelligent Systems and Systems of Ethics. *Ethics and Information Technology,* pp.1–12. Available from: https://doi.org/10.1007/s10676-018-9448-6.

Bryson, J.J., Diamantis, M.E. and Grant, T.D., 2017. Of, For, and By the People: The Legal Lacuna of Synthetic Persons. *Artificial Intelligence and Law,* 25(3), pp.273–291. Available from: https://doi.org/10.1007/s10506-017-9214-9.

Bryson, J.J. and Kime, P.P., 2011. Just an Artifact: Why Machines are Perceived as Moral Agents. *Proceedings of the 22nd international joint conference on artificial intelligence.* Barcelona: Morgan Kaufmann, pp.1641–1646.

Bryson, J. and McGonigle, B., 1998. Agent Architecture as Object Oriented Design. In: M. Singh, A. Rao and M. Wooldridge, eds. *Intelligent agents IV agent theories, architectures, and languages. ATAL 1997. Lecture notes in computer science (lecture notes in artificial intelligence).* Berlin, Heidelberg: Springer, vol. 1365, pp.15–29. Available from: https://doi.org/10.1007/BFb0026747.

Bryson, J.J. and Stein, L.A., 2001. Modularity and Design in Reactive Intelligence. *International joint conference on artificial intelligence.* Lawrence Erlbaum Associates Ltd, vol. 17, pp.1115–1120. Available from: ftp://www.ai.mit.edu/people/joanna/ijcai01.pdf.

Bryson, J.J. and Winfield, A.F.T., 2017. Standardizing Ethical Design for Artificial Intelligence and Autonomous Systems. *Computer*, 50(5), pp.116–119. Available from: http://ieeexplore.ieee.org/stamp/stamp.jsp?tp={&}arnumber=7924235.

BSI, 2016. *Robots and Robotic Devices: Guide to the Ethical Design and Application of Robots and Robotic Systems*. London, UK: BSI Standards Ltd.

Burkart, J.M., Allon, O., Amici, F., *et al.*, 2014. The Evolutionary Origin of Human Hyper-Cooperation. *Nature Communications*, 5, pp.1–9. Available from: https://doi.org/10.1038/ncomms5747.

Caliskan-islam, A., Bryson, J.J. and Narayanan, A., 2017. Semantics Derived Automatically From Language Corpora Necessarily Contain Human Biases. *Science*, 356(6334), pp.183–186.

Calo, R., 2017. Artificial Intelligence Policy: A Primer and Roadmap. *UCDL Review*, 51, pp.399–435. Available from: https://lawreview.law.ucdavis.edu/issues/51/2/Symposium/51-2_Calo.pdf.

Cameron, D., Collins, E.C., Chua, A., *et al.*, 2015. Help! I Can't Reach the Buttons: Facilitating Helping Behaviors Towards Robots. *Lecture notes in computer science (including subseries lecture notes in artificial intelligence and lecture notes in bioinformatics)*. vol. 9222, pp.354–358. Available from: https://doi.org/10.1007/978-3-319-22979-9_35.

Caminada, M., Kutlak, R., Oren, N. and Vasconcelos, W.W., 2014. Scrutable Plan Enactment via Argumentation and Natural Language Generation. *Proceedings of the 2014 international conference on autonomous agents and multi-agent systems*, pp.1625–1626. Available from: http://dl.acm.org/citation.cfm?id=2616095.

Caporeal, L.R. and Heyes, C.M., 1997. Why Anthropomorphize? Folk Psychology and Other Stories. In: R. Mitchell, N. Thompson and H. Miles, eds. *Anthropomorphism, anecdotes, and animals*. New York, NY, USA: State University of New York Press, pp.59–73.

Carlsmith, K.M., 2006. The Roles of Retribution and Utility in Determining Punishment. *Journal of Experimental Social Psychology*, 42(4), pp.437–451. Available from: https://doi.org/10.1016/j.jesp.2005.06.007.

Carsten Stahl, B., 2004. Information, Ethics, and Computers: The Problem of Autonomous Moral Agents. *Minds and Machines*, 14(1), pp.67–83. Available from: https://doi.org/10.1023/B:MIND.0000005136.61217.93.

Centre de Recherche en Éthique, 2017. *Montréal Declaration on Responsible AI*. Unpublished. Available from: https://www.montrealdeclaration-responsibleai.com/the-declaration.

Charisi, V., Dennis, L., Fisher, M., *et al.*, 2017. *Towards Moral Autonomous Systems*. Available from: http://arxiv.org/abs/1703.04741.

Churchland, P.S., 2011. *Braintrust: What Neuroscience Tells Us About Morality*. Princeton, NJ, USA: Princeton University Press.

Coeckelbergh, M., 2010. Moral Appearances: Emotions, Robots, and Human Morality. *Ethics and Information Technology*, 12(3), pp.235–241. Available from: https://doi.org/10.1007/s10676-010-9221-y.

Coeckelbergh, M., 2019. Artificial Intelligence, Responsibility Attribution, and a Relational Justification of Explainability. *Science and Engineering Ethics*, 7. Available from: https://doi.org/10.1007/s11948-019-00146-8.

Collett, T.H.J. and MacDonald, B.A., 2006. Developer Oriented Visualisation of a Robot Program an Augmented Reality Approach. *HRI '06 proceedings of the 1st ACM SIGCHI/SIGART conference on human-robot interaction*, pp.49–56. Available from: https://doi.org/10.1145/1121241.1121252.

Collins, E.C., 2017. Vulnerable Users: Deceptive Robotics. *Connection Science*, 29(3), pp.223–229. Available from: https://doi.org/10.1080/09540091.2016.1274959.

Committee on Legal Affairs, 2016. *Draft Report With Recommendations to the Commission on Civil Law Rules on Robotics (2015/2103(INL))*. Brussels: European Parliament. Available from: http://www.europarl.europa.eu/sides/getDoc.do?pubRef=-//EP//NONSGML+COMPARL+PE-582.443+01+DOC+PDF+V0//EN&language=EN.

Cramer, H.S.M., 2007. Interaction With User-Adaptive Information Filters. *CHI 2007 extended abstracts on human factors in computing systems*, p.1633. Available from: https://doi.org/10.1145/1240866.1240870.

Crump, M.J.C., McDonnell, J.V. and Gureckis, T.M., 2013. Evaluating Amazon's Mechanical Turk as a Tool for Experimental Behavioral Research. *PLoS One*, 8(3). Available from: https://doi.org/10.1371/journal.pone.0057410.

Curtis, J., 2019. *British American Tobacco Hit With $436m Damages Claim in Canada*. Available from: https://www.cityam.com/british-american-tobacco-hit-436m-damages- claim-canada/ [Accessed 2019-12-2].

Danaher, J., 2017. The Rise of the Robots, and the Crisis of Moral Patiency. *AI and Society*. Available from: https://doi.org/10.1007/s00146-017-0773-9.

Dautenhahn, K., 2007. Methodology & Themes of Human-Robot Interaction: A Growing Research Field. *International Journal of Advanced Robotic Systems*, 4(1 SPEC. ISS.), pp.103–108.

Dawkins, R., 1982. *The Extended Phenotype: The Gene as the Unit of Selection*, Popular Science From Oxford. Oxford, UK: W.H. Freeman & Company. Available from: http://books.google.co.uk/books?id=Sfl91UOCKUsC.

Dennett, D.C., 1989. *The Intentional Stance*. Cambridge, MA: MIT Press.

Dennett, D.C., 1996. *Kinds of Minds*. New York, NY, USA: HarperCollins.

Dennett, D.C., 2007. *Breaking the Spell: Religion as a Natural Phenomenon*. London, UK: Penguin Adult. Available from: https://books.google.co.uk/books?id=bFeXs5vrTXEC.

Dennett, D.C., 2015. *Elbow Room: The Varieties of Free Will Worth Wanting*. New ed. Cambridge, MA, USA; London, England: MIT Press.

Dignum, V., 2018. Ethics in Artificial Intelligence: Introduction to the Special Issue. *Ethics and Information Technology*, 20(1), pp.1–3. Available from: https://doi.org/10.1007/s10676-018-9450-z.

Dignum, V., 2019. Artificial Intelligence: Foundations, Theory, and Algorithms. *Responsible artificial intelligence: How to develop and use AI in a responsible way*. Springer International Publishing. Available from: https://books.google.co.uk/books?id=mPERyAEACAAJ.

DiSalvo, C. and Gemperle, F., 2003. From Seduction to Fulfillment: The Use of Anthropomorphic Form in Design. *Proceedings of the 2003 international conference on designing pleasurable products and interfaces*, pp.67–72. Available from: https://doi.org/10.1145/782896.782913.

DiSalvo, C.F., Gemperle, F., Forlizzi, J. and Kiesler, S., 2002. All Robots Are Not Created Equal: The Design and Perception of Humanoid Robot Heads. *Conference on designing interactive systems processes practices methods and techniques*, pp.321–326. Available from: https://doi.org/10.1145/778712.778756.

Donnelly, P., 2017. *Machine Learning: The Power and Promise of Computers that Learn by Example*. London, UK: The Royal Society. Available from: https://royalsociety.org/~/media/policy/projects/machine-learning/publications/machine-learning-report.pdf.

Dörnyei, Z. and Taguchi, T., 2009. *Questionnaires in Second Language Research: Construction, Administration, and Processing*. New York, NY, USA: Routledge.

Dunbar, R.I., 1998. The Social Brain Hypothesis. *Evolutionary Anthropology: Issues, News, and Reviews, 6(5)*, pp.178–190.

Durrant-Whyte, H. and Bailey, T., 2006. Simultaneous Localization and Mapping (SLAM): Part I The Essential Algorithms. *Robotics & Automation Magazine*, 2, pp.99–110. Available from: https://doi.org/10.1109/MRA.2006.1638022.

Epstein, S., 1998. *Cognitive-Experiential Self-Theory*. Boston, MA: Springer US, pp.211–238. Available from: https://doi.org/10.1007/978-1-4419-8580-4_9.

Fieser, J., 2017. *Internet Encyclopedia of Philosophy*. Available from: http://www.iep.utm.edu/ethics/.

Fiori, M. and Shuman, V., 2017. The Joint Contribution of Activation and Inhibition in Moderating Carryover Effects of Anger on Social Judgment. *Frontiers in Psychology*, 8(SEP), pp.1–12. Available from: https://doi.org/10.3389/fpsyg.2017.01435.

Fisher, M., Dennis, L. and Webster, M., 2013. Verifying Autonomous Systems. *Communications of the ACM*, 56(9), pp.84–93. Available from: https://doi.org/10.1145/2494558.

Fong, T., Nourbakhsh, I. and Dautenhahn, K., 2003. A Survey of Socially Interactive Robots: Concepts, Design, and Applications. *Robotics and Autonomous Systems*, 42(3–4), pp.143–166. Available from: https://doi.org/10.1016/S0921-8890(02)00372-X.

Gaudl, S., 2016. Building Robust Real-Time Game AI: Simplifying and Automating Integral Process Steps in Multi-Platform Design. Ph.D. University of Bath. Available from: http://swen.fairrats.eu/research/papers/Gaudl-PhD-Robust GameAI.pdf.

Gaudl, S. and Bryson, J.J., 2014. The Extended Ramp Goal Module: Low-Cost Behaviour Arbitration for Real-Time Controllers Based on Biological Models of Dopamine Cells. *Computational Intelligence in Games*. Available from: http://opus.bath.ac.uk/40056/.

Gee, F., Browne, W. and Kawamura, K., 2005. Uncanny Valley Revisited. *IEEE RO-MAN 2005*. Nashville, TX, USA: IEEE, pp.151–157. Available from: https://doi.org/10.5143/JESK.2007.26.1.047.

Georgeon, O.L., Marshall, J.B. and Gurney, K., 2013. The Small Loop Problem: A Challenge for Artificial Emergent Cognition. *Advances in intelligent systems and computing*, 196 AISC, pp.137–144. Available from: https://doi.org/10.1007/978-3-642-34274-5_27.

Ghallab, M., Nau, D.S. and Traverso, P., 2004. *Automated Planning: Theory and Practice*, Morgan Kaufmann Series in Artificial Intelligence. Elsevier/Morgan Kaufmann. Available from: https://books.google.co.uk/books?id=eCj3cKC_3ikC.

Gjersoe, N. and Wortham, R.H., 2019. What Behaviours Lead Children to Anthropomorphise Robots? *Movement that shapes behaviour 2019, AISB convention 2019*. Falmouth, UK, pp.7–10. Available from: http://aisb2019.machinemovementlab.net/MTSB2019_Gjersoe_Wortham.pdf.

Goetz, J., Kiesler, S. and Powers, A., 2003. Matching Robot Appearance and Behavior to Tasks to Improve Human-Robot Cooperation. *The 12th IEEE international workshop on robot and human interactive communication (RO-MAN 2003)*. Millbrae, CA, USA: IEEE.

Goulden, M., Tolmie, P., Mortier, R., Lodge, T., Pietilainen, A.K. and Teixeira, R., 2017. Living With Interpersonal Data: Observability and Accountability in the Age of Pervasive ICT. *New Media & Society*. Available from: https://doi.org/10.1177/1461444817700154.

de Graaf, M.M. and Malle, B., 2017. *How People Explain Action (and Autonomous Intelligent Systems Should Too)*. Providence, RI, USA: Brown University.

Greene, J., 2014. *Moral Tribes: Emotion, Reason and the Gap Between Us and Them*. EBL ebooks online. London, UK: Atlantic Books. Available from: https://books.google.co.uk/books?id=xIeAAgAAQBAJ.

Greene, J. and Haidt, J., 2002. How (and Where) Does Moral Judgement Work? *Trends in Cognitive Sciences*, 6(12), pp.517–523. Available from: https://doi.org/10.1016/s1364-6613(02)02011-9.

Gunkel, D.J., 2017. Mind the Gap: Responsible Robotics and the Problem of Responsibility. *Ethics and Information Technology*, pp.1–14. Available from: https://doi.org/10.1007/s10676-017-9428-2.

Gunkel, D.J., 2018. The Other Question: Can and Should Robots Have Rights? *Ethics and Information Technology*, 20(2), pp.87–99. Available from: https://doi.org/10.1007/s10676-017-9442-4.

Gurney, K.N., Prescott, T.J. and Redgrave, P., 1998. The Basal Ganglia Viewed as an Action Selection Device. *Eighth international conference on artificial neural networks*. London, UK: Springer, pp.1033–1038. Available from: http://www.shef.ac.uk/~abrg/publications/icann98.pdf.

Guthrie, S., 1997. Anthropomorphism: A Definition and a Theory. In: R. Mitchell, N. Thompson and H. Miles, eds. *Anthropomorphism, anecdotes, and animals*. New York, NY, USA: State University of New York Press, pp.50–58.

Haidt, J., 2006. *The Happiness Hypothesis: Finding Modern Truth in Ancient Wisdom*. London, UK: Basic Books. Available from: https://books.google.co.uk/books?id=Suw3DgAAQBAJ.

Haidt, J., 2012. *The Righteous Mind: Why Good People Are Divided by Politics and Religion*. London, UK: Penguin Books Limited. Available from: https://books.google.co.uk/books?id=y9-GG5gPzgwC.

Haidt, J., Graham, J. and Joseph, C., 2009. Above and Below Left-Right: Ideological Narratives and Moral Foundations. *Psychological Inquiry*, 20(2–3), pp.110–119. Available from: https://doi.org/10.1080/10478400903028573.

Haikonen, P.O.A., 2013. Consciousness and Sentient Robots. *International Journal of Machine Consciousness*, 05(01), pp.11–26. Available from: https://doi.org/10.1142/S1793843013400027.

Hall, E.T., 1989. *Beyond Culture*. Revised ed. New York, NY, USA: Anchor Books. Available from: https://books.google.co.uk/books?id=reByw3FWVWsC.

Hamilton, W., 1964. The Genetical Evolution of Social Behaviour. I. *Journal of Theoretical Biology*, 7(1), pp.1–16. Available from: https://doi.org/10.1016/0022-5193(64)90039-6.

Hancock, P.A., Billings, D.R. and Schaefer, K.E., 2011. Can You Trust Your Robot? *Ergonomics in Design*, 19(3), pp.24–29. Available from: http://erg.sagepub.com/content/19/3/24.full.pdf.

Harris, S., 2011. *The Moral Landscape: How Science Can Determine Human Values*. New York, NY, USA: Free Press. Available from: https://books.google.co.uk/books?id=5FRW30QaDQwC.

Hauser, M., 2006. *Moral Minds: How Nature Designed Our Universal Sense of Right and Wrong*. HarperCollins. Available from: https://books.google.co.uk/books?id=shacaSCF3igC.

Holland, J.H., 2000. *Emergence: From Chaos to Order*. Popular Science/Oxford University Press. Available from: https://books.google.co.uk/books?id=VjKtpujRGuAC.

Holland, J.H., 2014. *Complexity: A Very Short Introduction*. Oxford University Press. Available from: https://books.google.co.uk/books?id=lmygAwAAQBAJ.

Horvitz, E., 2017. AI, People, and Society. *Science*, 357(6346), pp.7. Available from: https://doi.org/10.1126/science.aao2466.

Humanists International, 1952. *Amsterdam Declaration 1952*. https://humanists.international/policy/amsterdam-declaration-1952/ [Accessed 2018-12-19].

Hume, D., 1738. *A Treatise of Human Nature*. London. Available from: https://en.wikipedia.org/wiki/A_Treatise_of_Human_Nature.

IEEE, 2016. *Ethically Aligned Design*. Unpublished. Available from: http://ieeexplore.ieee.org/stamp/stamp.jsp?tp={&}arnumber=7924235.

IEEE, 2017. *Ethically Aligned Design – Version 2*. Unpublished. Available from: http://standards.ieee.org/develop/indconn/ec/ead_v2.pdf.

Innovate UK, 2015. *The UK Landscape for Robotics and Autonomous Systems*. Horsham, UK: Innovate UK. Available from: http://connect.innovateuk.org/web/ras-sig.

Johnson-Laird, P.N., 1983. *Mental Models: Towards a Cognitive Science of Language, Inference, and Consciousness*. Cambridge, MA, USA: Harvard University Press, vol. 6.

Jones, T.M., 1991. Ethical Decision Making by Individuals in Organizations. *The Academy of Management Review*, 16(2), pp.366–395. Available from: https://doi.org/10.5465/AMR.1991.4278958.

Kahneman, D., 2012. *Thinking, Fast and Slow*. London, UK: Penguin Books. Available from: https://books.google.co.uk/books?id=AV9x8XakdV0C.

Kahneman, D. and Tversky, A., 1996. On the Reality of Cognitive Illusions. *Psychological Review*, 103(3), pp.582–591. Available from: https://doi.org/10.1037/0033-295X.103.3.582.

Kamewari, K., Kato, M., Kanda, T., Ishiguro, H. and Hiraki, K., 2005. Six-and-a-Half-Month-Old Children Positively Attribute Goals to Human Action and to Humanoid-Robot Motion. *Cognitive Development*, 20(2), pp.303–320. Available from: https://www.gutenberg.org/files/5682/5682-h/5682-h.htm.

Kant, I., 1785. *Fundamental Principles of the Metaphysics of Morals*. Available from: https://ebooks.adelaide.edu.au/k/kant/immanuel/k16prm/chapter1.html.

Kaplan, F., 2004. Who is Afraid of the Humanoid? Investigating Cultural Differences in the Acceptance of Robots. *International Journal of Humanoid Robotics*, 1(3), pp.1–16. Available from: https://csl.sony.fr/downloads/papers/2004/kaplan-04e.pdf.

Keilthy, L., June 2008. ANPR System Performance. *Parking Trend International*. Available from: http://nebula.wsimg.com/1205ba4f6f448b01cb774681f96b7b0a?AccessKeyId=4CB8F2392A09CF228A46.

Kempen, G., Olsthoorn, N. and Sprenger, S., 2012. Grammatical Workspace Sharing During Language Production and Language Comprehension: Evidence From Grammatical Multitasking. *Language and Cognitive Processes*, 27(3), pp.345–380.

Kiesler, S. and Goetz, J., 2002. Mental Models of Robotic Assistants. *CHI '02 extended abstracts on human factors in computing systems*. Minneapolis, MN, USA: ACM New York, p.576. Available from: https://doi.org/10.1145/506443.506491.

Kim, T. and Hinds, P., 2006. Who Should I Blame? Effects of Autonomy and Transparency on Attributions in Human-Robot Interaction. *Proceedings – IEEE international workshop on robot and human interactive communication*, pp.80–85. Available from: https://doi.org/10.1109/ROMAN.2006.314398.

Klamer, T. and Ben Allouch, S., 2010. Acceptance and Use of a Social Robot by Elderly Users in a Domestic Environment. *2010 4th international conference on pervasive computing technologies for healthcare*, pp.1–8. Available from: https://doi.org/10.4108/ICST.PERVASIVEHEALTH2010.8892.

Kollanyi, P. and Howard, N., 2016. *Bots and Automation Over Twitter During the U.S. Election | Political Bots*. Oxford, UK: Oxford Internet Institute. Available from: http://comprop.oii.ox.ac.uk/2016/11/17/bots-and-automation-over-twitter-during-the-u-s-election/.

Kornuta, T. and Zieliński, C., 2013. Robot Control System Design Exemplified by Multi-Camera Visual Servoing. *Journal of Intelligent and Robotic Systems: Theory and Applications*, 77(3–4), pp.499–523. Available from: https://doi.org/10.1007/s10846-013-9883-x.

Krizhevsky, A., Sutskever, I. and Hinton, G.E., 2012. ImageNet Classification With Deep Convolutional Neural Networks. *Advances in Neural Information Processing Systems*, pp.1–9. 1102.0183. Available from: http://papers.nips.cc/paper/4824-imagenet-classification-with-deep-convolutional-neural-networ.

Langley, P., Laird, J.E. and Rogers, S., 2009. Cognitive Architectures: Research Issues and Challenges. *Cognitive Systems Research*, 10(2), pp.141–160. Available from: https://doi.org/10.1016/j.cogsys.2006.07.004.

Lawrence, S., Giles, C.L., Tsoi, A.C. and Back, A.D., 1997. Face Recognition: A Convolutional Neural-Network Approach. *IEEE Transactions on Neural Networks*, 8(1), pp.98–113. Available from: https://doi.org/10.1109/72.554195.

Lee, M.K. and Makatchev, M., 2009. How Do People Talk With a Robot ? An Analysis of Human-Robot Dialogues in the Real World. *CHI 2009 spotlight on works in progress*, pp.3769–3774. Available from: https://doi.org/10.1145/1520340.1520569.

Li, D., Rau, P.L.P. and Li, Y., 2010. A Cross-Cultural Study: Effect of Robot Appearance and Task. *International Journal of Social Robotics*, 2(2), pp.175–186. Available from: https://doi.org/10.1007/s12369-010-0056-9.

Lieto, A., Chella, A. and Frixione, M., 2016. Conceptual Spaces for Cognitive Architectures: A Lingua Franca for Different Levels of Representation. *Biologically Inspired Cognitive Architectures*, pp.1–9. Available from: https://doi.org/10.1016/j.bica.2016.10.005.

Lillicrap, T.P., Hunt, J.J., Pritzel, A., *et al.*, 2016. Continuous Control With Deep Reinforcement Learning. *International conference on learning representations 2016*. San Juan, Puerto Rico. 1509.02971. Available from: http://arxiv.org/abs/1509.02971.

Lim, C.U., Baumgarten, R. and Colton, S., 2010. Evolving Behaviour Trees for the Commercial Game DEFCON. *Lecture notes in computer science (including subseries lecture notes in artificial intelligence and lecture notes in bioinformatics)*, 6024 LNCS(PART 1), pp.100–110. Available from: https://doi.org/10.1007/978-3-642-12239-2-11.

Ling, S., 2012. Attention Alters Appearance. *Journal of Vision*, 12(9), pp.1387–1387. NIHMS150003. Available from: https://doi.org/10.1167/12.9.1387.

Linville, P.W., Fischer, G.W. and Salovey, P., 1989. Perceived Distributions of the Characteristics of In-Group and Out-Group Members: Empirical Evidence and a Computer Simulation. *Journal of Personality and Social Psychology*, 57(2), pp.165–188. Available from: https://doi.org/10.1037/0022-3514.57.2.165.

Lohse, M., Hegel, F. and Wrede, B., 2008. Domestic Applications for Social Robots – An Online Survey on the Influence of Appearance and Capabilities. *Journal of Physical Agents*, 2(2), pp.21–32.

Lyons, J.B., 2013. Being Transparent About Transparency: A Model for Human-Robot Interaction. *Trust and autonomous systems: Papers from the 2013 AAAI spring symposium. Association for the Advancement of Artificial Intelligence,* pp.48–53.

Macke, S., 2014. *Dia Diagram Editor*. Available from: http://dia-installer.de/.

Malle, B., Scheutz, M., Scheutz, M. and Forlizzi, J., 2016. Which Robot Am I Thinking About? The Impact of Action and Appearance on People's Evaluations of a Moral Robot. *The eleventh ACM/IEEE international conference on human robot interaction*. Christchurch, New Zealand: IEEE, pp.125–132. Available from: https://doi.org/10.1109/HRI.2016.7451743.

Malle, B.F. and Knobe, J., 1997. The Folk Concept of Intentionality. *Journal of Experimental Social Psychology*, 33(2), pp.101–121. Available from: https://doi.org/10.1006/jesp.1996.1314.

Marx, K., 1867. Capital, vol. 1, trans. *Ben Fowkes (New York, NY, USA: Vintage, 1977)*, 382, p.154.

Matz, S.C., Kosinski, M., Nave, G. and Stillwell, D.J., 2017. Psychological Targeting as an Effective Approach to Digital Mass Persuasion. *Proceedings of the National Academy of Sciences*. Available from: https://doi.org/10.1073/pnas.1710966114.

McAndrew, F.T. and Koehnke, S.S., 2016. On the Nature of Creepiness. *New Ideas in Psychology*, 43, pp.10–15. Available from: https://doi.org/10.1016/j.newideapsych.2016.03.003.

McBride, J., 2017. Robotic Bodies and the Kairos of Humanoid Theologies. *Sophia*, pp.1–14. Available from: https://doi.org/10.1007/S11841-017-0628-3.

McCarthy, J., Minsky, M.L., Rochester, N. and Shannon, C.E., 2006. A Proposal for the Dartmouth Summer Research Project on Artificial Intelligence. *AI Magazine*, 27(4), pp.12–14. 9809069v1. Available from: http://www-formal.stanford.edu/jmc/history/dartmouth/dartmouth.html.

Mikolov, T., Chen, K., Corrado, G. and Dean, J., 2013. Distributed Representations of Words and Phrases and Their Compositionality. *Nips proceedings*. Lake Tahoe, USA. 1310.4546. Available from: https://doi.org/10.1162/jmlr.2003.3.4-5.951.

Miller, G., 2008. The Roots of Morality. *Science*, 320(5877), pp.734–737. Available from: http://science.sciencemag.org/content/320/5877/734/tab-pdf.

Miller, T., Howe, P. and Sonenberg, L., 2017. Explainable AI: Beware of Inmates Running the Asylum. *IJCAI-17 workshop on explainable AI (XAI)*. Melbourne, Australia, pp.36–42. 1712.00547. Available from: https://arxiv.org/pdf/1712.00547.

Minsky, M., 2007. *The Emotion Machine: Commonsense Thinking, Artificial Intelligence, and the Future of the Human Mind*. Simon & Schuster. Available from: https://books.google.co.uk/books?id=OqbMnWDKIJ4C.

Mitchell, R.W., Thompson, N.S. and Miles, H.L., 1997. *Anthropomorphism, Anecdotes, and Animals*, SUNY Series in Philosophy and Biology. State University of New York Press. Available from: https://books.google.co.uk/books?id=1kWZt3de0loC.

Morgan Wortham, S., 2010. *The Derrida Dictionary*. Bloomsbury Academic. Available from: https://books.google.co.uk/books?id=PVtjXOyPSMAC.

Morris, D., 2019. Burning Down the House: Bitcoin, Carbon-Capitalism, and the Problem of Trustless Systems. *AI and Society*, 34(1), pp.161–162. Available from: https://doi.org/10.1007/s00146-018-0870-4.

Mueller, E.T., 2016. *Transparent Computers: Designing Understandable Intelligent Systems*. San Bernardino, CA: Erik T. Mueller.

Murphy, K.P., 2012. Machine Learning: A Probabilistic Perspective. Cambridge, MA, USA: MIT Press. Available from: https://books.google.co.uk/books?id=RC43AgAAQBAJ.

Nakhaeinia, D., Payeur, P., Hong, T.S. and Karasfi, B., 2015. A hybrid Control Architecture for Autonomous Mobile Robot Navigation in Unknown Dynamic Environment. *2015 IEEE international conference on automation science and engineering (CASE)*, vol. 5, pp.1274–1281. Available from: https://doi.org/10.1109/CoASE.2015.7294274.

National Science and Technology Council, 2016. *Preparing for the Future of Artificial Intelligence*. Washington, DC, USA: National Science and Technology Council.

Nikolai, C. and Madey, G., 2009. Tools of the Trade: A Survey of Various Agent Based Modeling Platforms. *Journal of Artificial Societies and Social Simulation*, 12(2). Available from: http://jasss.soc.surrey.ac.uk/12/2/2.html.

Nilsson, N.J., 1984. *Shakey the Robot*. Technical Note 323. Menlo Park, CA, USA: SRI International.

Nisbett, R.E. and Wilson, T.D., 1977. The Halo Effect: Evidence for Unconscious Alteration of Judgments. *Journal of Personality and Social Psychology*, 35(4), pp.250–256. Available from: https://doi.org/10.1037/0022-3514.35.4.250.

Novikova, J. and Watts, L., 2014. A Design Model of Emotional Body Expressions in Non-Humanoid Robots. *The second international conference on human-agent interaction*. Tsukuba, Japan. Available from: http://people.bath.ac.uk/jn352/docs/HAI2014_NovikovaWatts.pdf.

Novikova, J. and Watts, L., 2015. Towards Artificial Emotions to Assist Social Coordination in HRI. *International Journal of Social Robotics*, 7(77). Available from: https://doi.org/10.1007/s12369-014-0254-y.

Otto, M., 2018. Regulation (EU) 2016/679 on the Protection of Natural Persons With Regard to the Processing of Personal Data and on the Free Movement of Such Data (General Data Protection Regulation – GDPR). *International and European Labour Law*, 2014, pp.958–981. Available from: https://doi.org/10.5771/9783845266190-974.

Perez Vallejos, E., Wortham, R.H. and Miakinkov, E., 2017. When AI Goes to War: Youth Opinion, Fictional Reality and Autonomous Weapons. *CEPE/ETHICOMP 2017*. Turin. Available from: http://opus.bath.ac.uk/55045/.

Pinker, S., 2008. *The Moral Instinct*. Available from: http://query.nytimes.com/gst/fullpage.html?res=9804EFDB1F3CF930A25752C0A96E9C8B63.

Pinker, S., 2018. *Enlightenment Now: The Case for Reason, Science, Humanism, and Progress*. New York, NY, USA: Penguin.

Prescott, T.J., 2013. The AI Singularity and Runaway Human Intelligence. In: N. Lepora, A. Mura, H. Krapp, P. Verschure and T. Prescott, eds. *Biomimetic and biohybrid systems: Second international conference, living machines 2013*. London: Springer, vol. 8064 LNAI, pp.438–440. Available from: https://doi.org/10.1007/978-3-642-39802-5-59.

Prescott, T.J., 2017. Robots Are Not Just Tools. *Connection Science*, 29(2), pp.142–149. Available from: https://doi.org/10.1080/09540091.2017.1279125.

Prescott, T.J., Bryson, J.J. and Seth, A.K., 2007. Introduction. Modelling Natural Action Selection. *Philosophical Transactions of the Royal Society of London. Series B, Biological Sciences*, 362(1485), pp.1521–1529. Available from: https://doi.org/10.1098/rstb.2007.2050.

Prescott, T.J., Epton, T., Evers, V., *et al.*, 2012. Robot Companions for Citizens: Roadmapping the Potential for Future Robots in Empowering Older People. *Proceedings of the conference on bridging research in ageing and ICT development (BRAID)*. Available from: http://www.iidi.napier.ac.uk/c/publications/publicationid/13371986.

Raspberry Pi Foundation, 2016. *Raspberry Pi Website*. Available from: https://www.raspberrypi.org/.

Rauwolf, P., 2016. *Understanding the Ubiquity of Self-Deception: The Evolutionary Utility of Incorrect Information*. Ph.D. University of Bath. Available from: http://opus.bath.ac.uk/51253/.

Rauwolf, P., Mitchell, D. and Bryson, J.J., 2015. Value Homophily Benefits Cooperation But Motivates Employing Incorrect Social Information. *Journal of Theoretical Biology*, 367, pp.246–261. Available from: https://doi.org/10.1016/j.jtbi.2014.11.023.

Reichardt, M., Föhst, T. and Berns, K., 2015. An Overview on Framework Design for Autonomous Robots. *Information Technology*, 57(2), pp.75–84. Available from: https://doi.org/10.1515/itit-2014-1065.

Relly, J.E. and Sabharwal, M., 2009. Perceptions of Transparency of Government Policymaking: A Cross-National Study. *Government Information Quarterly*, 26(1), pp.148–157. Available from: https://doi.org/10.1016/j.giq.2008.04.002.

Rendall, D., Owren, M.J. and Ryan, M.J., 2009. What Do Animal Signals Mean? *Animal Behaviour*, 78(2), pp.233–240. Available from: https://doi.org/10.1016/j.anbehav.2009.06.007.

Ribeiro, M.T., Singh, S. and Guestrin, C., 2016. Model-Agnostic Interpretability of Machine Learning. Available from: https://doi.org/10.1145/2858036.2858529.

Richardson, K., 2015. The Asymmetrical 'Relationship': Parallels Between Prostitution and the Development of Sex Robots. *ACM SIGCAS Computers and Society*, 45(3), pp.290–293. Available from: https://doi.org/10.1145/2874239.2874281.

Robins, B., Dautenhahn, K., Te Boekhorst, R. and Billard, A., 2004. Robots as Assistive Technology-Does Appearance Matter? *Proceedings of the 2004 IEEE international workshop on robot and human interactive communication*. Kurashiki, Okayama, Japan: IEEE, pp.277–282. Available from: https://doi.org/10.1109/ROMAN.2004.1374773.

Robins, B., Dautenhahn, K., Te Boekhorst, R. and Billard, A., 2005. Robotic Assistants in Therapy and Education of Children with Autism: Can a Small Humanoid Robot Help Encourage Social Interaction Skills? *Universal Access in the Information Society*, 4(2), pp.105–120. Available from: https://doi.org/10.1007/s10209-005-0116-3.

Rohlfshagen, P. and Bryson, J.J., 2010. Flexible Latching: A Biologically-Inspired Mechanism for Improving the Management of Homeostatic Goals. *Cognitive Computation*, 2(3), pp.230–241. Available from: https://doi.org/10.1007/s12559-010-9057-0.

Rotsidis, A., 2018. *Improving Robots' Transparency With Mobile Augmented Reality Alexandros Rotsidis Master of Science The University of Bath*. M.Sc. University of Bath. Available from: https://researchportal.bath.ac.uk/files/190425734/thesis.pdf.

Rotsidis, A., Theodorou, A., Bryson, J.J. and Wortham, R.H., 2019. Improving Robot Transparency: An Investigation With Mobile Augmented Reality. *2019 28th IEEE international symposium on robot and human interactive communication (RO-MAN)*. Delhi, India: IEEE. Available from: https://researchportal.bath.ac.uk/en/publications/improving-robot-transparency-an-investigation-with-mobile-augment.

Ruse, M. and Wilson, E.O., 1986. Moral Philosophy as Applied Science. *Philosophy*, 61(236), pp.173–192. Available from: http://www.jstor.org/stable/3750474.

Russell, S. and Norvig, P., 2016. *Artificial Intelligence: A Modern Approach, Global Edition*. Pearson Education Limited. Available from: https://books.google.co.uk/books ?id=_BV6DAAAQBAJ.

Ryle, G., 1949. *The Concept of Mind*. London: Hutchinson.

Salem, M., Eyssel, F., Rohlfing, K., Kopp, S. and Joublin, F., 2013. To Err is Human(-like): Effects of Robot Gesture on Perceived Anthropomorphism and Likability. *International Journal of Social Robotics*, 5(3), pp.313–323. Available from: https://doi.org/10.1007/s12369-013-0196-9.

Salem, M., Lakatos, G., Amirabdollahian, F. and Dautenhahn, K., 2015. Would You Trust a (Faulty) Robot?: Effects of Error, Task Type and Personality on Human-Robot Cooperation and Trust. *Proceedings of the tenth annual ACM/IEEE international conference on human-robot interaction – HRI '15*. pp.141–148. Available from: https://doi.org/10.1145/2696454.2696497.

Samek, W., Binder, A., Montavon, G., Lapuschkin, S. and Muller, K.R., 2016. Evaluating the Visualization of What a Deep Neural Network Has Learned. *IEEE Transactions on Neural Networks and Learning Systems*, 28(11), pp.2660–2673. 1509.06321. Available from: https://doi.org/10.1109/TNNLS.2016.2599820.

Samsonovich, A.V., 2013. Extending Cognitive Architectures. *Advances in intelligent systems and computing*, 196 AISC, pp.41–49. Available from: https://doi.org/10.1007/978-3-642-34274-5_11.

Santoni de Sio, F. and Di Nucci, E., 2017. Pushing the Margins of Responsibility: Lessons From Parks' Somnambulistic Killing. *Neuroethics*. Available from: https://doi.org/10.1007/s12152-017-9311-1.

Saxe, R., Schulz, L.E. and Jiang, Y.V., 2006. Reading Minds Versus Following Rules: Dissociating Theory of Mind and Executive Control in the Brain. *Social Neuroscience*, 1(3–4), pp.284–298. Available from: http://www.ncbi.nlm.nih.gov/pubmed/18633794.

Scholl, B.J. and Gao, T., 2013. Perceiving Animacy and Intentionality: Visual Processing or Higher-Level Judgment? In: M. Rutherford and V.A. Kuhlmeier, eds. *Social perception: Detection and interpretation of animacy, agency, and intention*. Boston, MA, USA: MIT Press, pp.197–230.

Schroeder, J. and Epley, N., 2016. Mistaking Minds and Machines: How Speech Affects Dehumanization and Anthropomorphism. *Journal of Experimental Psychology: General*, 145(9), pp.1–11. Available from: https://doi.org/10.1037/xge0000214.

Schwab, P. and Hlavacs, H., 2015. Capturing the Essence: Towards the Automated Generation of Transparent Behavior Models. *Proceedings, the eleventh artificial intelligence and interactive digital entertainment international conference (AIIDE – 15)*. Santa Cruz, CA USA: AAAI, pp.184–190. Available from: https://www.aaai.org/ocs/index.php/AIIDE/AIIDE15/paper/view/11519/11377.

Sengers, P., 1998. Do the Thing Right: An Architecture for Action Expression. In: K.P. Sycara and M. Wooldridge, eds. *Proceedings of the second international conference on autonomous agents*. Minneapolis, MN, USA: ACM Press, pp.24–31.

Seth, A.K., 2007. The Ecology of Action Selection: Insights from Artificial Life. *Philosophical Transactions of the Royal Society of London. Series B, Biological Sciences*, 362(1485), pp.1545–1558. Available from: https://doi.org/10.1098/rstb.2007.2052.

Sharkey, A. and Sharkey, N., 2012. Granny and the Robots: Ethical Issues in Robot Care for the Elderly. *Ethics and Information Technology*, 14(1), pp.27–40. Available from: https://doi.org/10.1007/s10676-010-9234-6.

Sherman, J.W., Gawronski, B. and Trope, Y., 2014. *Dual-Process Theories of the Social Mind*. New York, NY, USA: Guilford Publications. Available from: https://books.google.co.uk/books?id=prtaAwAAQBAJ.

Shostak, S., 2013. Braintrust: What Neuroscience Tells Us About Morality. *The European Legacy*, 18(4), pp.527–528. Available from: https://doi.org/10.1080/10848770.2013.791461.

Silver, D., Huang, A., Maddison, C.J., *et al.*, 2016. Mastering the Game of Go With Deep Neural Networks and Tree Search. *Nature*, 529(7587), pp.484–489. 1610.00633. Available from: https://doi.org/10.1038/nature16961.

Skinner, B.F.B.F., 1973. *Beyond Freedom and Dignity*, Pelican. Harmondsworth: Penguin Books.

Smith, M.J. and Harper, D., 1995. Animal Signals: Models and Terminology. *Journal of Theoretical Biology*, 177(3), pp.305–311. Available from: https://doi.org/10.1006/jtbi.1995.0248.

Snow, C.P., 1959. *The Two Cultures and the Scientific Revolution*. New York, NY, USA: Cambridge University Press. Available from: https://books.google.co.uk/books?id=RUBdAAAAQBAJ.

Soares, N., 2015. *The Value Learning Problem*. Berkley, CA, USA: Machine Intelligence Research Institute. Available from: http://intelligence.org/files/ValueLearningProblem.pdf.

Sperber, D. and Wilson, D., 1986. Relevance: Communication and Cognition. Oxford, UK: Blackwell. Available from: http://books.google.co.uk/books?id=2sOKgpYuX4wC.

Stubbs, K., Hinds, P.J. and Wettergreen, D., 2007. Autonomy and Common Ground in Human-Robot Interaction: A Field Study. *IEEE Intelligent Systems*, 22(2), pp.42–50.

Syrdal, D.S., Dautenhahn, K., Woods, S.N., Walters, M.L. and Koay, K.L., 2007. Looking Good? Appearance Preferences and Robot Personality Inferences at Zero Acquaintance. In: A. Tapus, M. Michalowski and S. Sabanovic, eds. *AAAI spring symposium: Multidisciplinary collaboration for socially assistive robotics*. Palo Alto, CA, USA: AAAI, pp.86–92.

Szollosy, M., 2017. EPSRC Principles of Robotics: Defending an Obsolete Human(ism)? *Connection Science*, 29(2), pp.150–159. Available from: https://doi.org/10.1080/09540091.2017.1279126.

Tajfel, H., 1970. Experiments in Intergroup Discrimination. *Scientific American*, 223(5), p.96.

Tapus, A. and Mataric, M.J., 2008. User Personality Matching With a Hands-Off Robot for Post-Stroke Rehabilitation Therapy. *Springer Tracts in Advanced Robotics*, 39, pp.165–175. Available from: https://doi.org/10.1007/978-3-540-77457-0_16.

Theodorou, A., 2016. ABOD3: A Graphical Visualization and Real-Time Debugging Tool for BOD Agents. *CEUR workshop proceeding*, vol. 1855. Available from: http://opus.bath.ac.uk/53506/.

Theodorou, A., Wortham, R.H. and Bryson, J.J., 2016. Why Is My Robot Behaving Like That? Designing Transparency for Real Time Inspection of Autonomous Robots. *AISB workshop on principles of robotics*. Sheffield, UK. Available from: http://opus.bath.ac.uk/49713/.

Theodorou, A., Wortham, R.H. and Bryson, J.J., 2017. Designing and Implementing Transparency for Real Time Inspection of Autonomous Robots. *Connection Science*, 29(3), pp.230–241. Available from: https://doi.org/10.1080/09540091.2017.1310182.

Tinbergen, N., 1951. *The Study of Instinct*. Oxford, UK: Oxford University Press. Available from: https://books.google.co.uk/books?id=WqZNkgEACAAJ.

Tinbergen, N. and Falkus, H., 1970. *Signals for Survival*. Oxford: Clarendon Press. Available from: http://books.google.co.uk/books?id=5LHwAAAAMAAJ.

Tipping, M., 2004. Bayesian Inference: An Introduction to Principles and Practice in Machine Learning. In: O. Bousquet, U. von Luxburg and G. Rätsch, eds. *Advanced lectures on machine learning: ML summer schools 2003, Canberra, Australia, February 2–14, 2003, Tübingen, Germany, August 4–16, 2003, revised lectures*. Springer Berlin Heidelberg, pp.41–62. Available from: https://doi.org/10.1007/978-3-540-28650-9_3.

Tufekci, Z., 2015. Algorithmic Harms Beyond Facebook and Google: Emergent Challenges of Computational Agency. *Journal on Telecommunications & High Technology Law*, 13(23), pp.203–216. arXiv:1011.1669v3. Available from: https://doi.org/10.1525/sp.2007.54.1.23.

UK Government Home Office, 2019. *Home Secretary Launches Windrush Compensation Scheme*. Available from: https://www.gov.uk/government/news/home-secretary-launches-windrush-compensation-scheme [Accessed 2019-12-04].

UNI Global Union, 2017. *Top 10 Principles for Ethical Artificial Intelligence*. Nyon, Switzerland: UNI Global Union. Available from: http://www.thefutureworldofwork.org/media/35420/uni_ethical_ai.pdf.

Valley, T.U., Mori, M. and Minato, T., 1970. The Uncanny Valley. *Energy*, 7(4), pp.1–2.

Vitale, J., Tonkin, M., Herse, S., *et al.*, 2018. Be More Transparent and Users Will Like You: A Robot Privacy and User Experience Design Experiment. *Proceedings of the 2018 ACM/IEEE international conference on human-robot interaction*. Chicago, IL, USA: ACM New York, pp.379–387.

Wachter, S., Mittelstadt, B. and Floridi, L., 2017. Transparent, Explainable, and Accountable AI for Robotics. *Science Robotics*, 2(6). Available from: https://doi.org/10.1126/scirobotics.aan6080.

Waddington, D.I., 2005. A Field Guide to Heidegger: Understanding 'The Question Concerning Technology'. *Educational Philosophy and Theory*, 37(4), pp.567–583. Available from: https://doi.org/10.1111/j.1469-5812.2005.00141.x.

Walden, J., Jung, E.H., Sundar, S.S. and Johnson, A.C., 2015. Mental Models of Robots Among Senior Citizens: An Interview Study of Interaction Expectations and Design Implications. *Interaction Studies: Social Behaviour and Communication in Biological and Artificial Systems*, 16(1), pp.68–88. Available from: https://doi.org/10.1075/is.16.1.04wal.

Walters, M., Koay, K., Syrdal, D., Dautenhahn, K. and Te Boekhorst, R., 2009. Preferences and Perceptions of Robot Appearance and Embodiment in Human-Robot Interaction Trials. *New frontiers in human-robot interaction: Symposium at AISB09 convention*. Edinburgh, UK, pp.136–143. Available from: http://uhra.herts.ac.uk/handle/2299/9642.

Walters, M.L., Syrdal, D.S., Dautenhahn, K., Te Boekhorst, R. and Koay, K.L., 2008. Avoiding the Uncanny Valley: Robot Appearance, Personality and Consistency of Behavior in an Attention-Seeking Home Scenario for a Robot Companion. *Autonomous Robots*, 24(2), pp.159–178. arXiv:1011.1669v3. Available from https://doi.org/10.1007/s10514-007-9058-3.

Wardle, H. and Obermuller, L., 2018. The Windrush Generation. *Anthropology Today*, 34(4), pp.3–4. Available from: https://doi.org/10.1111/1467-8322.12445.

Weiner, N., 1948. *Cybernetics: Or Control and Communication in the Animal and the Machine*. Cambridge, MA, USA: MIT Press.

Winfield, A.F.T., 2017. *How Intelligent Is Your Intelligent Robot?* Unpublished. Available from: https://arxiv.org/pdf/1712.08878.

Winfield, A.F.T., Blum, C. and Liu, W., 2014. Towards an Ethical Robot: Internal Models, Consequences and Ethical Action Selection. In: M. Mistry, A. Leonardis, M. Witkowski and C. Melhuish, eds. *Advances in autonomous robotics systems*. Switzerland: Springer International Publishing, pp.85–96. Available from: http://link.springer.com/content/pdf/10.1007{%}2F978-3-319-10401-0_8.pdf.

Woods, S., 2006. Exploring the Design Space of Robots: Children's Perspectives. *Interacting with Computers*, 18(6), pp.1390–1418. Available from: https://doi.org/10.1016/j.intcom.2006.05.001.

Wortham, R.H., 2016. Book Review: In Our Own Image by George Zarkadakis (2015). *AISB Quarterly*, 143, pp.14–16. Available from: http://www.aisb.org.uk/publications/aisbq/AISBQ143.pdf.

Wortham, R.H. and Bryson, J.J., 2016. A Role for Action Selection in Consciousness: An Investigation of a Second-Order Darwinian Mind. *CEUR workshop proceedings*, vol. 1855, pp.25–30. Available from: http://ceur-ws.org/Vol-1855/.

Wortham, R.H. and Bryson, J.J., 2018. Communication. In: T.J. Prescott, N.F. Lepora and P.F.M.J. Verschure, eds. *Living machines: A handbook of research in biomimetic and biohybrid systems*. Oxford: Oxford University Press, chap. 33.

Wortham, R.H., Gaudl, S.E. and Bryson, J.J., 2016. Instinct: A Biologically Inspired Reactive Planner for Embedded Environments. *Proceedings of ICAPS 2016 PlanRob workshop*. London, UK. Available from: http://icaps16.icaps-conference.org/proceedings/planrob16.pdf.

Wortham, R.H., Gaudl, S.E. and Bryson, J.J., 2019. Instinct: A Biologically Inspired Reactive Planner for Intelligent Embedded Systems. *Cognitive Systems Research*, 57, pp.207–215. Available from: https://doi.org/10.1016/j.cogsys.2018.10.016.

Wortham, R.H. and Rogers, V.E., 2017. The Muttering Robot: Improving Robot Transparency Though Vocalisation of Reactive Plan Execution. *26th IEEE international symposium on robot and human interactive communication (RO-MAN) workshop on agent transparency for human-autonomy teaming effectiveness*. Lisbon. Available from: http://opus.bath.ac.uk/56760/.

Wortham, R.H. and Theodorou, A., 2017. Robot Transparency, Trust and Utility. *Connection Science*, 29(3), pp.242–248. Available from: https://doi.org/10.
1080/09540091.2017.1313816.

Wortham, R.H., Theodorou, A. and Bryson, J.J., 2016. What Does the Robot Think?
Transparency as a Fundamental Design Requirement for Intelligent Systems. *IJCAI-
2016 ethics for artificial intelligence workshop*. New York, NY, USA. Available
from: http://opus.bath.ac.uk/50294/1/WorthamTheodorouBryson_EFAI16.pdf.

Wortham, R.H., Theodorou, A. and Bryson, J.J., 2017. Improving Robot Transparency:
Real-Time Visualisation of Robot AI Substantially Improves Understanding in Naive
Observers. *2017 26th IEEE international symposium on robot and human interactive
communication (RO-MAN)*. Lisbon: IEEE.

Zarkadakis, G., 2015. *In Our Own Image: Will Artificial Intelligence Save or
Destroy Us?* Ebury Publishing. Available from: https://books.google.co.uk/books
?id=teAtBQAAQBAJ.

Zhao, X., Phillips, E. and Malle, B.F., 2019. *How People Infer a Humanlike Mind From
a Robot Body*. Available from: https://doi.org/10.31234/osf.io/w6r24.

Zwetsloot, R. and Dafoe, A., 2019. *Thinking About Risks From AI: Accidents, Misuse and
Structure*. Lawfare. Available from: https://www.lawfareblog.com/thinking-about-
risks-ai-accidents-misuse-and-structure.

Index